CHILD SEXUAL ABUSE
A Handbook for Health Care and Legal Professionals

CHILD SEXUAL ABUSE

A Handbook for Health Care and Legal Professionals

by

Diane H. Schetky, M.D.

and

Arthur H. Green, M.D.

with chapters by

Martin A. Finkel, D.O.
Judith V. Becker, Ph.D.
Meg S. Kaplan, Ph.D.

BRUNNER/MAZEL, *Publishers* • New York

Library of Congress Cataloging-in-Publication Data

Schetky, Diane H.
  Child sexual abuse.

  Includes bibliographies and index.
  1. Child molesting. 2. Sexually abused children.
I. Green, Arthur H. II. Title. [DNLM: 1. Child Abuse,
Sexual. WA 320 S319c]
RC560.C46S38 1988   614.1   87-31987
ISBN 0-87630-495-1

Copyright © 1988 by Diane H. Schetky and Arthur H. Green

Published by
BRUNNER/MAZEL, INC.
19 Union Square
New York, New York 10003

MANUFACTURED IN THE UNITED STATES OF AMERICA

10 9 8 7 6 5 4 3 2

Foreword

This is an important and timely book. Diane Schetky and Arthur Green have provided us with a comprehensive and comprehensible current account of what is known and what is not known on the subject of child sexual abuse. Drs. Schetky and Green, both highly skilled and talented child psychiatrists, have a wealth of information and experience that they share with us in an admirably straightforward and sensible way. They pull no punches. They provide us with the available data, and where no adequate scientific data are available, they draw on their considerable practical knowledge. Each problem area is faced directly and forthrightly, making this book the single-most useful volume for all health care and legal professionals who work with sexually abused children and their families.

The size of the problem they address is large. The annual number of new sexual abuse cases in children under the age of 18 years is in the range of 150,000 to 200,000. Reported cases continue to increase each year, in some years by as much as 25%. Yet until recently most cases were never reported and the majority of victims never told anybody about their sexual abuse. Nevertheless, whether or not the experience is reported, the harm that is done remains.

Drs. Schetky and Green bring their clinical insights and developmental perspective to bear on the many difficult and complex issues involved in evaluating and treating the child and his or her family. They also provide a valuable approach to the sometimes daunting problems that face expert witnesses when a case of alleged child sexual abuse is heard in a court of law.

Drs. Schetky and Green, together with their colleagues Martin Finkel, Judith Becker, and Meg Kaplan, are to be congratulated for having the courage to set down their conclusions and recommendations. Their aim is to help all professionals who are involved at various points in the evaluation of allegations of sexual abuse and in the treatment of sexually victimized children and their families. They have succeeded in this aim. We will all benefit from their wisdom, experience, and knowledge.

Melvin Lewis, M.D.
Professor of Pediatrics and Psychiatry
Yale University Child Study Center
New Haven, CT

v

Contents

Acknowledgments

The authors wish to express their appreciation to the attorneys Robert Crotty of Tacoma, Washington, and Cynthia George of Stamford, Connecticut, for their helpful comments, and to James A. Browning of Rockport, Maine, for editorial assistance.

Introduction

Child sexual abuse involves the exploitation of a child for the sexual gratification of an adult. A narrower form of child sexual abuse is incest, which refers to the sexual exploitation of the child by another family member. The term *incest* derives from the latin word *incestum*, which means unchaste or low. The legal definition of incest is cohabitation between persons related to a degree wherein marriage would be prohibited by law. However, in its common usage incest also includes stepparents and relatives by marriage and sexual acts short of penetration, such as exhibitionism, touching, and fondling, as well as intercourse.

Incest has received much more attention in the literature than extrafamilial sexual abuse and many have pondered the reasons for the existence of the incest taboo and for its violation. Whereas most authors refer to the universality of the incest taboo, Masters (1964) counters this notion, citing many African and Eastern societies whose peoples engage in incestuous practices without seeming to suffer any guilt or damage. However, these are the exceptions, and among most civilizations today the incest taboo remains in effect. The origins of the taboo are felt to be rooted in biological, psychological, and sociological factors. Fear of damaged offspring through inbreeding is often cited as a reason for the incest taboo, as a group practicing incest may be selectively disadvantaged if lesser fitness results from inbreeding (Lindzey, 1967). The Zulus have an interesting variant on this which holds that children of such unions are normal at birth but are later changed into monsters by outraged ancestral spirits (Masters, 1964, p. 45). Sociological reasons for the taboo stem from the need to strengthen the tribe through forming new alliances. This was very simply and eloquently stated to Margaret Mead by an elderly member of the Arapesh of New Guinea, who replied in response to her query about incest, "What, you would like to marry your sister! Don't you want a brother-in-law? Don't you realize that if you marry another man's sister and another man marries your sister, you will have at least two brothers-in-law while if you marry your own sister you will have none? With whom will you hunt, with whom will you garden, whom will you go to visit?" (Mead, 1950, p. 68).

Psychological reasons for the incest taboo include the need to maintain order and roles in the family. Weinberg (1955) notes that incest undermines both the social intimacy and sexual distance that are necessary to preserve family unity. Parsons (1954) stresses that the taboo permits for the socialization of children. The child is first bonded to the parent but then must separate from the parent and subordinate sexual needs to social regulation. Parsons believes that incest undermines the parent's authority and leads to special treatment of the victim.

The strongest prohibitions exist against incest with mothers. Herman (1981) notes that this is an affront to the father's prerogatives, whereas if the father violates his daughter, "No particular man's rights are offended" (p. 62). Herman adds, "The man who has the power to give a woman away also has the power to take her for himself. That power can be contested only by other men, not by the women who are given or taken. No kinsman, and certainly no man outside the family, is in a position to challenge a father's power over his daughters" (p. 62).

Finkelhor (1982) offers a different interpretation of why women are much less prone than men to sexually abuse children. He believes that women are much better able to distinguish between sexual and nonsexual forms of affection and that because men are not allowed many legitimate outlets for nurturing, they may seek it in inappropriate relationships. Finkelhor also notes that heterosexual success is much more important to men's gender identities than it is to women's and that many men seek sexual outlets devoid of relationships. Finally, he comments on the fact that men are socialized to seek sexual partners who are younger and smaller than themselves, whereas women tend to seek men who are older and larger.

There are several organizations in existence with strong followings who are lobbying for the legalization of sexual relations between adults and children. NAMBLA (North America Man-Boy Love Association) views sex with children as an act of love and the René Guyon Society believes in "sex before eight or it's too late." Guyon (1934) argues that "when we arrive at the stage of social development at which taboos are asked to show their raison d'être we soon discover that, in this particular matter of incest at any rate, no solid grounds at all can be produced. There are no logical, or physiological arguments of any kind available" (in Masters, 1964, pp. 3-4).

In the half century since Guyon wrote this, there have emerged many cogent arguments against using children as sex objects which go far beyond moral objections. Incest represents an abuse of the father's power. Ethical objections relate to the fact that children, by their nature, are incapable of giving informed consent to sex with adults (Finkelhor,

1979). The conditions of true consent require that one know what he or she is consenting to and be free to say yes or no. Children lack the information necessary to make informed decisions. Further, children do not have the freedom to say yes or no to sex with adults, particularly if they are physically and emotionally dependent upon them. Incest, as noted, undermines family structure and controls and also deprives the child of a normal father-daughter relationship. Sexual abuse also causes excessive premature sexual stimulation of the child and teaches her to use sex as a means of getting nurturance. Finally, as will be discussed later, we now know that sexual abuse of any kind leads to feelings of being damaged, used, and deceived and is associated with numerous problems in later life.

The number of cases of reported child sexual abuse continues to rise and threatens to tax the available resources for dealing with them. Whereas reported cases in the early 1970s probably represented the tip of the iceberg, we are now at a point where heightened public awareness of the problem has led to frequent overreporting. Between 1983 and 1984 reports of child sexual abuse rose by 59% (*New York Times*, March 19, 1986, p. C14). However, if one looks at all reported cases of child abuse, about 55% per year remain unsubstantiated (American Humane Society, personal communication, 1986). Professionals dealing with these cases have weighty decisions to make, balancing the need to protect children at risk against the danger of possibly unwarranted intrusion into the private lives of families. An additional problem arises from the burden put on understaffed child protective agencies by spurious reports of child sexual abuse.

ABOUT THIS BOOK

This volume is designed to help those professionals involved at various points in the evaluation of allegations of sexual abuse and the treatment of sexually victimized children and their families. While the book offers much practical advice to the clinician, it is hoped that the more general and theoretical parts will be of interest to the legal profession and general audience as well. We shall be addressing various aspects of both incest and child sexual abuse. Although some studies cited refer only to incest, these findings may often be applicable to child sexual abuse in general. When we use the term *sexual abuse*, it may be assumed that this generally includes incest. In view of the fact that most victims of sexual abuse are female, we refer to the victim as "she." Likewise, we refer to the offender as "he" but we recognize that women may also sexually abuse children. For the sake of simplicity, we have chosen to refer to the clinician as "he" and the attorney or judge as "she."

We begin with an *Overview* section, which looks at child sexual abuse in the context of normal psychosexual development and then in an historical perspective. Following is a survey of the literature on child sexual abuse and a summary of the current state of knowledge regarding psychodynamics and aftereffects. The next section on *Evaluation* deals with the clinical evaluation of the child, including the psychiatric and medical evaluation and the complex problems brought about by false allegations of sexual abuse. Special issues such as sibling incest, male victims of sexual abuse, and institutional abuse of children are also discussed, followed by a chapter on the evaluation and treatment of the male sexual offender. The third section of the book, *Legal Issues*, includes chapters on child pornography and child prostitution, the child as a witness, and the role of the clinician as an expert witness in court. The fourth section, *Treatment and Prevention*, considers the many issues involved in treating the sexually abused child and offers some thoughts on prevention. An appendix follows which provides a list of source materials that may be used in prevention, training, and treatment programs.

Research into the area of child sexual abuse is rapidly expanding. In this book we try to bring together current research and our own clinical insights which have resulted from many years of evaluating and treating sexually abused children in diverse settings (an inner-city child abuse nursery, child psychiatry clinics, and private practice in urban, suburban, and rural settings) and testifying in court. We also bring to the book our unique perspective as child psychiatrists stressing developmental and psychodynamic issues, the need for indepth evaluation of the child and her family, and appropriate treatment. It is hoped that this book will familiarize the reader with what the important issues are and render the evaluation and treatment of sexually abused children less formidable. Although these cases are often complex and confusing, they can also be challenging, and it can be gratifying seeing them through to a just resolution.

Diane H. Schetky, M.D.

REFERENCES

Guyon, R. (1934). *The Ethics of Sexual Acts.* New York: Knopf.
Finkelhor, D. (1979). What's wrong with sex between adults and children? *Am. J. Orthopsychiat.,* 49(4):692–697.

Finkelhor, D. (1982). Sexual abuse: A sociological perspective. *Child Abuse and Neglect*, 6:97–102.

Herman, J. (1981). *Father-Daughter Incest.* Boston: Harvard University Press.

Lindzey, G. (1967). Some remarks concerning incest, the incest taboo and psychoanalytic theory. *Amer. J. Psychol.*, 22:1051.

Masters, R.E.L. (1964). *Patterns of Incest.* New York: The Julian Press.

Mead, M. (1950). *Sex and Temperament.* New York: Mentor.

Parsons, T. (1954). The incest taboo in relation to social structure and the socialization of the child. *Br. J. Sociol.*, 5:101–117.

Weinberg, S.K. (1955). *Incest Behavior.* New York: Citadel Press.

CHILD SEXUAL ABUSE
A Handbook for Health Care and Legal Professionals

Section I

OVERVIEW

1

Overview of Normal Psychosexual Development

Arthur H. Green

Freud's theories of infant and childhood sexuality (1905) at the turn of this century were initially received in a climate of disbelief. It was presumed at that time that children were sexually naive and inactive. Freud's lifting of the taboos against childhood sexuality paved the way for the scientific documentation of infant and child sexual behavior by large numbers of clinicians and researchers. Children are now regarded as sexual creatures capable of their own style of developmentally determined sexual behaviors and fantasies. The recent media explosion on the sexual abuse and exploitation of children and increased reporting of child sexual abuse are causing child care professionals to review our knowledge of childhood sexuality. So often, sex play in a child is interpreted as a symptom of sexual molestation and will initiate an investigation by child protective services and/or criminal prosecution. On the other hand, sexual or seductive behavior in a child might be used by a perpetrator to justify the molestation.

This chapter describes the range and varieties of sexual behavior in normal boys and girls from infancy through adolescence and focuses on the interaction between biological, cognitive, and emotional factors. This knowledge should help us identify potential pathological alterations in childhood sexuality resulting from premature and inappropriate sexual contact with an adult. A review of the psychoanalytic theory of psychosexual development will help us understand how children of varying ages might perceive and react to sexual molestation by a parent or caretaker.

INFANCY

Kinsey and coworkers (1948, 1953) reported that male babies are capable of penile erections from birth, and female babies of vaginal

5

lubrication. Halverson (1940) observed that penile erections in young infants are usually associated with bladder and bowel distention. They appear to be reflex-like and often cause displeasure. When infants touch and rub their genitals during general body exploration, they respond with greater pleasure. Newson and Newson (1963) reported that 36% of the mothers of 1-year-olds observed genital play in their children. Manipulation of the penis in boys was more common than genital stimulation by girls. Kinsey and coworkers (1948, 1953) observed masturbation in infants under 12 months old, and they suggested that some of the infantile genital stimulation leads to an orgastic response. Newton and Newton (1967) described a release in tension in the infant during nursing akin to a sexual, erotic experience. Spitz (1965) regarded infantile genital play as one of a series of rhythmic, autoerotic behaviors which include thumbsucking, rocking, and hairpulling. According to Roiphe and Galenson (1981), boys begin sporadic self-stimulation between 7 and 10 months of age, while in girls this behavior begins near the end of the first year. The earlier onset of genital play in boys may be due to the fact that the male genitals are more exposed and may receive greater stimulation during diapering and bathing.

Roiphe and Galenson (1981) also described an early genital phase in girls and boys at about 18 months, characterized by a heightened genital sensitivity which produces a more intense, focused pleasure than the earlier forms of genital self-stimulation had provided. During the early weeks of this increased genital sensitivity, Roiphe and Galenson observed that both boys and girls carried out repetitive and intense genital self-stimulation either manually or by indirect means, such as rocking and thigh pressure. Both boys and girls attempted visual exploration as well. There was evidence of accompanying erotic arousal, including pleasurable facial expression and autonomic excitation, and penile erections in the boys. Galenson and Roiphe (1979) also witnessed an inward gaze in the children and a facial expression indicating self-absorption. From this, they inferred that a true fantasy feeling state accompanies that genital self-stimulation, which they equated with true masturbation.

TODDLERHOOD AND PRESCHOOL PERIOD

Sexual and genital interest increases considerably during ages 2 through 5. Sears, Maccoby, and Levin (1957) found that about half of a group of middle-class preschool children engaged in sex play or genital handling. Levy (1928) documented masturbatory activities in 55% of boys, but only 16% of the girls were involved in genital play. This discrepancy might be due to a greater amount of "indirect" genital stimulation in girls in the form of thigh rubbing. Sex play involving undressing and sexual exploration is common by the age of four (Isaacs, 1933). Isaacs described exhibitionistic and voyeuristic activities with other children and adults during the sex games of these preschool children. Gundersen, Melas, and Skar (1981) observed the sexual behavior of a large population of preschool children in Bergen, Norway. They noted frequent genital fondling and exhibitionism in the children, who also demonstrated a keen interest in the genitals of others. Many of these children masturbated, with some experiencing orgasm.

Sex differences in behavior, i.e., gender role behavior, become apparent during the toddler–preschool years. Boys are more involved in rough-and-tumble physical activity and play more with trucks, cars, guns, and fire engines. They like to build with blocks and Lego. Girls prefer doll play, sewing, drawing, and homemaking games. These differences may be observed as early as 1 year (Maccoby & Jacklin, 1975) and are well delineated by ages 3 to 4.

Core gender identity is well established by the ages of 3 to 4, when children tend to play with same-sex peers and show preferences for same-sex adults as role models. This process begins, however, during the beginning of the second year. Lewis and Weinraub (1974) demonstrated that 13-month-old infants preferred to gaze at other infants of the same sex. Lewis (1975) also described how infants were more likely to crawl toward their same-gender companion. Same-sex preferences occur earlier and more strongly in boys than in girls (Rutter, 1971). At first, children use clothing and hair as cues for defining sex. It is not until about age 7 that most children are able to discriminate on the basis of genital cues. It is clear that a child's gender identity is developed before he or she is aware of sex differences and long before there is an appreciation of the genital basis of sexual identity.

Although infants and preschool children have the capacity to respond in a sexual manner, the earliest sexual behavior appears to be more reflexive and associated with the exploration of the body. The ensuing pleasurable feelings tend to be repeated and self-reinforced, and can subsequently come under voluntary control. The actual onset of true erotic feelings in the child, i.e., when a child becomes conscious of erotic desire and erotic pleasure and seeks it from his/her own body and from others, is difficult to assess. Martinson (1976) estimated that a 5-year-old is capable of true autoerotic feelings, while Freud and other psychoanalytic observers would consider the blissful nursing and sucking experiences in the infant to be truly erotic. The ability of the infant and toddler to achieve a "true" awareness of erotic stimulation is severely limited by cognitive immaturity, which mires his/her thinking in the preoperational mode. Therefore, infantile sexual experiences remain primitive and unassimilated by adult standards.

SCHOOL-AGE OR LATENCY PERIOD

The time span between the age of 6 and the onset of puberty was called the latency period by Freud because of the relative suppression or concealment of sexual interests and activities. Boys and girls prefer to socialize with children of their own sex. The curbing of sexual and aggressive impulses is associated with a greater interest in learning, which in turn is facilitated by advances in cognitive development. However, in sexually permissive cultures, sex play and heterosexual intercourse take place between children of latency age (Ford & Beach, 1951). Even in western societies, sexual activities are widespread during this period. Janus and Bess (1976) documented overt sexual preoccupations and interest in children attending kindergarten through sixth grade by analyzing their drawings and compositions. Ramsey (1943) observed the incidence of masturbation in 7-year-old boys to be 10%, in 8-year-olds, 14%. The incidence of masturbation rose steadily at each successive age so that 85% of the 13-year-olds engaged in this practice. Data on overt heterosexual play also challenge the concept of a latency period. Ramsey's (1943) study indicated that heterosexual play rose from less than 5% at age 5 to about 33% at age 8 and 67% at age 13. Broderick and Rowe (1968) found that a majority of children between ages 10 and 12 claimed to have a sweetheart. By 10 years of age 67% of them had been kissed; this increased to 83% at age 12. McNab (1976) demonstrated that parents' attitudes toward sex impact strongly on their children. He administered tests of sexual attitude to 172 children and their parents and found a strong correlation between the scores of parents and their children. Parents also influence the sexual attitudes of their children by the way they handle sexual issues in the home, i.e., nudity, discussions of sexual matters, bathroom habits, degree of sexual privacy, and manner of expressing affection. Children's sexuality is also influenced by peer group attitudes and the overall societal values pertaining to sexual behavior.

Erikson (1950) described significant sex differences in play between preadolescent boys and girls. He observed that boys constructed high towers or fallen-down structures and erected fewer enclosures. Girls rarely built towers; instead, they built house interiors surrounded by simple enclosures with low walls and elaborate gates. The masculine variables of "high" and "low" are contrasted with the feminine variables of "open" and "closed." Erikson postulated that these sex differences in spatial organization are influenced by the morphology of the sex organs, i.e., the external male organ is erectable and intrusive in character, conducting mobile sperm cells, while the internal organs of the female have a vestibular access leading to expectant ova. The sex-related spatial modes are also related to social roles, i.e., boys are aggressive, mobile, and independent, while girls are preoccupied with taking care of a home and raising children. Erikson believed that these spatial and thematic differences result from an interaction of biological, cultural, and psychological forces rather than from simple adherence to cultural values.

PUBERTY AND ADOLESCENCE

Puberty can be defined as a transition period that takes the individual from biological immaturity to maturity. Dramatic physical changes take place during this period, such as acceleration in growth and the development of secondary sex characteristics. These physical changes are mediated by hormonal mechanisms. According to Marshall (1975), the average age at menarche is 13 years, while Zacharias and Wurtman (1969) reported the mean age at menarche in the United States to be 12.65. The onset of puberty in boys is about two years later than in girls, i.e., age 14½.

Tanner (1962, 1975) described the consistent acceleration of the onset of puberty in western countries during the last 150 years. The age of menarche has fallen from 17 to 13 years during this period. This trend has been attributed to improvement in nutrition and social conditions. The tendency toward earlier menarche has also been observed in oriental countries.

While childhood sexual activities are often exploratory and sporadic, in adolescence sexual preoccupations exert a powerful influence on everyday fantasies, behavior, and object relationships. Kinsey et al.'s investigation (1948) revealed that by age 15, 82% of boys had masturbated to orgasm, 8% had experienced orgasm during heterosexual petting, and 39% had experienced premarital intercourse. In contrast, only 20% of females had masturbated to orgasm, 4% had experienced orgasm through heterosexual petting, and 3% had engaged in premarital intercourse (Kinsey et al., 1953). However, this marked discrepancy between adolescent male and female sexual activity has not been documented in more recent studies. In 1972, Zelnick and Kantner (1971) reported that 14% of girls had coitus by age 15, 21% by age 16, 27% by age 17, 37% by age 18, and 46% by age 19. In a subsequent study, Zelnick and Kantner (1977) found an increased prevalence of sexual activity. By age 19, 55% of unmarried teenage women had experienced sexual intercourse. Jessor and Jessor (1975) carried out a four-year longitudinal study of 432 high school students and 205 college students. In their sample, 21% of tenth-grade males had experienced intercourse at least once, with increases to 28% and 33% in the eleventh and twelfth grades, respectively. A larger percentage of females at each grade level had experienced intercourse: 26%, 40%, and 55% for tenth, eleventh, and twelfth grades, respectively. By the fourth year of college, 82% of males and 85% of females were no longer virgins.

This apparent trend toward earlier and more frequent sexual activity among adolescents in recent years has been the topic of several sociological surveys. Sorensen (1973) described "the new sexual relationship"—serial monogamy without marriage—as a close sexual relationship of uncertain duration between two unmarried adolescents from which either party may depart when he or she desires, often to participate in another such relationship. Sorensen's survey revealed that 21% of American adolescents were involved in such an arrangement. Some 62% of the total adolescent sample said, "So far as sex is concerned, I do what I want to regardless of what society thinks." Wall and Kaltreider (1977) documented this "new morality" in a survey of gynecology clinic patients. They found a decrease in formal marriage, a reduction in the wish for children, and an attitudinal shift toward acceptance of a bisexual adaptation. Other studies of middle-class adolescent populations have described a reduced interest in marriage and family as life goals (Chess, Thomas, & Cameron, 1976; Hendin, 1975). Esman (1979) maintains that the predominant shift in the "new morality" sanctioning freer sexuality in adolescents has been in the values of adolescent girls, who now feel permitted to do what had previously been forbidden them.

HORMONAL INFLUENCES IN SEXUAL DEVELOPMENT

The highest level of hormonal control resides in the hypothalamus, which influences the pituitary gland. This, in turn, regulates the ovaries and testes and the adrenal gland to produce the sex hormones, androgens, estrogens, and progestins, which mediate most of the physical changes of puberty.

The testis produces androgens during fetal life which influence the development of male or female reproductive structures. High levels of androgens will cause male sexual differentiation in the fetus, while lower levels will result in female sexual differentiation. Fetal hormones also act on the hypothalamus, causing the pituitary to release gonadotrophic hormones. Androgen production by the testis stops at the time of birth, and thereafter until puberty there are no significant differences in sex hormone production. Prior to the onset of puberty, there is an increase in pituitary gonadotrophins which leads to a rise in adolescent hormone production by the gonads. The production of androgens increases in boys and girls at 8 to 10 years, with a much greater increase in adolescence. This increase is more dramatic in boys than in girls. The production of estrogens gradually rises in boys and girls from about the age of 7, with a large increase in girls and a small increase in boys. In addition to the importance of fetal androgens in sexual differentiation, there is evidence to believe that they also influence psychosexual behavior. Ehrhardt, Epstein, and Money (1968) reported that a high percentage of girls who were fetally androgenized by the adrenogenital syndrome manifested tomboyism with a high energy level and a minimal interest in doll play, dresses, and girls' activities.

In boys, pubertal development is associated with rising levels of testosterone production by the testes, which stimulates the growth of the male accessory sex organs (the prostate, seminal vesicles, and epididymis). The increasing secretion of testosterone in boys during puberty also leads to facial and axillary hair growth, and growth of the testes and scrotum, penis, and pubic hair. A deepening of the voice occurs due to enlargement of the larynx and thickening of the vocal cords. Between 10 and 17 years, plasma testosterone produced by the testes increases twentyfold (Faiman, Winter, & Reyes, 1976). Androgens produced by the adrenals also show a marked increase in both sexes at puberty. The production of sperm in the boy occurs at about age 14½, with a range from ages 12½ to 16½. The average onset of puberty in boys is 14.

The secretion of estrogens by the ovaries increases in girls at puberty and continues to accelerate after menarche until menstrual cycles are established. The physical signs associated with the onset of puberty in girls is development of the breasts, followed by the appearance of pubic hair, which usually precede menarche. The increase in estrogen is much smaller for boys, but small amounts of estrogen are secreted by the adrenal cortex and the testes in males during adolescence and adulthood.

PSYCHOANALYTIC THEORY OF PSYCHOSEXUAL DEVELOPMENT: CONCEPTUAL FRAMEWORK

Freud (1905) hypothesized a progression of "libidinal" stages in which psychic organization forms around different constellations of pleasurable strivings directly linked with the process of biological maturation. These constellations, or "phases," become increasingly more complex as the child grows older. This concept of sexual development is not confined to genital sensations, but extends to all the pleasure-seeking drives relating to the body. Each new phase occurs as the result of the resolution of conflicts during the preceding phase, which is based on a concept of developmental progression.

The Oral Phase (Birth to 1½ Years)

The oral phase of development is characterized by the dominance of oral activity, both pleasure-seeking and aggressive. In infancy, the mothering figure is the most crucial presence in the infant's environment. The mouth is an important organ for the satisfaction of both nutritive and nonnutritive needs. For the infant, being held, caressed, and soothed are connected with the feeding experience. A relationship develops between being gratified and loved, and the ingestion of food. The mouth is also used extensively for the active exploration of the environment, and for autoerotic gratification in biting and thumbsucking. The oral phase is also characterized by object dependency and the emergence of a primitive ego equipment. The infant is able to differentiate between pleasure and pain, and between states of satiation and tension. Memory traces emerge in connection with pleasure–pain experiences with the primary caretaker and give rise to mental representations of the maternal object, the outside world, and the self. Some conflicts originating in this phase of development are overeating or food avoidance, thumbsucking or nail biting, depressions associated with maternal loss, or character traits of excessive dependency and demandingness.

The Anal Phase (1½ to 3 Years)

During this phase, the child's pleasure-seeking activities are focused on the anal zone and its functions. This is reinforced by toilet training, by which the child learns to control his or her anal sphincter. This concept of control is generalized to permit a gradual acquisition of autonomy and independence from the caregiver, which is, in turn, facilitated by rapid progress in motor development and language. There is a heightened pleasure in physical activity and in the achievement of mastery and independence. The child frequently expresses negativism and oppositionalism in his or her bid to achieve autonomy. These behaviors often alternate with clinging, dependent behaviors. Symptoms of constipation, encopresis, and enuresis may have origins in anal-phase conflicts, while character traits such as compulsivity, cleanliness, and stinginess, and their opposites of messiness, rebelliousness, and sado-masochistic behavior may have similar roots in this phase. Excessive or abnormal anal stimulation from constipation, laxatives, enemas, or sexual abuse (i.e., sodomy) may give rise to anal symptoms and/or

anally focused sexual behavior. During this phase, the child might perceive a sexual encounter primarily as an aggressive or sadistic act.

The Phallic Phase (3 to 4½ Years)

Sexuality becomes increasingly genital or "phallic" during this period. Children become more interested in their genitals and masturbate more frequently. They are interested in the genital differences between boys and girls, and between mothers and fathers, and in the origins of babies. Castration anxiety is manifested at this time. The 3- to 4-year-old boy, who is very proud and exhibitionistic about his penis, develops castration anxiety when he sees female genitalia. He fears losing his own genitals. Castration anxiety in little girls is derived from the perception that they lack the visible organ that boys have. A girl might feel that she lost a penis or has been damaged in some way. She might also believe that she could be injured by sexual contact with older males because of their large penises. Freud developed the concept of "penis envy," which refers to the fantasy of possessing a hidden penis in little girls.

The Oedipal Phase (4½ to 6½ Years)

During the oedipal stage of development, children exhibit a possessive attitude toward the opposite-sex parent, which leads to rivalry with the parent of the same sex. In the boy, the sexual yearnings for the mother propel him into a competitive relationship with his father. He wants to become bigger and stronger than his father, but fears retaliation in the form of physical punishment and castration. According to Freud (1905), castration anxiety terminates the Oedipus complex in boys. The boy ultimately gives up the struggle with his father and develops an identification with him, incorporating his masculine qualities.

For a girl, the experience of castration and feelings of deprivation will motivate her to turn away from her mother and toward her father, from whom she might obtain the fantasied penis, or baby. This, however, leads to conflict with the girl's dependency on the mother. The risk of alienating the mother is too great, so the girl ultimately resolves the oedipal conflict by renouncing the desire for exclusive possession of the father and proceeds to identify with her mother, with the hope of getting a man like her father in the future. Some girls pass through a tomboy stage, attempting a masculine identification with the father in latency and early adolescence. The shift back to the mother occurs later in adolescence. A major difference between boys and girls in their negotiation of the oedipal conflict is that boys retain their mother as the primary love object, while girls shift their attachment from the mother to the father.

Latency Period (6½ to 10 Years)

The latency period refers to the relative diminution of sexual and aggressive drives following the resolution of the oedipal conflict. The curbing of these drives enhances learning. Learning is also strengthened by maturational changes in cognitive development. Children achieve the state of concrete operations during latency. Latency-age boys are often preoccupied with "superheroes" with magical powers who fight evil. A subtheme is their avoidance of heterosexual activity, which parallels their own avoidance of girls. This may be understood as an attempt to loosen the attachment to the mother and to consolidate a masculine identification. Latency-age girls, however, continue to express romantic fantasies and show more interest in boys. Both girls and boys demonstrate a heightened interest in peer group activities during this period, establishing friendships primarily with children of the same sex. There is a rapid development of superego functions during latency, as values stemming from school, peers, and significant adults are internalized. Defense mechanisms are strengthened and there is a greater emphasis on secondary process thinking, all of which result in a greater mastery over impulses and drives. This, in turn, frees up energy for learning, exploring, and establishing social relationships.

The suppression of overt sexual fantasy and behavior during latency is greatly influenced by cultural and environmental factors. In cultures that condone or promote sexual activity among children, or where children are sexually molested, the latency period will be disrupted. Freud (1905) described the pathological impact of these environmental factors:

> The external influences of seduction are capable of provoking interruptions of the latency period or even its cessation, and that in this connection the sexual instinct of children proves in fact to be polymorphously perverse; it seems, moreover, that any such premature sexual activity diminishes a child's educability. (p. 111)

Puberty and Adolescence

Puberty begins with the occurrence of menarche in the girl and seminal emissions in the boy, with the development of secondary sexual characteristics under the influence of hormonal change. At this time, physical maturation occurs in almost every system in the body in both the boy and the girl. These secondary sexual characteristics, together with the achievement of menstruation and sperm production, serve as organizers for gender identification in the adolescent.

Puberty signals the beginning of early adolescence, which is a period of turmoil, characterized by rapid shifts in mood and behavior. Rebelliousness and rejection of parental values alternate with conformity to peer group ideals. Egocentric behavior might suddenly give way to altruistic preoccupations, often with social or political causes. There are simultaneous urges to be independent and to preserve childhood parental attachments.

In adolescence, there is a shifting of love interest to someone of the opposite sex who is closer in age. These first sexual relationships are often based upon a narcissistic object choice. Narcissistic and sexual gratification eclipse tender and affectionate feelings in importance, especially in boys. Adolescent boys split off sexual feelings from love as a defense against unresolved oedipal strivings toward the mother or sister. Girls are less conflicted about heterosexual fantasies, which serve to counteract the regressive pull toward the mother. These narcissistically tinged relationships are often followed by highly idealized, romantic liaisons with dramatic overtones, which might be considered the precursors of adult sexuality. Adolescents gradually learn to integrate feelings of love and tenderness with sexuality, but this is usually not accomplished until later in adolescence. Masturbation remains an important sexual outlet during adolescence until a true love relationship is established. Masturbation is often a source of guilt to the adolescent, which is usually related to the aggressive, exploitative, or grandiose accompanying fantasies, rather than to the act itself.

The achievement of genitality, or the capacity for heterosexual relationships outside of the family, is a major developmental task of adolescence. The other major tasks for this period are independence from childhood parental relationships and the consolidation of a firm sense of identity.

SUMMARY

Sexual activity is commonly observed in infants and preschool children, and steadily increases during the school years and adolescence. Sexual behavior consists of masturbation during infancy and extends to genital play with peers and sexual curiosity about parents and other adults, which may lead to genital touching and exhibitionism. Many of these children experience orgasm. Children's early capacity for sexual responsiveness exceeds their cognitive and emotional capacity to process these events; therefore, children can be easily seduced and pressured into sexual contact by peers, older children, and adults. The capacity to integrate these sexual experiences is not fully developed until late adolescence.

The theory of psychosexual development provides a framework for understanding the pathological impact of child sexual abuse. The child's response to adult-initiated sexual activity depends upon the child's level of psychosexual development and on whether or not the genital contact is welcomed or rejected. For example, an infant or preschool child might regard the sexual stimulation as a pleasurable event, due to a lack of awareness of the deviant nature of the act. Unwanted sexual contact with an adult at this age might be construed as a primarily aggressive act, rather than a sexually stimulating event. An incestuous experience in an oedipal-phase child would probably intensify normal oedipal guilt with a fear of retaliation and lead to unresolved oedipal fixations. A similar intensification of oedipal conflict would be expected in preadolescent and adolescent incest victims. In addition, these children would be compromised in their ability to establish future extrafamilial sexual relationships. Molestation by the same-sex parent or adult might impair the development of heterosexual object ties and promote homosexual arousal patterns. Children experiencing deprivation and unresolved dependency needs during the oral and anal periods might be more vulnerable to sexual victimization because the sexual contact might be the only form of emotional nurturance available to the child. Sexual acting out by the incest victim might be reinforced by the pleasurable nature of the genital stimulation, the secondary gain provided by the associated physical contact and dependency gratification, and the tendency to repeat and reenact the molestation as a means of mastering the traumatic experience. A more detailed discussion of the pathogenesis and sequelae of child sexual abuse will be presented in Chapter 3.

REFERENCES

Broderick, C., & Rowe, G. (1968). A scale of preadolescent heterosexual development. *J. Marriage and the Family*, 30:97–101.

Chess, S., Thomas, A., & Cameron, M. (1976). Sexual attitudes and behavior patterns in a middle class adolescent population. *Amer. J. Orthopsychiat.*, 46:689–701.

Ehrhardt, A., Epstein, R., & Money, J. (1968). Fetal androgens and female gender identity in the early-treated adrenogenital syndrome. *Johns Hopkins Med. J.*, 122:160–167.

Erikson, E. (1950). *Childhood and Society*. New York: W.W. Norton.

Esman, A. (1979). Adolescence and "The New Sexuality." In T. Karasu & C. Socarides (Eds.), *On Sexuality*. New York: International Universities Press, pp. 19–28.

Faiman, C., Winter, J., & Reyes, F. (1976). Patterns of gonadotrophins and gonadal steroids throughout life. *Clin. Obstet. Gynaecol.*, 3:467–483.

Ford, C., & Beach, F. (1951). *Patterns of Sexual Behavior*. New York: Harper.

Freud, S. (1905). Three essays on the theory of sexuality. In J. Strachey (Ed.), *The Standard Edition of the Complete Works of Sigmund Freud*, Vol. 7, pp. 125–143. London: Hogarth Press, 1953.

Galenson, E., & Roiphe, H. (1979). The development of sexual identity: Discoveries and implications. In T. Karasu & C. Socarides (Eds.), *On Sexuality*. New York: International Universities Press, pp. 1–17.

Gundersen, B., Melas, P., & Skar, J. (1981). Sexual behavior of preschool children: Teachers' observations. In L. Constantine & F. Martinson (Eds.), *Children and Sex*. Boston: Little, Brown, pp. 45–61.

Halverson, H. (1940). Genital and sphincter behavior of the male infant. *J. Genet. Psychol.*, 56:95–136.

Hendin, H. (1975). *Youth in Crisis*. New York: Norton.

Isaacs, S. (1933). *Social Development in Young Children*. London: Routledge and Kegan Paul.

Janus, S., & Bess, B. (1976). Latency: Fact or fiction. *Amer. J. Psychoanal.*, 36:339–346.

Jessor, S., & Jessor, R. (1975). Transition from virginity to nonvirginity among youth: A social-psychological study over time. *Dev. Psychol.*, 11:473–484.

Kinsey, A., Pomeroy, W., & Martin, C. (1948). *Sexual Behavior in the Human Male*. Philadelphia: W.B. Saunders.

Kinsey, A., Pomeroy, W., Martin, C., & Gebhardt, P. (1953). *Sexual Behavior in the Human Female*. Philadelphia: W.B. Saunders.

Levy, D. (1928). Fingersucking and accessory movements in early infancy: An ethologic study. *Amer. J. Psychiat.*, 7:881–918.

Lewis, M. (1975). Early sex differences in the human: Studies of socioemotional development. In E. Rubinstein, R. Green, & E. Brecher (Eds.), *New Directions in Sex Research*. New York: Plenum.

Lewis, M., & Weinraub, M. (1974). Sex of parent x sex of child: Socioemotional development. In R. Friedman, R. Richart, & R. Van de Wiele (Eds.), *Sex Differences in Behavior*. New York: John Wiley, pp. 165–189.

Maccoby, E., & Jacklin, C. (1975). *The Psychology of Sex Differences*. London: Oxford University Press.

Marshall, W. (1975). Growth and sexual maturation in normal puberty. *Clin. Endocrinol. & Metabol.*, 4:3–25.

Martinson, F. (1976). Eroticism in infancy and childhood. *J. Sex Res.*, 12:251–262.

McNab, W. (1976). Sexual attitude development in children and the parents' role. *J. School Health*, 46:537–542.

Newson, J., & Newson, E. (1963). *Patterns of Infant Care in an Urban Community*. London: Allen and Unwin.

Newton, N., & Newton, M. (1967). Psychological aspects of lactation. *New England J. Med.*, 277:1179–1188.

Ramsey, C. (1943). The sexual development of boys. *Am. J. Psychol.*, 56:217–233.

Roiphe, H., & Galenson, E. (1981). *Infantile Origins of Sexual Identity*. New York: International Universities Press.

18   *Child Sexual Abuse*

Rutter, M. (1971). Normal psychosexual development. *J. Child Psychol. & Psychiat.*, 11:259-283.

Sears, R., Maccoby, E., & Levin, H. (1957). *Patterns of Child Rearing.* New York: Harper and Row.

Sorenson, R. (1973). *Adolescent Sexuality in Contemporary America.* New York: World.

Spitz, R. (1965). *The First Year of Life.* New York: International Universities Press.

Tanner, J. (1962). *Growth at Adolescence* (2nd Ed.). Oxford, England: Blackwell Scientific Publications.

Tanner, J. (1975). Growth and endocrinology of the adolescent. In L. Gardner (Ed.), *Endocrine and Genetic Diseases of Childhood and Adolescence* (2nd Ed.). Philadelphia: W.B. Saunders, pp. 14-64.

Wall, S., & Kaltreider, N. (1977). Changing social-sexual patterns in gynecological practice. *J.A.M.A.*, 237:565-568.

Zacharias, L., & Wurtman, R. (1969). Age at menarche: Genetic and environmental influences. *New England J. Med.*, 280:868-875.

Zelnick, M., & Kantner, J. (1971). Sex and contraception among unmarried teenagers. In C. Westcoff (Ed.), *Toward the End of Growth.* Englewood Cliffs, N.J.: Prentice-Hall.

Zelnick, M., & Kantner, J. (1977). Sexual and contraceptive experiences of young unmarried women in the United States, 1976 and 1977. *Family Planning Perspectives*, 9:55-73.

2

Child Sexual Abuse in Mythology, Religion, and History

Diane H. Schetky

Oh most wicked speed to post with such dexterity to incestuous sheets. It is not nor it cannot come to good. But break, my heart, for I must hold my tongue.—*Hamlet*, Act 1, Sc. 2

This chapter will explore sexual abuse as depicted in mythology and the Bible and will attempt to summarize the history of child sexual abuse. It is hoped that history may lend some perspective on the problem and that through understanding the past we may be better able to deal with the future.

MYTHOLOGY

Mythology provides us with a projective screen for man's instinctual wishes and, as Hamilton (1942) notes, "Mythology is generally supposed to show us the way the human race thought and felt untold ages ago" (p. 13). If "the Greeks made their gods in their own image" (p. 16), as Hamilton suggests, then incest was as prevalent then as it is now.

Zeus was insatiable in his sexual appetites and knew none of the constraints of the incest taboo. Conceived out of the incestuous union of Cronun to his sister Rhea, Zeus married, among others, his own sister Hera. This was a tumultuous marriage marked by spouse abuse on both sides and vindictive behavior on the part of Hera, who was fiendishly jealous of Zeus's many lovers. Zeus's progeny is said to have been enormous, and among his conquests were numerous married women, his granddaughter Thalia, his aunt Leto, his sister Demeter (whom he raped in the form of a bull when she repulsed him), and several young girls. He also used his bull disguise to rape young Europa, daughter of the king of Sidon, who was quite taken by Zeus: "He is so mild and dear and gentle to behold. He is not like a bull but like a good true man, except he cannot speak" (Hamilton, 1942, p. 81). His seduction tactics were similar to those used by present-day pedophiles who first win the child's trust, then employ gentle persuasion. Persephone was conceived as a result of this relationship and Zeus went on to rape her as well. Another pedophiliac conquest was Danae, whose father, Acrisius, had locked her and her nurse into a bronze underground chamber because an oracle had told him she would bear a son who would overpower him. Zeus was not deterred by the bronze chamber or the nursemaid and succeeded in impregnating Danae. When she gave birth to their son, Perseus, her father was terrified by this miracle and threw mother and child to sea in a chest.

The fear of the son overpowering the father permeates Greek mythology. Zeus himself was fortunate to have survived, as an oracle told his father that he would be supplanted by one of his children; so Cronun proceeded to swallow each of his children at birth. Poor Rhea was overcome with grief and when Zeus was born she sequestered him and presented her husband instead with a large stone wrapped in swaddling cloth which he swallowed. Zeus was later to vanquish his father by giving him an emetic and forcing him to bring up the stone and all of his ingested children. Cronun seems to have started a family tradition, as Zeus was also warned that if he had a child by Metis, goddess of wisdom and his first wife, this child would be more powerful than he and dethrone him. Rather than take this risk, Zeus swallowed Metis and her unborn child, thereby incorporating her wisdom while also identifying with his aggressor father. He later gave birth to this child, Athene. Hera, infuriated, was spurred on to give birth unaided to Typhon, "scourge of mankind" (New LaRousse Encyclopedia of Mythology, 1968).

King Laius of Thebes was also warned by a prophet that he would die at the hands of his son and so he tried to get rid of his son, Oedipus, at birth. As is well known, Oedipus kills a stranger who happens to be his father and marries (unbeknownst to him) his mother, Jocasta. Oedipus's horror on learning of the crimes he has committed suggests the incest taboo was in effect then and that perhaps people in these times were aware of the genetic disadvantages of inbreeding. In Sophocles' play, Oedipus relates how the oracle at Delphi told him that he would kill his father, marry his mother "and have children men would shudder to look upon" (Hamilton, 1942, p. 259). Ironically, it is as Oedipus is trying to flee his home and this prophecy that he kills his unknown father. Oedipus, overwhelmed by what he has done, then blinds himself. Jocasta hangs herself, their two sons kill each other, and their daughters are buried alive. Violence then, much as today, was a not uncommon sequela of incest.

The Phaedra complex is the counterpart to the Oedipus complex in stepfamilies (Messer, 1969). In the legend by Euripides, Phaedra marries the much older Theseus, king of Athens, and finds herself attracted to his son, Hippolytes. Upon learning of this, Hippolytes is appalled and flees their home. Feeling rejected, Phaedra kills herself and leaves a note saying she has been violated by Hippolytes. Theseus banishes his son and invokes the wrath of Poseidon, which leads to Hippolytes' violent death. Only later does Theseus learn of his son's innocence.

Incestuous themes are also present in Norse mythology. Volsung is killed by his son-in-law, who also captures Volsung's son, Sigmund. Sigmund's sister Signy devises a plan to save her brother by going to him in disguise and becoming impregnated by him. She gives birth to their son, Sinfiotli, whom she hopes, as one of their own blood, will help them. He subsequently avenges Volsung's death by killing Signy's husband, the murderer of his grandfather, Volsung, and his half-siblings with the help of Sigmund. Signy chooses to die in their burning house with her husband which suggests that although her incestuous motives were ostensibly altruistic she may have also experienced some guilt over her actions.

In Indian mythology Brahma is considered to be the first of the gods. He faced a problem similar to Adam in the Bible, which he solved by creating a female partner out of his own flesh with whom he then fell in love. With this wife/daughter he went on to create the human race. The god Shiva is said to have sprung from Brahma's fifth head which he later lost to Shiva's arrow when Shiva became angered with Brahma for drunkenly committing incest with his daughter (Ions, 1983). One of the more popular Indian gods is Ganesha, who has the head of an elephant. Numerous explanations exist as to how he came by this elephant head. One version holds that his father went away on a long trip and upon returning home was angered to find his wife in bed with a young man. Failing to recognize his son, the father cut off his son's head. Overcome with remorse, he then declared he would replace it with the first head he saw, which happened to be the head of an elephant.

Brother-sister incest was quite common among Egyptian deities, with Nut, the goddess of the sky, marrying her twin brother, Geb. Ra, god of the sun, was infuriated by this and decreed that Nut could not bear children in any given month. However, Thoth, the moon god, took pity on her and by creating five additional days in the year enabled her to successively give birth to five children. The children of Nut and Geb proceeded to intermarry, with Osiris taking his sister Isis as his queen and Nephthys marrying her brother Set. The latter union was to be barren and Nephthys then conspired to bear a child by her brother Osiris which she did by getting him drunk. Set, who had been jealous of his older brother all along, eventually murdered him. Incest among the gods is said to have inspired the Pharaohs to do likewise, the most notable of these unions being the marriage of Cleopatra to her brother. One rationalization offered for this custom was the need to preserve the purity of the royal blood.

THE BIBLE

The Old Testament reminds us that we are all children of incest in that the children of Adam and Eve were left no other choices if they were to perpetuate the species. Noah and his clan faced a similar problem following the flood. The story of Lot provides a paradigm for incest as a form of family dysfunction. Lot's wife was unavailable because she had been turned into a pillar of salt and, as is often the case in incestuous families, Lot's facilities were impaired by alcohol. Lot's daughters are portrayed as the aggressors but their motives were noble: "Come let us make our father drink wine, and we will lie with him, that we may preserve the seed of our father. And they made their father drink wine that night: and the first born went in, and lay with her father; and he perceived not when she lay down nor when she arose" (*Genesis*, 19:32–33). God apparently regarded drunken irresponsibility as a sound defense and Lot was absolved of any blame. Prohibitions against incest are found in the Book of Leviticus:

The man who lies with his father's wife has uncovered his father's nakedness; both of them shall be put to death, their blood is upon them. (*Leviticus*, 20:11)

If a man lies with his daughter-in-law both of them shall be put to death; they have committed incest, their blood is upon them. (*Leviticus*, 20:12)

Disher (1984) speculates that these prohibitions were intended to castigate the Egyptians and Canaanites, "who worshipped and deified sex" (p. 22), and to prevent the Hebrews from being absorbed and corrupted by other cultures. Curiously, although Leviticus goes into great detail regarding prohibited sexual relationships with assorted relatives and animals, there is no mention of father-daughter incest, which suggests that it may not have been a problem and certainly not as prevalent as brother-sister incest. The theme of brother-sister incest again appears in the second Book of Samuel, with Ammon, son of David, forcing himself upon his half-sister, Tamar, rendering her desolate and incurring the wrath of David (*II Samuel*, 13:9-21).

Child sexual abuse as we know it today is not mentioned in the Bible, although in many ancient cultures the belief persisted that sexual contact with a virgin could cure the maladies of old age. As David grew infirm in latter years, his servants suggested restoring him with a virgin: "So they sought for a beautiful maiden throughout all the territory of Israel, and found Abishag the Shunammite, and brought her to the king. The maiden was very beautiful" (*I Kings*, 1:1-4).

Under Hebrew customs a father could sell his daughter to a prospective bridegroom providing she was a virgin. If for any reason she were defiled, she was held responsible for this and could be stoned to death along with the rapist. Brownmiller (1975) notes the reasoning was that if the daughter had protested by screaming she would have been rescued. However, if she were beyond the city where her screams could not be heard, her life was spared and the rapist had to pay compensation to her father.

The New Testament is relatively tame compared to the Old Testament. Disher (1984) notes, "The major difference regarding sex in the Old and New Testaments is that in the Old they did it, while in the New they just talked about it" (p. 51). Incest does not appear to have been a pressing issue for the Apostles. The emphasis of the church fathers was on repression or control of sexual instincts, and some, like St. Augustine, viewed sexual intercourse as "fundamentally disgusting" (Tannahill, 1979, p. 132) and held celibacy to be morally superior. Tannahill observes, "Their deliberations—products often of a highly personal and highly prejudiced view of life and society—took on an aura of revealed truth, and their morality, almost entirely relative in its origins, achieved the status of the absolute" (1979, p. 127).

To summarize, incest as portrayed in mythology and the Bible, with the exception of Zeus, seems to have involved primarily siblings. In several instances the woman is the perpetrator and, rather than feeling victimized by the experience, she emerges with what she wanted—a child. Inasmuch as brother-sister incest involves less abuse of power and more often a degree of informed consent, at least on the part of the woman, it follows that she is less likely to be traumatized by this experience than by father-daughter incest. We are left to speculate how the drunken male partners of these women reacted to these incestuous experiences or whether they had any recall at all. Interestingly, the role of alcohol in biblical and mythological incest was to render the male victim amnestic, rather than to lessen the offender's inhibitions as it may do today.

On the other hand, we must remember that these stories are written from a male perspective and that women and children were regarded as property and thus were not viewed as victims.

CHILD SEXUAL ABUSE IN HISTORY

In writings on early history, children are notable by their absence. What little information we have on them suggests they were regarded as disposable and were treated with a singular lack of empathy. Apart from the Christ child, they were rarely depicted in art prior to the sixteenth century, suggesting they were not considered very important. The few pictures that include children portray them as mini adults, implying that the distinctions between children and adults were not great.

Children were not seen to have special needs or rights, and in ancient Greece fathers were permitted to practice infanticide (Durant, 1939). In this context, it is not surprising that children were often used sexually to gratify adults and that boy brothels thrived in Athens from the sixth to fourth centuries B.C. The Greeks rationalized pederasty as a form of education, and Sophocles viewed it as "the cultivation of moral perfection in the beloved" (Tannahill, 1981). Aristotle believed that masturbating boys would hasten their manhood (DeMause, 1974, p. 46). Legislation regulating man-boy relationships emerged in the sixth century B.C. under Solon, who was himself a pederast. He imposed the death penalty for any adult male found (without permission) on the premises of a school for preadolescent boys, and the penalty for soliciting a free boy was loss of civil rights for life (Tannahill, 1981). However, Tannahill suggests that these laws did not act as a deterrent and in fact were often overlooked.

Incest was widely practiced in Persia around the same time and even regarded as highly desirable, although some contend it was primarily a practice of rulers and priests (Masters, 1964). The Romans prohibited incest on the grounds that it would narrow the family's social contacts, but this sanction was often ignored by nobility. In the case of the Emperor Caligula, he had the senators bend the law so as to enable him to marry his niece (Masters, 1964). Under the influence of Christianity, homosexuality began to wane and in 538 A.D., Emperor Justinian declared that homosexuality could be punished by castration followed by public exhibition of the offender (Tannahill, 1981, p. 143).

Infanticide continued to be practiced until the nineteenth century and females were more likely to be killed than males, resulting in a sizable imbalance of males to females (DeMause, 1974). Exposure was a convenient means of getting rid of children who were sickly, deformed, unwanted, or of the "wrong" sex. Killing an infant became a crime in Rome in 374 A.D., although the practice was to continue. Other common abuses of children included selling them or using them as hostages in Babylonian times, sedating them with opium, restraining them in swaddling clothes, and even castrating them. The latter was done by parents in the hope that their children might gain political favor or in order to use their genitals for medicinal or magical purposes. Some castrated boys were favored by pedophiles. The Emperor Constantine passed laws against castration but the practice is said to have grown under his successors (DeMause, 1974, p. 47).

Tuchman (1978) reminds us that in the Middle Ages there were few boundaries between the world of children and adults and that those children who managed to survive to age 7 were then apprenticed out into a world of adult ribaldry and debauchery. Sex play between adults and children was common. Aries (1962) describes how Louis XIII "laughed uproariously when his nanny wiggled his cock" (p. 100) and how at less than one year of age he would delight in doing the same to others and make them kiss his penis. Apparently such fondling was considered harmless and even the queen mother engaged in it and joked with her son saying, "I am holding your spout" (Aries, 1962, p. 101).

Postman (1982) contends that it was not until the sixteenth century that childhood emerged as a distinct phase of development. He credits this to the arrival of the printing press and literacy, which enabled adults to be privy to information not accessible to children, and also to the Jesuits. The latter stressed the notion of childhood innocence, shame, modesty, the need to protect children from adult secrets, and the schooling of children. The Jesuits began to view children with compassion, urged speaking decently to them, ended the practice of children and adults sleeping together, and prohibited familiarity between servants and children (Aries, 1962). As children became literate, the Jesuits also advocated censoring their reading material.

Masters (1964) notes that "Christianity extended its definition of incestuous relationships to preposterous lengths" (p. 27), such that in rural villages where most people were related in some degree, marriage became impossible. Masters feels that this encouraged furtive incest and cites the sharing of wives among brothers unable to find wives of their own. Accusations of incest were also used for political ends to assure imprisonment or execution of one's enemies.

During the Renaissance, homosexuality became "almost an obligatory part of the Greek revival" (Durant, 1953, p. 576). Prostitution also flourished along with the arts in Italy, but in new form with courtesans versed in literature, culture, and manners. Marriages were arranged and some girls betrothed as early as age 3 to be married at age 12. (Early betrothals were a way of guaranteeing virginity.) An unmarried daughter of 15 years was considered a disgrace to her family (Durant, 1953). Adultery was common among both husbands and wives, and it was tolerated. Amidst this climate of promiscuity the clergy freely engaged in incest and orgies. Pope Alexander VI not only seduced his daughter but also is said to have turned the Vatican into a brothel; and Pope John XXII sodomized boys and had sexual relations with some 200 girls, women, and nuns (Masters, 1964).

Although the sexual misuse of children persisted into the eighteenth and nineteenth centuries, children became more valued and, for some, an economic advantage and even objects of conspicuous consumption. John Locke urged abandoning physical punishment in favor of mental constraints (severe punishment was commonly employed in attempt to curb masturbation). Rousseau attacked the persistent practice of swaddling infants and stressed children's innate capacity for reason. High infant mortality continued to be a problem and this, combined with the long-standing practice of farming out children to wet nurses, surely impeded bonding between mother and child. However, in general more attention was paid to children and their education was stressed. Orphanages and foundling homes emerged as alternatives to abandoning or killing children. In 1885 the Society for Prevention of Cruelty to Children was established in England. As in the United States, societies for protecting children were preceded by those protecting animals.

In the nineteenth century, Puritan morality gave way to Victorian ideals, in which courtly love was resurrected and along with it middle-class women's distaste for sex. Concomitantly, prostitution thrived and venereal disease became epidemic. The fear of venereal disease created a great demand for virgin prostitutes. Like present-day prostitutes, these were often innocent young women recruited in railway stations or parks who offered their services for financial reward. Virgin brothels sprang up in London, although more often than not they featured patched-up virgins who were adept at losing their virginity several times a week. Child brothels existed in London during the eighteenth century and featured 14- and 15-year-old girls, some of whom had been sent out by their parents to seek their fortunes. The demand for child prostitutes increased, and it is estimated that in 1869 in one English seaport there were 1,500 child prostitutes at work, at least one-third of whom were under age 13 (Tannahill, 1981, p. 358). There was also a revival of pederasty under a group of poets known as the Uranians who, like their Greek models, argued that they were providing working-class boys with love, protection, and guidance (Tannahill, 1981, p. 360). It was not until 1885 that the English Parliament passed legislation protecting women and children from prostitution and suppressing brothels.

The situation in nineteenth century France was not much better, and according to Bernard (1886), a French physician, between 1827 and 1876 there were 36,176 reported cases of "rape and assaults on the morality" of children 15 years of age and younger. Bernard noted that children as young as 4 years of age were vulnerable to such attacks and that when they occurred "their parents would rather remain silent" (p. 49). Another physician, Brouardel, noted that convicted rapists were often family men and that "sexual assaults are crimes of the home" (1909, p. 8). Tardieu (1857) also commented on the frequency of sexual assaults on young children, in particular fathers abusing their daughters. He countered claims by authorities that children were making up these allegations for material gain; he cited physical findings, the victims' reluctance to tell, physiological effects of the act, and convincing details as all supportive of their allegations. Magnan (1893) was one of the first to describe the behavioral aftereffects of child sexual abuse. He presented a case of a 5-year-old girl who had been sexually assaulted and subsequently became highly eroticized to the point where she was making aggressive sexual advances on adults and ultimately had to be put in an institution for the insane.

Masson (1984) believes that Freud was well aware of the above-mentioned studies by Bernard, Brouardel, and Tardieu when he formulated his theory of premature sexual experiences as an etiological factor in hysteria. Freud stated, "The behavior of patients while they are reproducing these infantile experiences is in every respect incompatible with the assumption that the scenes are anything else than a reality which is being felt with distress and reproduced with greatest reluctance" (Freud, 1896, p. 199). As is well known, Freud later abandoned these ideas in pursuit of his patients' fantasies and the child's desire rather than real life events and the adult's capacity for committing incest. Given the frequency of hysteria, Freud could not fathom the idea that sexual perversions could be that widespread or that fathers (including his own) could have such inclinations (Freud, 1897, p. 5).

In contrast, Freud's colleague and close friend, Ferenczi, held firm to his belief that his patients' reports were "the terrible truth" not fantasy

(Masson, 1984, p. 176). In an eloquent paper presented in 1932 entitled, "Confusion of Tongues between Children and Adults," he described the effects of sexual abuse on the child's psyche. He noted, "The overwhelming power and authority of the adults render them silent: often they are deprived of their senses. Yet that very fear, when it reaches its xenith, forces them automatically to surrender to the will of the aggressor, to anticipate each of his wishes and to submit to them; forgetting themselves entirely to identify totally with the aggressor" (cited in Masson, 1984, p. 298). Ferenczi further noted that the child's relationship with the mother was often not intimate enough to permit her to confide in her or turn to her for help and that if she did the mother might reject her claims as nonsense. Ferenczi also described how the child might attempt to deal with the trauma by developing dissociative symptoms.

Sadly, Ferenczi was ridiculed by his colleagues, including Freud, who could not tolerate his dissension. They accused him of being paranoid and claimed his patients' accounts were mere fairy tales. Clearly, Freud at this point in time had much invested in maintaining his theories and, as stated by Anna Freud, "keeping up the seduction theory would mean to abandon the Oedipus complex, and with it the whole importance of phantasy life, conscious or unconscious phantasy. In fact, I think there would have been no psychoanalysis afterwards" (Masson, 1984, p. 113). The medical community, which had been offended by Freud's earlier seduction theory, readily embraced his new position. Because of his stature, Freud had considerable influence upon members of the medical community. They succeeded in suppressing Ferenczi's paper and even destroyed the proofs. The paper was to lie dormant for 16 years until an English translation was published. Thus, what became a giant step forward in the development of psychoanalysis became a giant step backward for women and children and the ability of professionals to recognize child sexual abuse.

The early twentieth century saw the continued interest in children as evidenced in child labor laws, public education, the child guidance movement, and children's aid societies. Children were no longer viewed as property and the courts began to recognize that children might have interests separate and beyond those of their parents, as was reflected in custody decisions based first on the tender years presumption and later the concept of the child's best interest. Further, the developing fields of child psychiatry and child psychology began to shed new light on children's sexuality and family dynamics. However, it was not until 1974 that laws were passed in the United States mandating the reporting of child abuse.

In summary, we need to look at the history of childhood in order to keep child sexual abuse in perspective. In doing so we realize that the sexual abuse of children has been with us since early mankind and that, until the past century, in most cultures abusive practices that we would not tolerate today were the norm. Although child sexual abuse may not have changed much over the last few thousand years, what has changed is our attitude toward children and sexual abuse: our society has an increased intolerance for sexual abuse and a willingness to tackle the problem.

REFERENCES

Aries, P. (1962). *Centuries of Childhood.* New York: Vintage Books, Random House.

Bernard, P. (1886). Des attentes à la pudeur sur les petites filles. In *Archives d'Anthropologie Criminelle et des Sciences Pénales.* Paris: Masson, p. 49.

Brouardel, P. (1909). *Les Attentes aux Moeurs.* Paris: J.B. Baillière, p. 3.

Brownmiller, S. (1975). *Against Our Will: Men, Women, and Rape.* New York: Simon & Schuster.

DeMause, L. (1974). *The History of Childhood.* New York: Psychotherapy Press.

Disher, A.D. (1984). *Sex in the Bible* (pamphlet). P.O. Box 1203, Winona, MN 55987.

Durant, W. (1939). *The Story of Civilization II: The Life of Greece.* New York: Simon & Schuster.

Durant, W. (1953). *The Story of Civilization V: The Renaissance.* New York: Simon & Schuster.

Edwards, C. (1921). *The Hammurabi Code.* London: Watt.

Freud, S. (1896). The etiology of hysteria. In E. Jones (Ed.), *Collected Papers, Vol. 1.* New York: Basic Books, 1959.

Freud, S. (1897). Letter to Wilhelm Fliess. In E. Jones (Ed.), *The Life and Works of Sigmund Freud, Vol. 2.* New York: Basic Books, 1954-57, p. 5.

Hamilton, E. (1942). *The Greek Myths.* New York: Mentor Books, New American Library.

Ions, V. (1983). *Indian Mythology.* New York: Peter Bedrick Books.

Magnan, V. (1893). *Leçons Cliniques sur les Maladies Mentales.* Paris: 2ème Bureau du Progrès Médical, p. 187.

Masson, J. (1984). *The Assault on Truth: Freud's Suppression of the Seduction Theory.* New York: Farrar, Strauss, & Giroux.

Masters, R.E.L. (1964). *Patterns of Incest.* New York: The Julian Press.

Messer, A. (1969). The Phaedra complex. *Arch. Gen. Psych.,* 21:213-218.

New LaRousse Encyclopedia of Mythology. (1968). Buffalo, NY: Prometheus Books.

Postman, N. (1982). *The Disappearance of Childhood.* New York: Delacorte Press.

Tannahill, R. (1981). *Sex in History.* London: Sphere Books (Abacus).

Tardieu, A. (1857). *Etude Medico-Légale sur les Attentats aux Moeurs.* Weimer: Voight, p. 62.

Tuchman, B. (1978). *A Distant Mirror.* New York: Alfred Knopf.

3

Overview of the Literature on Child Sexual Abuse

Arthur H. Green

PREVALENCE OF SEXUAL ABUSE

The true incidence of sexual abuse and incest is difficult to determine, due to the sensitive nature of the problem. Weinberg (1955) estimated that there was one case of incest per million persons per year in English-speaking countries. In 1972, Ferracuti made a worldwide estimate of between one and five cases per million. However, other investigators produced much higher estimates of incest and sexual abuse as a result of surveying specific populations. C. Landis et al. (1940) surveyed 142 psychiatric patients and determined that 24% of these women had been sexually abused by an adult before puberty. About half of them were abused by a family member. Husain and Chapel (1983) reported that 14% of adolescent girls admitted to a psychiatric hospital were incest victims. Kinsey et al. (1953) also found that 24% of a population of 4,441 women had experienced sexual abuse during childhood. Of these women, 6.5% were victimized by family members, including 1% by a father or stepfather. J. Landis's (1956) survey of 1,028 female college students revealed that 35% had been sexually abused by an adult during childhood and adolescence. Sixteen percent of these women were involved in direct sexual contact with the perpetrators, while the remaining 19% were victims of exhibitionists. A survey by Gagnon (1965) on more extensive data derived from 1,200 women in Kinsey's group indicated that 28% of the population had been sexually abused by an adult before puberty, with 0.6% victimized by fathers or stepfathers. Finkelhor's (1979) survey of 530 female college students documented a 19% incidence of sexual abuse during childhood and adolescence. Nine percent of a population of 266 male students had also been victimized. These surveys were rather consistent in that one-fifth to one-third of adult women reported sexual contact with an adult male as a child.

30

These surveys are somewhat flawed by a sampling bias reflected by predominately white, middle-class populations. A more representative, random sample of 930 adult women in San Francisco was obtained by Russell (1983). She determined that 16% of the women reported at least one experience of intrafamilial sexual abuse before the age of 18 years. Twelve percent of these women had been sexually abused by a relative before 14 years of age. Thirty-one percent of the sample reported at least one experience of sexual abuse by a nonrelative before the age of 18, with 20% of the women reporting victimization by a nonrelative before 14 years of age. When both intrafamilial and extrafamilial child sexual abuse are combined, 38% of the 930 women reported at least one experience of sexual abuse before the age of 18, and 28% reported sexual victimization before the age of 14. A similar type of random survey was carried out by Finkelhor (1984), who interviewed 521 parents in the Boston area who had children between the ages of 6 and 14. These parents had a total of 1,428 children. Four-and-one-half percent of the parents reported that their children had been victims of sexual abuse, while another 4.5% revealed that their children were targets of attempted sexual abuse. About 10% of the reports identified parents or relatives as the perpetrator, while the majority of the children were victims of strangers or acquaintances. The actual incidence of sexual molestation in this population is likely to be higher because many children never disclose their abuse and the parents would be unlikely to report sexual contact initiated by themselves. Fifteen percent of the mothers and 6% of the fathers reported that they themselves had been sexually abused during childhood.

One of the largest and most systematic efforts to collect information on cases of child abuse in the United States was the National Incidence Study carried out in 1979 and 1980. Data on all forms of child maltreatment, including sexual abuse, were gathered from 26 counties within 10 states (National Center for Child Abuse and Neglect, 1981). A total of 652,000 cases of child abuse and neglect were projected in the United States for the year May 1979 through April 1980. Approximately 7% of these cases were of sexual abuse, suggesting that 44,700 cases of sexual abuse were known to professionals during the study year. The National Incidence Study was criticized by Finkelhor and Hotaling (1984) for not including cases of extrafamilial sexual abuse and failing to include unreported cases in the estimate. These researchers project the annual number of new sexual abuse cases to be 150,000 to 200,000, based upon the 1979 census estimate of 60 million children under the age of 18, and a 5% victimization rate by parents and caretakers.

New York State Central Registry for Child Abuse (1983, 1984) reported 4,331 cases of child sexual abuse in 1983, and 6,859 cases in

1984, an increase of 23% in one year. The 6,859 cases of sexual abuse in 1984 represented 8.5% of all cases of child abuse (81,056) for that year.

It is clear that a large discrepancy exists between reporting rates of child sexual abuse and the much higher estimates of victimization obtained from retrospective surveys of adults. This suggests that most cases of child sexual abuse are never reported to public agencies such as child protective services or the police. This is congruent with the low reporting rates in the surveyed populations; i.e., in Russell's (1983) study only 2% of the intrafamilial and 6% of the extrafamilial sexual abuse cases were reported to the police. In the Kinsey-Gagnon survey (Gagnon, 1965), 6% of the cases were reported. In fact, the majority of the victims never tell anybody about their sexual abuse. In Finkelhor's (1979) college student survey, 63% of the females and 73% of the males who had been victimized never told anyone prior to the survey. In Herman's (1981) sample of formerly molested women in psychotherapy, 58% had disclosed their abuse for the first time during their treatment. It would be important to study the differences between "disclosing" and "nondisclosing" victims of child sexual abuse. One might speculate that the unreported cases were the least harmful or violent. On the other hand, it might be argued that the inability to disclose the incest "secret" is associated with a more pathological and unsupportive family structure.

PARTICIPANTS IN FATHER-DAUGHTER INCEST

Fathers

Fathers or stepfathers who sexually abuse the children in their care are difficult to study for numerous reasons. First of all, the majority of these men are never apprehended because of the failure of the child and/or mother to disclose the molestation. Second, even when the incest is disclosed, the child might not be believed or supported by the family, so that a formal report will not be lodged with the child protective services or the police. Finally, if the cases are reported and the father is prosecuted, he is still unlikely to admit the molestation, so that attempts to gather meaningful data directly from sexually abusive fathers and stepfathers is virtually impossible, unless they are incarcerated or participating in a treatment program. Therefore, a good deal of information about these men is derived from their victims and other family members. The following characteristics have been frequently attributed to sexually abusing fathers or stepfathers:

Domineering and tyrannical. The sexually abusing father typically maintains his dominant position in the family through violence or threats. Weinberg (1955), Herman (1981), and Meiselman (1978) described the controlling and intimidating characteristics of these men, who frequently resorted to physical abuse to maintain their power over the family. Paranoid personality traits are often associated with their wishes for domination and control, as described by Cavallin (1966), Raphling, Carpenter, and Davis (1967), and Weinberg (1955). Meiselman reported paranoid thinking in 10 of 13 fathers interviewed by a therapist during a study of 58 women involved in psychotherapy who had been incest victims during childhood.

Alcohol abuse. Alcohol abuse has been frequently cited as a precipitating factor to the incest behavior. Kaufman, Peck, and Tagiuri (1954) diagnosed 73% of incestuous fathers as alcoholics. Cavallin (1966) reported a 33% incidence of alcoholism in incestuous fathers, while Gebhard and colleagues (1965) cited a 25% incidence of alcoholism in fathers imprisoned for sexual relations with prepubertal daughters. Virkkunen (1974) found alcoholism in 48.9% of 45 case reports of incest in Helsinki, Finland. The use of alcohol itself cannot explain incest behavior; however, it may act as an inhibition-releasing influence.

Unstable employment. Unemployment or unstable employment history has been suggested as a major attribute of incestuous fathers by several investigators (Kaufman, Peck, & Tagiuri, 1954; Lukianowicz, 1972; Weinberg, 1955). Other observers have found them to be responsible workers who were often quite successful in their jobs or careers (Herman, 1981; Meiselman, 1978). It is possible that this discrepancy is related to socioeconomic differences among the different study populations, where lower-class perpetrators are more likely to have histories of unemployment or underemployment.

Lower socioeconomic status. There is some evidence that sexual abuse is more prevalent among the lower social classes, although it is amply represented in the middle and upper classes. Sexual abuse cases reported to the National Incidence Study came from families with median incomes of $9,285, 10% higher than families involved in physical abuse and neglect, but considerably lower than the median income for U.S. families ($19,661) in 1979 (National Center for Child Abuse and Neglect, 1981). Gebhard et al. (1965) compared incestuous fathers with other imprisoned sex offenders and demonstrated that economic deprivation is a special characteristic of the incest group. The National Incidence

Study also reported that boys who are sexually abused by fathers and stepfathers come more from lower-income and broken families. In Finkelhor's (1979) college student survey, father-daughter incest was overrepresented in the lower-income families.

Social and physical isolation. Weinberg (1955) described an "endo-gamic" type of incestuous father who is unable to establish gratifying social relationships outside of the family. Should the marital relationship fail to satisfy his sexual need, he will turn toward his children rather than seek out adult extramarital contacts. Many of these men are devoutly religious and moralistic with regard to conventional sexuality, according to Gebhard et al. (1965). Despite their tyrannical façade, they are extremely dependent upon their spouses and fear separation and divorce. The incestuous relationship provides these men with a certain degree of sexual and emotional fulfillment which is otherwise unavailable from their wives, while insuring the intactness of the family. They usually manifest a personality disorder (Meiselman, 1978).

Another type of endogamic incest occurs in socially isolated subcultures, in which physical isolation and increased tolerance to incest tend to create ingrown endogamic families. Riemer (1940) described incestuous fathers in rural areas of Sweden with poor social skills. Summit and Kryso (1978) referred to incest occurring in a "rustic environment" where families accept intrasibling and intragenerational incest as natural practices. Bagley (1969) cited the frequent occurrence of incest in association with polygamy among the nineteenth-century Mormons. Cultural attitudes seem to play a greater role than personality factors in the etiology of this type of incest.

The importance of social and physical isolation as a contributing factor to sexual victimization is supported by Finkelhor's (1979) college student survey, which indicated that incest and sexual abuse were higher in rural areas. The group of girls who spent their childhood on farms demonstrated the highest rates of sexual victimization. These children were over two-and-one-half times more likely than the rest of the sample to have had an incestuous experience.

Sexual deviation. Gebhard and colleagues (1965) described a pathological obsession with sex in incestuous fathers, which expressed itself in excessive sexual fantasy and sexual activity, excessive nudity bordering on exhibitionism, and preoccupation with oral–genital contact. Weinberg (1955) reported that most incestuous fathers went through a period of hypersexuality before initiating incest. Lukianowicz (1972), Shelton

(1975), and Weiner (1962) also cited hypersexual behaviors in incestuous fathers.

Gebhard and colleagues (1965) and Weinberg (1955) maintained that pedophiles constituted a distinct category of incest offenders. However, Meiselman (1978) did not encounter pedophiles among the fathers of her sample of incest victims. She concluded that pedophilia is seldom a factor in father-daughter incest. Groth (1982) made a distinction between "fixated" and "regressed" sexual offenders. The fixated offenders manifest an arrest in their psychosexual development and maintain a primary psychological and sexual interest in young children who are prepubertal. They rarely engage in sexual relationships with peers, and seldom marry. The regressed offenders, on the other hand, primarily focus their sexual interest on agemates. They frequently marry and appear to have adequate relationships with their wives and children. They become sexually attracted to children when their adult relationships become conflictual. According to Groth, the fixated offenders are more likely to victimize boys, while the regressed offenders usually select girl victims. The fixated offenders first manifest their pedophilia during adolescence, while the regressed offenders' pedophilic interests emerge in adulthood and are usually precipitated by stressful events. Groth further subdivides regressed offenders into passive–dependent and aggressive–dominant types. Groth's typology would include some sexually abusing fathers and stepfathers in the category of regressed offenders. He posits an overlap between incest offenders and pedophiles. Abel and colleagues (1981) found that incest offenders were sexually aroused by young children other than their daughters or stepdaughters, and found them similar to heterosexual pedophiles. Finkelhor (1984) would abolish the dichotomy between incest and pedophilia by placing offenders on a continuum regarding (a) the strength of their sexual interest in children and (b) the exclusivity of their sexual interest in children as opposed to adults.

It is likely that there exists a wide variety of incest offenders. They may be differentiated by their preference for boys or girls, use of force, strength and exclusivity of their sexual interest in children, level of adult heterosexual adjustment, and use of alcohol. Most are not psychotic and would fit into the category of personality disorders.

Background of emotional deprivation and physical and sexual victimization. Gebhard and colleagues (1965) compared incestuous fathers with other imprisoned sex offenders and observed that economic deprivation was a special characteristic of the incest group. Emotional deprivation in childhood was cited in the backgrounds of incestuous fathers by Lustig and coworkers (1966) and Weiner (1962). Groth and Burgess (1979) found that 32% of a group of 106 child molesters reported sexual victimization during their childhood compared to 3% of a comparison group of 64 police officers. Langevin and colleagues (1983) found over five times as many childhood sexual abuse incidents in the backgrounds of incest offenders as compared to nonoffender controls. Disturbed parent–child relationships and physical and sexual abuse were also described in the early histories of sexual abusers by Cavallin (1966), Kaufman, Peck, and Tagiuri (1954), Justice and Justice (1979), and Maisch (1972). Meiselman (1978) theorized that the early exposure to sexual victimization forced on these men or members of their families provides an "incestuous model," which teaches that other family members may be used as sexual partners.

Mothers

There has been increasing evidence that mothers play an important role in facilitating the incestuous union between the father/stepfather and daughter. They may be physically or emotionally unavailable to their daughters, which forces them into a greater dependency and intimacy with their fathers. They often ignore evidence of the incest and are frequently incapable of protecting their daughters from their spouses before or even after disclosure of the victimization. Clinical studies of these women reveal several important characteristics:

Background of emotional deprivation. Kaufman, Peck, and Tagiuri (1954) indicated that the mother's relationship with her own mother is often characterized by rejection and hostility. Maisch (1972) reported that 10% of the mothers in his sample spent all or part of their childhood in orphanages. Institutionalization and desertion have been cited by Eist and Mandel (1968) and Lustig and colleagues (1966). These mothers may have been deprived of a sound maternal role model due to the absence of or rejection by their mothers.

Absence or illness. Absence of the mother due to death, desertion, or illness has been described by Meiselman (1978) and Maisch (1972). Finkelhor (1979) reported that girls living without a natural mother in the home were 200% more likely to experience sexual abuse than girls living with their mothers. He also found maternal alcoholism to be a risk factor for incest. Mothers of incest victims were frequently reported to be depressed (Browning & Boatman, 1977; Herman, 1981; Justice & Justice, 1979). Absent mothers and mothers who are physically or emotionally depleted by illness or depression will clearly be unable to protect their daughters from incest or sexual victimization. Such unresponsiveness by the mothers might also increase their daughters' dependency on the father, which, in turn, would make it more difficult for these children to report the incest.

Passivity, dependency, and masochism. The characteristics of passivity, dependency, and masochism have often been cited in the descriptions of the wives of incestuous fathers (Herman, 1981; Lukianowicz, 1972; Meiselman, 1978; Weinberg, 1955). These women are often married to tyrannical and domineering men who behave sadistically toward them. The powerlessness and dependency of these women prevent them from challenging the pathological behavior of their spouses. They are willing to "look the other way" in order to save their marriage.

Aversion to sexuality. Frigidity, denial of sexual relations, and lack of sexual response have been described in mothers of incest victims (Weiner, 1962; Cormier, Kennedy, & Sangowicz, 1962; Lustig et al., 1966; Meiselman, 1978). The sexual unavailability of these mothers may act as a trigger for incestuous behavior in fathers who would prefer to use their children as sexual outlets rather than seek extramarital sexual relationships. Some of these mothers will consciously or unconsciously reverse roles with their daughters, allowing them to assume the role of companion and sexual partner to the father.

Childhood history of physical and/or sexual abuse. Goodwin, McCarthy, and DiVasto (1982) reported that mothers whose children had been abused or neglected were eight times more likely to have had prior incestuous experiences themselves than were women in a comparison group from the general population. Summit and Kryso (1978) also described an extremely high incidence of childhood sexual abuse in mothers seeking help at a child abuse treatment program. Gelinas (1983) described how the former incest victim tends to repeat the incestuous family constellation in which her husband will sexually abuse one or more of their daughters. The repetition of the incest experience is felt to be associated with an untreated traumatic neurosis.

Daughters

The sexual abuse literature has attempted to identify certain characteristics of female incest victims that might play a role in their molestation. Some observers speculated about the degree of compliance

exhibited by some of the victimized daughters. In those studies relying
on retrospective descriptions of the incest, it is often difficult to differentiate the predisposing factors in the child from those resulting
from the trauma.

Age. Most studies indicate that the eldest daughter in the family is
the most vulnerable to incest. Weinberg (1955) reported that 64% of
the incest victims in his sample were the eldest daughters. In most of
the remaining cases, the father attempted incest with the oldest daughter
and then turned his attention to a younger daughter if the oldest
rejected him or left home. Other investigators (Goodwin et al., 1982;
Herman, 1981; Meiselman, 1978) observed a similar predilection for the
oldest or only daughter to be victimized. The incestuous activity typically
begins when the child is between 8 and 12 years old (De Young, 1982;
Goodwin et al., 1982; Herman, 1981). The incest often begins with
genital fondling or oral-genital stimulation and may proceed to intercourse when the child reaches puberty.

Appearance. Female incest victims have frequently been described
as physically attractive by virtue of their good looks or early sexual
development. (Bender & Blau, 1937; Gebhard et al., 1965). Some of
these girls demonstrate "pseudomature" or "little mother" personality
traits (Kaufman, Peck, & Tagiuri, 1954; Rhinehart, 1961). On the other
hand, two recent studies have described a high incidence of physical
disability in their samples of incest victims. Davies (1979) reported
that 77% of a sample of incest victims displayed abnormal EEG results
compared with 5%–30% of children in the general population. Browning
and Boatman (1977) described a significant incidence of physical disability in their population of incest victims. Some daughters may be
promiscuous and play an active role in the sexual relationship (Mrazek
& Kempe, 1981; Weinberg, 1955).

Alienation from the mother. Most investigators agree that the majority of female incest victims experience rejection, hostility, and abandonment at the hands of their mothers, which is likely to result in a
heightened compensatory attachment to their fathers (Herman, 1981;
Meiselman, 1978; Mrazek & Kempe, 1981). The resulting sense of
alienation makes it difficult for the child to report the incest to her
mother. For some of these girls, the incestuous relationship represents
an oedipal triumph over their mothers.

Family Dynamics of Incest

The incestuous family has been universally regarded as disturbed and dysfunctional. A rigid, patriarchal family structure, cloaked in secrecy, is commonly observed, with the father maintaining his dominant position through force and coercion (Herman, 1981; Meiselman, 1978; Swanson & Biaggio, 1985). The marital relationship is unable to satisfy the strong dependency needs of the mother and father, who were often deprived during their own childhood. The family system is closed, and outsiders are often viewed with suspicion. (Sgroi, 1982). Role confusion is common, with the mother delegating her marital and homemaking responsibilities to the daughter (Meiselman, 1978). The father is often given the nurturing, maternal role, but he provides this in a sexual context (Mrazek, Lynch, & Bentovim, 1981). Indeed, the incestuous sexual relationship might be the only source of intimacy and affectionate contact for the child.

Boundaries are not respected in the incestuous family. There is little respect for one's physical space, privacy, and belongings. There is often a lack of modesty concerning nudity and toileting, and poor limit setting (Sgroi, 1982). While the father/perpetrator violates intergenerational boundaries, the mother often fails to protect the child. Denial is a prominent defense mechanism used by all of the family members. The father may rationalize the incest by regarding it as "sex education" for his daughter. The mother is unable to recognize the molestation because this would jeopardize the relationship with her husband. The child fails to perceive the true nature of her behavior through a numbing denial and constriction of affect. Expressing her outrage would threaten the shaky equilibrium of the family.

The child who is enmeshed in the incestuous relationship is unable to develop peer relationships and fails to become adequately socialized. The child may cling to the incestuous relationship because of the special power derived from being the father's favorite, as well as from the fear that the family would disintegrate should he/she abandon the role of the victim. In effect, by meeting the pathological needs of the father, mother, and child, the incest functions to keep the family intact.

The dynamic issues are altered for families headed by a stepfather. The presence of a stepfather increases the risk for sexual molestation, according to Finkelhor (1979) and de Young (1982). The lack of blood ties might weaken the incest barrier. At the same time, role confusion often is present in a newly reconstituted family. The absence of the stepfather's participation in the early physical care of his stepdaughter may interfere with the usual desexualization of parent-child physical contact. The vulnerability of the stepdaughter could be increased by the affective deprivation associated with the loss of her father and her mother's intense preoccupation with a new lover.

The risk factor for sexual abuse in stepfathers is supported in a recent study by Parker and Parker (1986) comparing the involvement of sexually abusing and nonabusing fathers recruited from prisons and mental health facilities in the early socialization of their daughters. The sexually abusing fathers were significantly less involved with the nurturance and care of their daughters than the nonabusing controls during the first three years and were subjected to more maltreatment during childhood. Nonbiological fathers were overrepresented among the sexual abusers, which was related to their more frequent absence from home during their daughters' early years. However, there was no difference in the incidence of sexual abuse among the biological and nonbiological fathers who were home during this period of time. These authors concluded that physical and psychological distance from the female child during the early years increases the probability of sexual abuse by producing a lower threshold for sexual arousal. Under ideal conditions of intense parent-child bonding, the father's heightened familiarity with the child will tend to inhibit his sexual interest. This study strongly suggests that the risk factor for sexual abuse in stepfathers is primarily related to the lack of early parental contact rather than in the "nonbiological" status.

PSYCHOLOGICAL IMPAIRMENT OF CHILD SEXUAL ABUSE VICTIMS

The existing literature on the impact of child sexual abuse and, more specifically, incest has been limited almost entirely to anecdotal clinical material and uncontrolled studies. Some observers (Bender & Blau, 1937; Burton, 1968; Landis, 1956; Rascovsky & Rascovsky, 1950; Yorukoglu & Kemph, 1966) have proposed that sexual exploitation of a child by an adult may not be psychologically damaging, while many others have noted the prevalence of psychological symptoms. While the latter group is constituted by most recent studies of child sexual abuse, methodological deficiencies render the findings confusing and inconclusive. A critical review of the literature reveals: 1) failure to employ comparison or control groups; 2) exceedingly small samples yielding inadequate statistical power; 3) lack of control for psychological impairment antedating any known sexual abuse; 4) confounding independent variables, e.g., physical abuse in addition to sexual abuse; 5) failure to match for the child's age or level of development; 6) use of unstandardized assessment instruments; and 7) lack of discrimination between acute and long-term psychological sequelae.

Despite a lack of methodological rigor reminiscent of the early child physical abuse literature, some consensus exists concerning immediate effects and two dimensions of long-term psychological impairment including general psychopathology and sexual behavior.

Short-term Effects

A rather consistent pattern of fearfulness and anxiety-related symptoms has been described in sexually abused children. Sleep disturbances, insomnia, and nightmares have been cited by Lewis and Sarrell (1969), Sgroi (1982), and Kempe and Kempe (1978). Somatic complaints and psychosomatic disorders were frequently observed (Adams-Tucker, 1982; Browning & Boatman, 1977; Lewis & Sarrell, 1969). Sgroi (1982) described fear reactions of sexual abuse victims extending to phobic avoidance of all males. These children also were afraid of physical injury as a consequence of sexual contact and feared retaliation by the perpetrators.

The degree of traumatization will be influenced by the age of the child, the extent of threats, coercion, or force, and concomitant physical injury. Severe traumatization can produce a full-blown post-traumatic stress disorder (to be described in the next section on long-term sequelae).

Long-term Sequelae

General psychopathology

Mistrust. Herman (1981), Knittle and Tuana (1980), and Sgroi (1982) have described the inability of sexually abused children to establish trusting relationships with adults. Their achievement of basic trust is compromised by the father's breach of his parental role and may be compounded by the mother's denial or failure to protect the child from incestuous activity. The child can no longer look to her parents for support and self-validation. Through the process of generalization, other adults and potential love objects might be considered untrustworthy and unpredictable.

Poor self-image. Sgroi (1982) refers to the "damaged goods" syndrome in which the sexually abused child feels physically damaged or altered by the sexual encounter. This is reinforced by critical and hostile responses from individuals in the environment. Sgroi also described reactions of shame and guilt in sexually abused children, as first noted by Sloane and Karpinski (1942). Shame and guilt are likely to be exacerbated when the child experiences sexual pleasure, which is heightened by gratification of phase-specific sexual fantasies. The child's fragile self-esteem is further eroded.

Depression. Depressive symptoms have been observed in sexually abused children by Kempe and Kempe (1978), Nakashima and Zakins (1977), Sgroi (1982) and Rosenfeld and colleagues (1977). McVicar (1979) indicated that adolescent sexual abuse victims were more vulnerable to depression than those of latency age. Nakashima and Zakins (1977), Kaufman, Peck, and Tagiuri (1954), and Lukianowicz (1972) described suicidal behavior in sexually abused adolescents, while Anderson (1981) reported case histories of four adolescent girls who attempted suicide following the disclosure of incest.

Hysterical symptoms and character traits. These have been noted by Rosenfeld (1979), Goodwin and colleagues (1982), and Lukianowicz (1972), while Gross (1979) found a prevalence of hysterical seizures in adolescent girls as a sequel to incest. Hysterical symptoms might represent the child's attempt to "wall off" traumatic impressions of the incest through primitive defenses such as denial, isolation of affect, and splitting. The most extreme dissociative reactions may result in multiple personality disorder. In fact, sexual and physical abuse are the most frequent antecedents to multiple personality (Kluft, 1985; Putnam, 1984).

Social withdrawal and impaired peer relations. Tsai and Wagner (1981), Adams-Tucker (1982), and Knittle and Tuana (1980) reported inadequate social skills, difficulties in interpersonal relationships, and social withdrawal in young sexual abuse victims. Sgroi (1982) described how incestuous families discourage separation–individuation of the target child and the attainment of peer relationships.

Impairment of body image. Sgroi (1982) also described the fear of physical damage present in sexually abused children, particularly in those cases where actual injury occurred. These children were preoccupied with concerns about permanent damage to their bodies and fears that they would be unable to experience normal sex lives and have babies in the future. Complications such as pregnancy or venereal disease as a result of incest further aggravate distorted bodily perceptions.

Poor school performance. Sudden drops in school performance have been observed by DeFrancis (1969), Goodwin and colleagues (1982),

Kaufman, Peck, and Tagiuri (1954), and Sgroi (1982). The sexually abused child might experience difficulty concentrating in the classroom due to preoccupation with the incest and family tensions. Social withdrawal extended to the school setting can progress to school refusal, while anxiety and guilt can lead to impulsive, acting-out behavior in the classroom.

Post-traumatic stress disorder (PTSD). Goodwin (1985) maintains that most incest victims who request treatment meet the criteria for PTSD, i.e., fear, startle reactions, anxiety, repetition, reenactment of or flashback to the trauma, sleep disturbance and depressive symptoms, ego constriction or regression, and explosive and maladaptive expressions of anger. These symptoms were first described in Kardiner's (1941) original studies of shell-shocked combat veterans. Goodwin (1985) also compared incest victims with rape victims afflicted with PTSD. However, she considers the symptoms in incest victims more severe and longer lasting because these children experience more numerous sexual assaults over a longer period of time.

Chronic or delayed PTSD may occur in adults who have been sexually molested during childhood. These men or women often seek psychiatric treatment for depression, sleep disturbance, and sexual or relationship problems. In the course of their therapy, they often appreciate for the first time the link between their current symptoms and prior victimization. Lindberg and Distad (1985) studied 17 adult women who entered individual therapy an average of 17 years after experiencing incest during childhood. They manifested such symptoms as intrusive imagery of the incest, feelings of detachment or constricted affect, sleep disturbance, guilt, and intensification of symptoms when exposed to events resembling the incest trauma. As a result, 16 of the 17 women experienced varying degrees of sexual dysfunction as adults.

Gelinas (1983) attributed the persisting negative effects of incest to a chronic traumatic neurosis. She described typical symptoms of denial alternating with repetitive intrusions of the traumatic experience, such as nightmares, hallucinations, and behavioral reenactments. Additional symptoms such as depression, impulsivity, and dissociative elements may also be present. Adult sexual behavior often triggers psychiatric symptoms because of its relationship to the prior incest experience.

Van der Kolk (1987) conceptualized a psychobiology of PTSD based on the animal model of inescapable shock. According to his theory, inescapable stress depletes norepinephrine (NE) and dopamine, which renders NE receptors hypersensitive to NE stimulation.

Kolb (1987) postulates that excessive stress and stimulus overload lead to synaptic changes in cortical neurones, leading to intense emotional arousal, which in turn disrupt learning and habituation, resulting in an intensification of symptoms. *Primary symptoms,* due to cortical neuronal change, are impairment of perceptual discrimination, poor impulse control, and increased sensitivity to external cues associated with the traumatic event. *Constant symptoms,* or "symptoms of release," are due to excessive activation of noradrenergic pathways which produce startle reactions, hyperalertness, intrusive thinking, nightmares, and psychophysiological symptoms of palpitations, nausea, vomiting, and diarrhea. *Reactive symptoms,* which present as social withdrawal and distancing behaviors, compulsive behaviors, and substance abuse, are defensive attempts to restore the body image and sense of self.

Drugs can reduce autonomic arousal at different levels in the nervous system. By inhibiting noradrenergic activity, clonidine, which blocks alpha-two receptors in the locus ceruleus, has been useful in reducing startle responses, explosiveness, intrusive reexperiencing, and nightmares. Beta-blockers, such as propranolol, have a selective sympatholytic action on the peripheral nervous system that reduces symptoms of anxiety.

Borderline personality disorder. Stone (1981) reported that a history of incest was common in adult patients with borderline personality disorder, particularly in females hospitalized for this condition. Stone and colleagues (1987) documented histories of childhood incest in 36% and 41% of recently hospitalized female patients diagnosed with borderline personality disorder in New York and Brisbane, Australia, respectively. Herman and van der Kolk (1987) attributed the higher incidence of borderline personality disorder in females to the more widespread sexual victimization of girls. They postulate that early experiences of violence occurring within the developing child's system of primary attachments may produce both psychological and psychophysiological disorders. These authors also cite the frequent history of physical abuse in the childhood of adult borderlines.

Disturbances in sexual behavior and gender role

On purely logical grounds, one would anticipate incestuous experiences to have an adverse impact on subsequent sexual functioning; therefore, it is not surprising that this finding is reported in many studies. Frigidity and promiscuity (Kempe & Kempe, 1978; Lukianowicz, 1972; Rosenfeld et al., 1977) are frequently noted, while Kempe and Kempe regarded incest as a training ground for prostitution. This hypothesis was corroborated by James and Meyerding (1977) in a retrospective study of adult female prostitutes. Thirty-six percent reported childhood incestuous experiences.

MacVicar (1979) described compulsive masturbation in several sexually abused girls of latency age and cited promiscuity as a common feature in adolescent victims. The latter often sought partners who resembled the original perpetrator. Two girls in MacVicar's sample engaged in homosexual fantasies and activities as a means of avoiding conflicts with men. Browning and Boatman (1977), Carper (1979), and Sloane and Karpinski (1942) hypothesized that the high incidence of promiscuity among incest victims represented the acting out of conflicts in lieu of the development of neurotic symptoms.

Yates (1982) described the eroticization of preschool children by incest, with the degree of eroticization proportional to the duration and intensity of the incestuous relationship. These young children were readily orgastic and/or maintained a high level of sexual arousal. Their highly cathected focus on sexual learning detracted from social learning. Many failed to differentiate affectionate relationships from sexual relationships and became aroused by routine physical or psychological closeness.

Brant and Tisza (1977) speculated that sexually abused children could be at risk for repeated sexual misuse. They maintained that these children provoked further sexual contact as a vehicle for obtaining pleasure and need satisfaction and as a means of mastering the original trauma. Katan's (1973) psychoanalytic treatment of six women who had been raped during childhood cited their tendency to repeat the traumatic events with adult partners or through their own children. Miller et al. (1978) demonstrated the vulnerability of incest victims to rape as adults, with a recidivist group reporting a significantly higher incidence of childhood sexual abuse.

At the other end of the spectrum are studies citing phobic reactions and sexual inhibition as long-term sequelae to incest. Alexander (1980) described the group therapy experiences of adult women who had been childhood incest victims. These women were unable to achieve fulfilling relationships with adults of either sex. Their marriages were unhappy, sexual pleasure was unobtainable, and intercourse typically avoided. Tsai et al. (1979) related the degree of sexual inhibition with the age, frequency, and duration of molestation and associated negative affects.

In essence, two contrasting adaptive styles in sexually abused children have been described in the literature: one seeking mastery through active repetition of the trauma, the other coping by avoidance of sexual stimuli.

CURRENT RESEARCH IN CHILD SEXUAL ABUSE

More systematic, controlled research designed to assess etiological factors, relevant demographic factors, and immediate and long-term effects of child sexual abuse is desperately needed in order to design syndrome-specific interventions for the growing numbers of sexual abuse victims. Some recent research along these lines will be described below.

Fish-Murray, Koby, and van der Kolk (1987) demonstrated that sexually and/or physically abused children between ages 6 and 11 lagged behind nontraumatized controls in intellectual and emotional development. The sexually/physically abused children were inferior in logical/operational thinking, they were impaired in their knowledge of self and others, their use of signs and symbols was infringed upon by the trauma, and they were impaired in their ability to accommodate or self-correct to stories elicited by the Thematic Apperception Test (TAT).

Gomes-Schwartz, Horowitz, and Sauzier (1985) assessed levels of emotional distress in 156 sexually abused children evaluated and treated at an outpatient treatment program over a two-year period. The children ranged in age between 4 and 18. The emotional distress was measured by the Louisville Behavior Checklist. The sample consisted of 78% girls and 22% boys. The scores of the sexually abused sample were compared to normative data for the general population and to norms for a child psychiatry clinic population. The sexually abused children were divided into preschool (ages 4 to 6), school age (ages 7 to 13), and adolescent groups (ages 14 to 18). Only 17% of the preschoolers met the criteria for clinically significant psychopathology, 20% demonstrated serious deficits in intellectual, physical, and social development, and 20% displayed severe anxieties, fears, or depression. As a group, the sexually abused preschool children manifested more behavioral problems than their normal peers but fewer behavioral problems than psychologically disturbed clinic children. The sexually abused school-age children manifested more signs of clinically significant pathology than did the sexually abused preschool children. Overall, 40% of the school-age youngsters were seriously disturbed in one or more areas of functioning. Common symptom patterns included angry destructive behavior, phobic reactions, neurotic behavior, and immaturity, but they were less disturbed than the child psychiatry clinic population. Twenty-four percent of the sexually abused adolescents showed clinically significant pathology on the neuroticism scale, which measures anxiety, depression, and obsessive concerns, and 21% displayed such pathology on the dependent–inhibited scale. These adolescents showed less pathology than the adolescents in the clinic population.

The relatively low proportions of preschool children having serious behavioral problems was attributed to their inability to comprehend the sexual nature of the experience. The more severe psychological difficulties in the 7-to-13-year-old group was explained by their greater awareness of the meaning of the sexual approaches. The fact that few adolescents exhibited severe psychopathology was felt to be a consequence of their greater ability to cognitively process the experience. An alternative explanation was the possibility that many of the more disturbed adolescents might have been placed in mental health, corrections, or social welfare institutions and, therefore, would have been less likely to reach an outpatient treatment program.

For children of all ages, the greater the violence associated with abuse, the more signs of emotional distress were exhibited. Children who had suffered physical injuries during the sexual abuse were more likely to exhibit behavioral problems in all of the areas measured by the Louisville scales. This study failed to find any relationship between the duration of abuse or the age at onset of abuse with subsequent psychopathology. A follow-up study of the entire sample 18 months later indicated that the children who were initially most disturbed were more likely to show improvement, while the children who were initially asymptomatic demonstrated more problems on follow-up. The rates of improvement were most dramatic for signs of anxiety such as sleep problems, nervousness, irritability, and signs of inner tension.

Conte and Schuerman (1987) studied 369 sexually abused children and compared them with controls. Again, the abused children fell between normal and emotionally disturbed children in terms of the psychopathology seen on a parent-completed behavior rating scale. Victims having supportive relationships with nonoffending adults or siblings were less affected, while victims living in more problematic families fared more poorly.

Tsai, Feldman-Summers, and Edgar (1979) examined factors contributing to the differential adjustment of women who were sexually molested as children. Three groups of 30 women each participated in the study: a clinical group consisting of women seeking therapy for problems associated with the molestation, a nonclinical group consisting of women molested as children who never sought therapy and considered themselves well adjusted, and a control group of women who had not been molested. The results indicated that the clinical group was significantly less well adjusted than either the nonclinical or control group on measures of psychosocial functioning and the MMPI. In addition, the women in the clinical group were significantly older at the time of their last molestation (mean age of 12 versus 9), and were more frequently molested for a longer duration of time (mean of 4.7 versus 2.5 years) than the nonclinical group. The clinical women also reported more negative feelings toward the molester, more painful responses and guilt during the molestation, and more coercion and pressure from the molester to maintain secrecy. The clinical women were more frequently victims of vaginal intercourse (70%) than women in the nonclinical group. The clinical women also displayed more disturbance in their current sexual adjustment. They reported less frequent orgasms during intercourse, a greater number of sexual partners, and less satisfaction with sexual relations than the nonclinical and control women. The limitations of this study are due to its inability to infer a causal relationship between the molestation variables and current psychological and sexual dysfunction, which may have been caused by pre- or post-molestation events. In addition, both groups of molested women were recruited by media advertisements and might not be representative of molested women in general.

A similar retrospective study by Herman, Russell, and Trocki (1986) compared the long-term impact of childhood incest on a sample of 53 women receiving outpatient therapy for their victimization and a non-clinical sample of 152 whose previous molestation was identified by a community survey. All of the women in the patient sample reported considerable or severe long-term effects from the incest, while only half of the victims in the community sample perceived long-term sequelae, such as negative feelings about men, sex, or themselves, anxiety, distrust, difficulty forming or maintaining intimate relationships, and sexual problems. The community subjects' perception of lasting harm was significantly associated with abuse experiences that had been forceful or violent, including vaginal, anal, or oral penetration, or had occurred over a prolonged period of time. Greater distress was correlated with a greater age difference between victim and perpetrator. Victimization by a father or stepfather was more likely to produce severe and long-lasting effects.

Bagley and McDonald (1984) conducted a follow-up study of 57 girls who were removed from home in childhood because of abuse, neglect, or family breakdown. Twenty of the girls experienced sexual abuse within the family before the age of 14. Eighteen of the girls were physically abused or neglected, and 19 were not maltreated. These maternally separated girls were compared with 30 normal controls. The subjects completed the Middlesex Hospital Questionnaire, which measures psychoneurosis (anxiety, phobia, depression, and obsessionality), a short version of the Coopersmith Self-Esteem Inventory, and Hudson's measure of psychosexual adjustment. A multiple regression analysis revealed that sexual abuse was the strongest predictor of impaired sexual adjustment, depression, and low self-esteem. Twenty-five percent of the sexually abused females made a suicidal gesture or attempt, while only 5% of the non-sexually abused separated children were suicidal. Fifty-five percent of the sexually abused girls had experienced beatings at the hands of a boyfriend, husband, or pimp, compared with 8% of the early separated nonabused group. The women who had been physically abused and neglected during childhood demonstrated higher scores for psychoneurosis than their sexually abused peers.

THEORETICAL ASPECTS OF TRAUMA IN SEXUAL ABUSE

Finkelhor and Browne (1986) proposed a model to explain the traumatic effects of sexual abuse. They identified four trauma-causing or "traumagenic" factors: traumatic sexualization, powerlessness, stigmatization, and betrayal.

Traumatic sexualization occurs through the sexual stimulation and reinforcement of the child's sexual response so that the child learns to use sexual behavior to gratify a variety of nonsexual needs. This leads to inappropriate and premature sexual activity, the misperception of sexual self-concept, and deviant patterns of sexual arousal.

Powerlessness refers to helplessness occurring during the sexual assault and the child's inability to stop it, leading to fear and anxiety.

Stigmatization describes the victim's sense of being "damaged" and blamed for the molestation, which is reinforced by peers and family members. This leads to shame, guilt, and low self-esteem, analogous to the concept of "scapegoating" in the literature on child physical abuse.

Betrayal occurs when the victim experiences cruelty and disregard at the hands of a trusted caretaker from whom love and protection are expected. Betrayal by a physically or sexually assaultive parent may lead to disillusionment, distrust of others, hostility, and anger.

This "traumagenic" model appears to be a useful tool in organizing our understanding of the impact of sexual abuse. This model might also be applied toward intervention and research in the field. Finkelhor and Browne did not differentiate acute and chronic stressors among the four factors. They emphasized the overdetermined relationships between the traumatic components of sexual abuse and the resulting symptoms, i.e., depression might be derived from a combination of stigmatization, betrayal, and helplessness.

It would be important to add a temporal perspective to the traumagenic model in order to explain the development of immediate and long-term sequelae. Child sexual abuse might be regarded as a periodic infliction of intense, overwhelming sexual and aggressive stimulation which is superimposed upon a chronic background of pathological family interaction, including stigmatization, betrayal, role reversal, chronic sexualization and seductiveness, and invasion of psychological and physical boundaries. The acute sexual assault, including traumatic sexualization and powerlessness, would produce fearfulness and anxiety-related symptoms such as nightmares, sleep disorders, hypervigilance, PTSD, and psychosomatic symptoms and dissociative responses. The underlying long-term family dysfunction, producing stigmatization and betrayal, would give rise to guilt, shame, low self-esteem, mistrust, paranoid symptoms, and pathological defenses. Disturbances in sexual behavior and gender identity might stem from the traumatic sexualization occurring in both the acute molestation and the chronic sexual overstimulation by the family. The tendency to actively or passively reenact or re-create the sexual encounter might be similarly derived from acute (PTSD) and long-term (identification with the aggressor) traumatic elements. The interaction between these acute and long-term variables is likely to potentiate their pathological impact. Differentiating the acute and chronic traumatic elements is consistent with psychoanalytic theories of shock and cumulative trauma.

Severity of both acute and long-term symptoms would vary as a function of the following: 1) age and developmental level of the child; 2) onset, duration, and frequency of the abuse; 3) degree of coercion and physical trauma; 4) relationship between the child and perpetrator; 5) child's preexisting personality; 6) familial response to disclosure; 7) institutional response; and 8) therapeutic intervention.

SUMMARY

Despite the relatively recent and often flawed clinical exploration of the child sexual abuse syndrome, a tentative but nevertheless compelling body of knowledge has been compiled in this area. Some consensus has been reached regarding the pathological characteristics of the participants in incest and their deviant family interaction. Our current knowledge of child sexual abuse has been largely based upon cases reported to child protective services or law enforcement agencies. The degree of impairment of these children ranges from slight to severe. The surprisingly high incidence of child sexual abuse among college students and randomly selected adults suggests, however, that most cases are never detected and remain untreated. When treated and untreated/unreported adult female victims of child sexual abuse were compared (Tsai, Feldman-Summers, & Edgar, 1979; Herman, Russell, & Trocki,

1986), the "clinical" population had experienced more frequent and longer-lasting molestation and exhibited more severe psychological impairment than their nonpatient peers. This suggests heterogeneity within the phenomenon of child sexual abuse with a continuum ranging from infrequent, more gentle fondling to more coercive and invasive sexual penetration in which lasting sequelae might be directly proportional to the severity and duration of the sexual contact.

A theoretical model for the pathogenesis of child sexual abuse as suggested by Finkelhor and Browne (1986) is described with some modification to reflect the interplay between immediate and long-term traumatic elements. Some examples of relevant research in this area have been described. However, it is obvious that research in child sexual abuse outcome is in its infancy, compared to the more rapid development of techniques for identification, reporting, and assessment. Clearly, more sophisticated and methodologically rigorous research is needed in order to design more logical intervention strategies.

REFERENCES

Abel, G., Becker, J., Murphy, W., & Flanagan, B. (1981). Identifying dangerous child molesters. In R.B. Stuart (Ed.), *Violent Behavior*. New York: Brunner/Mazel.

Adams-Tucker, C. (1982). Proximate effects of sexual abuse in childhood: A report on 28 children. *Amer. J. Psychiat.*, 139:1252-1256.

Alexander, H. (1980). Personal communication.

Anderson, L. (1981). Notes on the linkage between the sexually abused child and the suicidal adolescent. *Journal of Adolescence*, 4:157-162.

Bagley, C. (1969). Incest behavior and incest taboo. *Social Problems*, 16:505-519.

Bagley, C., & McDonald, M. (1984). Adult mental health sequelae of child sexual abuse, physical abuse, and neglect in maternally separated children. *Canadian Journal of Community Mental Health*, 3:15-26.

Bender, L., & Blau, A. (1937). The reaction of children to sexual relations with adults. *Amer. J. Orthopsychiat.*, 7:500-518.

Brant, R., & Tisza, V. (1977). The sexually misused child. *Amer. J. Orthopsychiat.*, 47:80-90.

Browning, D., & Boatman, B. (1977). Incest: Children at risk. *Amer. J. Psychiat.*, 134:69-72.

Burton, L. (1968). *Vulnerable Children*. New York: Schocken Books.

Carper, J. (1979). Emergencies in adolescents: Runaways and father-daughter incest. *Pediat. Clin. North Amer.*, 26:883-893.

Cavallin, H. (1966). Incestuous fathers: A clinical report. *Amer. J. Psychiat.*, 122:1132-1138.

Conte, J., & Schuerman, J. (1987). Factors associated with an increased impact of child sexual abuse. *Child Abuse and Neglect*, 11:201-211.

Cormier, B., Kennedy, M., & Sangowicz, J. (1962). Psychodynamics of father-daughter incest. *Canadian Psychiatric Assn. Journal*, 7:203-217.

Davies, R. (1979). Some neuropsychiatric findings. *The International Journal of Psychiatry in Medicine*, 9:115-121.

DeFrancis, V. (1969). *Protecting the Child Victim of Sex Crimes Committed by Adults*. Denver: American Humane Association.

De Young, M. (1982). *The Sexual Victimization of Children*. Jefferson, N.C.: McFarland.

Eist, H., & Mandel, A. (1968). Family treatment of ongoing incest behavior. *Family Process*, 7:216-232.

Ferracuti, F. (1972). Incest between father and daughter. In H. Resnick & M. Wolfgang (Eds.), *Sexual Behaviors: Sexual, Clinical, and Legal Aspects*. Boston: Little, Brown.

Finkelhor, D. (1979). *Sexually Victimized Children*. New York: Free Press.

Finkelhor, D. (1984). *Child Sexual Abuse: New Theory and Research*. New York: Free Press.

Finkelhor, D., & Browne, A. (1986). Initial and long-term effects: A conceptual framework. In D. Finkelhor (Ed.), *Sourcebook on Child Sexual Abuse*. Beverly Hills: Sage Publications.

Finkelhor, D., & Hotaling, G. (1984). Sexual abuse in the national incidence study of child abuse and neglect. *Child Abuse and Neglect*, 8:22-32.

Fish-Murray, C., Koby, E., & van der Kolk, B. (1987). Evolving ideas: The effect of abuse on children's thought. In B. van der Kolk (Ed.), *Psychological Trauma*. Washington, D.C.: American Psychiatric Press.

Gagnon, J. (1965). Female child victims of sex offenses. *Social Problems*, 23:176-192.

Gebhard, P., Gagnon, J., Pomeroy, W., & Christenson, C. (1965). *Sex Offenders: An Analysis of Types*. New York: Harper & Row.

Gelinas, D. (1983). The persisting negative effects of incest. *Psychiatry*, 46:312-332.

Gomes-Schwartz, B., Horowitz, J., & Sauzier, M. (1985). Severity of emotional distress among sexually abused preschool, school-age and adolescent children. *Hosp. & Comm. Psychiatry*, 36:503-508.

Goodwin, J. (1985). Post-traumatic symptoms in incest victims. In S. Eth & R. Pynoos (Eds.), *Post-Traumatic Stress Disorder in Children*. Washington, D.C.: American Psychiatric Press.

Goodwin, J., McCarthy, T., & DiVasto, P. (1982). Physical and sexual abuse of the children of adult incest victims. In J. Goodwin (Ed.), *Sexual Abuse: Incest Victims and their Families*. Boston: John Wright-PSC.

Groth, A.N. (1982). The incest offender. In S. Sgroi (Ed.), *Handbook of Clinical Intervention in Child Sexual Abuse*. Lexington, MA: Lexington Books.

Groth, A.N., & Burgess, A. (1979). Sexual trauma in the life histories of rapists and child molesters. *Victimology: An International Journal*, 4:10-16.

Gross, M. (1979). Incestuous rape: A cause for hysterical seizures in four adolescent girls. *Amer. J. Orthopsychiat.*, 49:704-708.

Herman, J. (1981). *Father-Daughter Incest*. Cambridge: Harvard University Press.

Herman, J. & van der Kolk, B. (1987). Traumatic antecedents of borderline personality disorder. In B. van der Kolk (Ed.), *Psychological Trauma*. Washington, D.C.: American Psychiatric Press.

Herman, J., Russell, D., & Trocki, K. (1986). Long-term effects of incestuous abuse in childhood. *Amer. J. Psychiat.*, 143:1293-1296.

Husain, A., & Chapel, J. (1983). History of incest in girls admitted to a psychiatric hospital. *Amer. J. Psychiat.*, 140:591-593.

James, J., & Meyerding, J. (1977). Early sexual experiences as a factor in prostitution. *Amer. J. Psychiat.*, 134:1381–1385.

Justice, B., & Justice, R. (1979). *The Broken Taboo.* New York: Human Sciences Press.

Kardiner, A. (1941). The traumatic neuroses of war. In S. Arieti (Ed.), *American Handbook of Psychiatry*, Vol. I. New York: Basic Books.

Katan, A. (1973). Children who were raped. In *The Psychoanalytic Study of the Child*, 28:208–224. New Haven & London: Yale University Press.

Kaufman, I., Peck, A., & Tagiuri, L. (1954). The family constellation and overt incestuous relations between father and daughter. *Amer. J. Orthopsychiat.*, 24:266–279.

Kempe, R., & Kempe, C. (1978). *Child Abuse.* Cambridge: Harvard University Press.

Kinsey, A., Pomeroy, W., Martin, C., & Gebhard, P. (1953). *Sexual Behavior in the Human Female.* Philadelphia: W.B. Saunders.

Kluft, R. (1985). *Childhood Antecedents of Multiple Personality.* Washington, D.C.: American Psychiatric Press.

Knittle, B., & Tuana, S. (1980). Group therapy as primary treatment for adolescent victims of intrafamilial sexual abuse. *Clinical Social Work Journal*, 8:236–242, 1980.

Kolb, L. (1987). A neuropsychological hypothesis explaining post-traumatic stress disorders. *Amer. J. Psychiat.*, 144:989–995.

Landis, C., Landis, A., Bolles, M., Metzger, H., Pitts, M., D'Esopo, D., Moloy, H., Kleegman, S., & Dickenson, R. (1940). *Sex in Development.* New York: Paul B. Hoebert.

Landis, J. (1956). Experiences of 500 children with adult sexual deviants. *Psychiat. Quart. Supplement*, 30:91–109.

Langevin, R., Handy, L., Hook, H., Day, D., & Russon, A. (1983). Are incestuous fathers pedophilic and aggressive? In R. Langevin (Ed.), *Erotic Preference, Gender Identity and Aggression.* New York: Erlbaum Associates.

Lewis, M., & Sarrell, P. (1969). Some psychological aspects of seduction, incest and rape in childhood. *J. Amer. Academy Child Psychiat.*, 8:606–619.

Lindberg, F., & Distad, L. (1985). Post-traumatic stress disorders in women who experienced childhood incest. *Child Abuse & Neglect*, 9:329–334.

Lukianowicz, N. (1972). Incest. *British J. Psychiat.*, 120:301–313.

Lustig, N., Dresser, J., Spellman, S., & Murray, T. (1966). Incest. *Archives of Gen. Psychol.*, 14:31–40.

Maisch, H. (1972). *Incest.* New York: Stein and Day.

MacVicar, K. (1979). Psychotherapy of sexually abused girls. *J. Amer. Acad. Child Psychiat.*, 18:342–353.

Meiselman, K. (1978). *Incest: A Psychological Study of Causes and Effects with Treatment Recommendations.* San Francisco: Jossey-Bass.

Miller, J., Moeller, R., Kaufman, A., DiVasto, P., Pathak, D., & Christy, J. (1978). Recidivism among sex assault victims. *Amer. J. Psychiat.*, 135:1103–1104.

Mrazek, P., & Kempe, H. (1981). *Sexually Abused Children and their Families.* New York: Pergamon Press.

Mrazek, P., Lynch, M., & Bentovim, A. (1981). Recognition of child sexual abuse in the United Kingdom. In P. Mrazek & H. Kempe (Eds.), *Sexually Abused Children and their Families.* New York: Pergamon Press.

Nakashima, I., & Zakins, G. (1977). Incest: Review and clinical experience. *Pediatrics*, 60:696–701.

National Center for Child Abuse and Neglect (NCCAN). (1981). Study findings: National study of incidence and severity of child abuse and neglect. Washington, D.C.: DHEW.

New York State Central Registry for Child Abuse (1983).

New York State Central Registry for Child Abuse (1984).

Parker, H., & Parker, S. (1986). Father-daughter sexual abuse: An emerging perspective. *Amer. J. Orthopsychiat.*, 56:531-549.

Putnam, F. (1984). The psychophysiologic investigation of multiple personality disorder. *Psychiat. Clin. North America*, 7:31-40.

Raphling, D., Carpenter, B., & Davis, A. (1967). Incest: A geneological study. *Arch. Gen. Psychiat.*, 16:505-511.

Rascovsky, M., & Rascovsky, A. (1950). On consummated incest. *Int. J. Psychoanal.*, 31: 42-47.

Rhinehart, J. (1961). Genesis of overt incest. *Comprehensive Psychiatry*, 2:338-349.

Riemer, S. (1940). A research note on incest. *American Journal of Sociology*, 45:566-575.

Rosenfeld, A. (1979). Incidence of a history of incest among 18 female psychiatric patients. *Amer. J. Psychiat.*, 136:791-795.

Rosenfeld, A., Nadelson, C., Kreiger, M., & Backman, J. (1977). Incest and sexual abuse of children. *J. Amer. Acad. Child Psychiat.*, 16:327-339.

Russell, D. (1983). Incidence and prevalence of intrafamilial and extrafamilial sexual abuse of female children. *Child Abuse and Neglect*, 7:133-146.

Sgroi, S. (1982). *Handbook of Clinical Intervention in Child Sexual Abuse.* Lexington, MA: Lexington Books.

Shelton, W. (1975). A study of incest. *Int. J. of Offender Therapy and Comparative Criminology*, 19:139-153.

Sloane, P., & Karpinski, F. (1942). Effects of incest on participants. *Amer. J. Orthopsychiat.*, 12:666-673.

Stone, M. (1981). Borderline syndromes: A consideration of subtypes and an overview, directions for research. *Psychiatr. Clin. North Amer.*, 4:3-13.

Stone, M., Unwin, A., Beacham, B., & Swenson, C. (1987, in press). Incest in female borderlines: Its frequency and impact. *Journal of Personality Disorders.*

Summit, R., & Kryso, J. (1978). Sexual abuse of children: A clinical spectrum. *Amer. J. Orthopsychiat.*, 48:237-251.

Swanson, L., & Biaggio, M. (1985). Therapeutic perspectives on father-daughter incest. *Amer. J. Psychiat.*, 142:667-674.

Tsai, M., Feldman-Summers, S., & Edgar, M. (1979). Childhood molestation: Variables related to differential impacts on psychosexual functioning in adult women. *J. Abnormal Psychology*, 88:407-417.

Tsai, M., & Wagner, N. (1981). Incest and molestation: Problems of childhood sexuality. *Medical Times* (Special Section), 16-22.

van der Kolk, B.A. (1987). *Psychological Trauma.* Washington, DC: American Psychiatric Press.

Virkkunen, M. (1974). Incest offenses and alcoholism. *Medicine, Science and Law*, 14:124-128.

Weinberg, K. (1955). *Incest Behavior.* New York: Citadel Press.

Weiner, I. (1962). Father-daughter incest. *Psychiat. Quart.*, 36:607-632.

Yates, A. (1982). Children eroticized by incest. *Amer. J. Psychiat.*, 139:482-485.

Yorukoglu, A., & Kemph, J. (1966). Children not severely damaged by incest with a parent. *J. Amer. Acad. Child Psychiat.*, 5:111-124.

Section II

EVALUATION

4

The Clinical Evaluation of Child Sexual Abuse

Diane H. Schetky

This chapter discusses the early stages of clinical intervention and outlines objectives for conducting the initial clinical evaluation of the sexually abused child and her family. Practical suggestions to the clinician are provided for interviewing the child. Formulating recommendations for treatment is also considered.

RECOGNITION OF CHILD SEXUAL ABUSE

"Recognition of sexual molestation in a child is entirely dependent on the individual's inherent willingness to entertain the possibility that the condition may exist" (Sgroi, 1975, p. 18). This means opening our minds to the fact that sexual abuse may occur in nice upper-middle-class families who are pillars of the community, as well as in multi-problem lower-class families. Further, it is important to bear in mind that children of all ages may be victimized and that boys are also at risk.

Discovering sexual abuse involves asking the right questions. This point was made to the author by a resident who always seemed to have an inordinately high number of patients in her caseload who had been sexually abused. When asked for possible reasons for this, she replied, "It's very simple. I routinely ask about sexual abuse." Such questions may be put to the new patient or older child while taking a history in the context of the review of systems. Questions such as, "How did you first learn about sex?" "Do you have any concerns about your body?" "Do you know of anyone who has ever experienced sexual abuse?" or "Has anyone ever touched you in a way that made you feel uncomfortable?" give the patient permission to talk about these concerns and signal that the clinician considers them important.

Sexual abuse may present itself in a variety of ways. The child may blow the whistle but is usually unlikely to do so until she approaches adolescence, at which time she is physically and emotionally less dependent upon the abuser if the abuse is within the family. Teenagers may also expose the family secret in response to a father's or stepfather's attempting intercourse or when he attempts to curtail their heterosexual activities. In one study (Sauzier, 1986), only 55% of victims revealed their sexual abuse. Those who never told either viewed the experience as insignificant or were involved in a complex relationship with the offender who was likely to be a family member.

When children do choose to talk about sexual abuse they are least likely to turn to a physician or nurse; rather, they are apt to confide in a neighbor, teacher, or trusted relative. Hence, it is most important to educate the public about how to respond in such situations. Sadly, one still hears of cases in which children are not believed or are told "Uncle Joe would never do a thing like that" and that they must have imagined it.

Sexual abuse may be discovered incidentally when a child displays a behavioral or physical problem (Table 1). Apart from gonorrhea in a child under age 14 (other than in a newborn), there are no absolute indicators of sexual abuse (Sgroi, 1977). Many physical findings are highly suggestive and will be discussed further in the chapter that follows. Behavioral manifestations are nonspecific and cover a wide spectrum from the withdrawing child to the more acting-out child (Table 1). Several studies suggest that sexually abused children fall between normal and emotionally disturbed children in terms of the psychopathology seen (Conte, 1985; Gomes-Schwartz, Horowitz, & Sauzier, 1985). How important the relationship with the offender was to the child and the mother's response to disclosure seemed to have bearing on the child's ensuing psychopathology.

Someone outside the family may suspect sexual abuse, as is becoming increasingly common given all the media attention to the problem. Such allegations require careful investigation to rule out the possibility of vindictiveness or projection. In many incestuous families, it is unusual for parents to make allegations of sexual abuse as the mother is often passive and feels at a loss to do anything about the situation, or her own dependency needs cause her to fear disruption of the family.

Fathers involved in incestuous relationships are usually loath to come forth because of shame, fear of incarceration, and job loss. Recently, there has been a proliferation of allegations of sexual abuse arising in the context of child custody and visitation disputes. Such charges may arise prior to separation or afterwards, at a point where the mother or

Table 1
Nonspecific Symptoms of Child Sexual Abuse

Physical Symptoms	Behavioral Symptoms
Pregnancy	Withdrawal
Genital lacerations	Anxiety, fearfulness
Rectal tears	Sleep disturbance
Inflamed genitalia	Somatic complaints
Discharge	Eroticization, increased sex play
Stomach aches	Self-destructive behaviors
Blood in stools	Acting-out behaviors
Bruising near genitals	School problems
	Depression, low self-esteem
	Poor peer relations

child feels safe in lodging them. A parent may bring about false allegations in an attempt to prevent the other parent from having access to the child, or possibly out of dissatisfaction with a custody decree. The complex issues in these cases will be discussed further in Chapter 6.

Clinicians need to be alert to factors that put a child at risk for sexual abuse. Among these are a stepfather in the home (Finkelhor, 1980; Russell, 1984) or living with a single mother (Sauzier, 1986). The latter puts a child at risk by exposing her to more caretakers and more of the mother's boyfriends.

THE INVESTIGATION OF CHILD SEXUAL ABUSE

The investigation of sexual abuse spans many disciplines including pediatrics, psychiatry, psychology, social work, guidance counselors, protective service workers, police, and attorneys. Often there will be duplication of efforts and the child is subjected to repeated interviews, some by skilled and others by less skilled persons. When not handled optimally, the process may be confusing to all the participants and traumatic to the child. Ideally, the investigation should be streamlined, with one mental health professional doing a videotaped interview of the child to be made available for others to see. Interviewers need to be skilled at evaluating and building rapport with young children and must possess a solid knowledge of child development, as well as an understanding of the dynamics of child sexual abuse. They need to be comfortable discussing sex with children and be aware of their own feelings and how they impact on the interview process. It is essential that they have access to the child and his family on several occasions.

The question of whether to undertake sexual abuse evaluations alone
or as a team is largely academic and a function of the context of the
clinician's practice. Obviously, if one is in solo practice in a rural area
one may not have the luxury of a team approach. The advantage of
doing the entire evaluation is that one has direct access to all parties
and can prepare a report based on direct observations. One must be
aware of countertransference issues and the attempts of various parties
to manipulate. In contrast, the team approach offers more opportunity
to discuss one's feelings about the case and provide support to one
another. Potential pitfalls exist however, as when team members take
sides or cannot arrive at a consensus of opinion and end up making
conflicting recommendations.

STRATEGIES FOR INITIAL INTERVENTION

Some clinicians may be reluctant to become involved in cases of
sexual abuse because they dislike dealing with crises or are uncertain
how to proceed. The following guidelines are offered to alleviate some
of these anxieties involved in dealing with incestuous families. Many
of the principles are applicable to extrafamilial abuse as well.

1. *Make the most of the crisis.* The Chinese character for crisis
combines the symbols for danger and opportunity. In crisis there is the
opportunity for change in the family structure and inserting oneself
into an otherwise closed system.

2. *Report and support.* Reporting of child sexual abuse cases or any
suspicion thereof is mandated in all states. Some well-intended professionals fear that reporting will only add to the family's stress. Although
this is a valid concern, it is at the same time naive to assume that
one can manage these cases single-handedly. The authoritarian backup
of the legal system is often critical to ensuring that incestuous families
remain in treatment. It is easiest to report sexual abuse immediately,
since the longer one waits the more likely one is to get dragged into
the family's pact of silence. The physician has an ethical obligation to
inform the parents that a report will be filed. Racusin and Felsman
(1986) point out that any deception undermines the possibilities for
therapeutic work and that informing parents serves to facilitate empathy
and render intervention more effective. Support means preparing the
family members for what lies ahead, being available to them, and
encouraging them to be responsive to the needs of the victim and other
children at risk.

3. *Give the most support and authoritarian protection to the family*

member who blew the whistle. Family members may turn on the child or pressure her to recant her allegations. Rather than deal with their own guilt, they may try to view the child making the allegations as the source of the problem. In one such case, parents accused their daughter of being a witch and physically and emotionally banished her from the family.

4. *Talk explicitly about what happened.* This diffuses the emotional impact of sexual abuse, avoids denial, and gives family members permission to talk about it.

5. *Monitor one's own feelings and nonverbal behavior and strive for a nonjudgmental stance.* For example, Chris, age 10, was asked why she had not been able to tell her caseworker about ongoing sexual abuse, and she replied, "Every time I tried to tell her, she got this weird expression on her face."

6. *Talk with family members individually.*

The Victim

In speaking with the victim, it is important to avoid overidentifying. One should not presuppose that the experience was all bad or painful for her or that she is necessarily angry with the offender, nor should one try to be angry for the victim. When the child is seen initially, the child's anger toward her mother over the issue of lack of protection and role reversal may be much closer to the surface than anger with the father. It is equally important not to view the child as the seductress or imply that she could have put a stop to the relationship, had she really wanted to. When the male therapist is confronted with a seductive child, he may be tempted to handle his own discomfort by casting the blame on the child. It is helpful to remember that seductive behavior is a learned behavior often reinforced by the offender.

It is important to take time to establish rapport with the child but not to "beat around the bush." If sexual abuse has already been uncovered, the child is likely to know why the clinician is seeing her. It is necessary to allow her to express her feelings in her own words and to avoid asking so many questions that she does not have a chance to give her view of what happened. The clinician can use the child's vocabulary but should clarify what the child means by specific terms.

It is useful to give the child an intellectual understanding of what occurred and reassure her that she did the right thing in telling about the sexual abuse. Two rationales that have proven helpful to child victims are that telling is the first step toward getting help for the offender and that it is a means of protecting other children at risk, such as younger siblings. Further, the child may be told that the secret is really the offender's secret, not hers. MacFarlane (1986) reassures the child by telling her that sharing a secret is like getting rid of a painful splinter.

The Nonoffender

The nonoffender will usually be the mother who may or may not have been aware of the ongoing sexual abuse. Anger toward her over her role in the abuse is not helpful; rather, one needs to look at her as a victim in need of support during a time of crisis. Common responses are shame, guilt, loss of self-esteem and family support, and feelings of helplessness. Some mothers may harbor intense anger toward men, which may make a male clinician uneasy. Typically, these women are passive and need to be helped to assume a more protective role toward their daughters and begin to assess their options in life. Activity may serve as a means of atoning for guilt and warding off depression, and the mother needs to be urged to help her daughter return to her usual activities. She will need support in dealing with the legal, social, economic, and emotional ramifications of sexual abuse that lie ahead. Specific assessment needs to be done in terms of what her own treatment needs might be and whether she is strong enough to offer her daughter needed protection.

The Offender

Incest serves to maintain a dysfunctional family system. Once the incest comes to light, the system is disrupted and families often fragment; thus, one may not have the opportunity to evaluate the offender. Overcoming antipathy toward the offender is not easy. Perhaps the best way is to get to know him and see him as troubled and a victim as well. Many offenders have been victims of past sexual abuse, poor parenting, emotional deprivation, and often male supremacist attitudes that have encouraged them to view females as sex objects and have left them confused about their own sexuality. For others, such as rapists, the dynamics may involve rage against women and a need to humiliate or overpower.

Common responses from the offender are denial or rationalization. For instance, a father who had abused his deaf daughter said he was only trying to teach her about sex in spite of the fact that they were both fluent in sign language. In some families where incest is multigenerational and part of the family norm, there may be no guilt expressed, only the rationalization, "If she ain't good enough for Dad, she ain't good enough for no man." Not uncommonly, the offender will try to place the blame on the child with excuses such as "she asked to see my penis."

Whether or not the offender is willing to assume responsibility for what occurred will be a factor in deciding whether it is safe for him and the victim to remain in the same home. Other critical factors to consider are whether the offender is amenable and willing to accept treatment and the presence of any psychiatric disorders. Many offenders will agree to therapy in the heat of the crisis. However, few are willing to stay with treatment once the crisis has passed and therapy begins to confront, hence the value of court-mandated treatment with a suspended sentence on condition that the offender remain in treatment.

Siblings

Often overlooked are siblings of sexually abused children. Brant and Sink (1984) note that the siblings' perspectives on the family conflicts can be useful in corroborating information provided by parents or the sexually abused child. In addition, the possibility that siblings have also been sexually abused must be considered. Tilelli, Turek, & Jaffe (1980), studying 130 sexually abused children, found that 17 siblings in seven families had also been sexually abused, suggesting that multiple abuse of siblings is not uncommon. Siblings may also require help in dealing with their feelings about the sexual abuse within the family.

OBJECTIVES OF THE CLINICAL EVALUATION

1. Understanding the Child and Allegations in the Context of Family Dynamics and the Child's Development

Most children are truthful in their allegations but some, particularly very young children, may be unduly influenced by allegations that are brought about by their parents. A second category concerns children who have been excessively sexually stimulated or abused previously and use allegations of sexual abuse for secondary gain. (These issues will be discussed in more detail in Chapter 6.) If allegations are felt to be unfounded, the clinician needs to come forth with a psychodynamic explanation for them, which necessitates a familiarity with the child's history and the family dynamics. For instance, mothers who have been sexually abused may be hypervigilant with regard to their daughters and mistrustful of men. On the other hand, a high percentage of mothers of sexually abused children have themselves been sexually abused (Goodwin et al., 1981). Thus, such a history is not necessarily indicative of a false allegation. Psychiatric diagnoses on parents may shed light on their perception of events, e.g., the hysterical or borderline mother may overreact or have distorted perceptions. The presence of a thought disorder per se does not mean allegations are delusional.

The clinician needs to allow parents the opportunity to express their feelings about the abuse. Guilt over lack of protection is common and some parents may attempt to compensate by becoming overprotective. Others may feel their child has been stigmatized and damaged. The therapist needs to provide families with support and education and guidelines about how to respond to the child's behaviors and concerns. At times, it may be necessary to check their fantasies of retaliating against the perpetrator. Venting their anger *and* allowing them to take constructive action are obviously a first step in this direction. Sexual abuse of a child may also activate unresolved feelings about similar abuse parents may have experienced and there may be a tendency to overidentify with the victim or try to work through their own past trauma through the child.

Developmental history should be obtained on the child with particular focus on past traumas or sexual abuse, level of functioning prior to abuse, cognitive development, and credibility. It is also helpful to inquire about the child's daily routine, who has access to the child, and family attitudes about nudity and sexuality.

Observing the young child with respective parents, particularly if there is the possibility that allegations in the context of a custody dispute may be false, can be very helpful. Custodial parents may protest vehemently, claiming it will traumatize the child and that the child has no relationship with the other parent or is terrified of him. Sometimes these concerns may be legitimate, whereas at other times they point to a parent trying to suppress certain information. The clinician will need to weigh the risks versus benefits of observing the child with the alleged perpetrator when he is a family member.

2. Validating Sexual Abuse (Table 2)

Factors enhancing a child's credibility include verification over time. The words that the child chooses to describe the abuse should change over time but the facts should remain the same. Verification may also occur through dreams, reenactment, and traumatic play (Terr, 1980). Most children who have been abused will show signs of stress in their daily life and during the evaluation, although some may remain asymp-

Table 2
Assessing Child's Credibility in Allegations of Sexual Abuse

Child	Enhance Credibility	Decrease Credibility
Language	Uses own vocabulary Vocabulary changes but not facts Tells from child's viewpoint	Adult terms Rote phrases Lack of detail
Affect	Consonant with allegations	Inappropriate to allegations
Behavior	Seductive, precocious, regressed, guarded somatic complaints	No behavioral changes
Cognitive Development	Differentiates fact from fantasy	Impaired reality testing
Memory	Good recall of details including sensorimotor Absence of denial Idiosyncratic detail	Vague/evasive Prior abuse may confuse picture
Motives	Absence of secondary gain	Possible secondary gain Manipulative, need to please parent
Play/drawings	Sexual themes May reenact trauma Exaggerates or avoids sexual features	Sexual themes absent
History	Progressive sexual activity over time Delayed disclosure Child threatened to keep secret Psychological coercion Sex rings, rituals, pornography	Other medical history to explain heightened sexual concerns
Physical	Gonorrhea under age 14 other than newborn Strong indicators: hymenal disruption, anal scars or relaxation, gonorrhea of rectum or vagina, other V.D.s	Normal P.E. in spite of history of penetration

tomatic. Verification may occur through outside clues and facts, such as another child who may have witnessed the abuse or physical evidence. Corroboration of behavioral changes and/or allegations may be obtained by reports from other sources such as pediatricians, teachers, and babysitters. Physical symptoms and findings, while helpful for corroborating sexual abuse, are not necessary.

Sgroi (1984) notes that incest usually involves multiple incidents over time with a progression of sexual activity toward more intimate and invasive contact. Commonly, elements of secrecy or psychological coercion accompany the sexual abuse.

The child's history of reliability and cognitive maturity should also be taken into consideration. Finally, the absence of possible motives for false allegations will usually enhance the child's credibility.

In some cases, false retractions of allegations may occur, as when the child fears sending her father to jail, her parents' anger, or destroying the family. She may also fear abandonment by the family or being sent into foster care. Families may pressure children to alter their testimony, as in one case when the child was told, "God wants you to lie in order to keep our family together!" If retractions occur, the examiner needs to try to find out why. The likelihood of false retraction will diminish if the child is provided with immediate support and told that she is believed.

3. Evaluating the Need for Treatment

Numerous factors need to be considered in assessing the child's response to sexual abuse and the need for treatment, including the child's age and emotional development. Chapter 1 presented psychoanalytic concepts of child sexual development. Using Erikson's schemata of psychosocial development which complements psychoanalytic theory, we will look at how sexual abuse impacts on various developmental tasks. According to Erikson (1950), the task of infancy is to establish basic trust. He noted,

> Parents must not only have certain ways of guiding by prohibition and permission, they must also be able to represent to the child a deep, an almost somatic conviction that there is a meaning to what they are doing. Ultimately, children become neurotic not from frustrations, but from the lack or loss of societal meaning in these frustrations. (1950, pp. 249–250)

How, we might ask, can any young child make sense out of sexual abuse when it totally undermines trust?

The task of the toddler is that of autonomy versus shame and doubt. Sexual abuse represents an attack on the child's autonomy and newly acquired control of his body. Loss of control is associated with a sense of shame, and an attack on the body is likely to be viewed as aggressive rather than sexual in nature. For instance, 3-year-old Megan spoke of her fears of being eaten up by her father when he was sexually abusing her. The preschooler has not yet internalized society's views about incest and so experiences less guilt than the older child. A greater trauma is likely to be the ensuing disruption of the family, given the preschooler's emotional and physical dependence on her parents.

The task of the oedipal child is initiative versus guilt, and Erikson (1950) referred to the child's "pleasure in attack and conquest" (p. 255). The oedipal child has increased awareness of sexuality and an active fantasy life and competes for a favored position vis-à-vis the opposite-sex parent. The male child may fear castration as punishment for his unacceptable oedipal wishes. If abused at this age (usually by a male), he is likely to feel that his equipment is inferior and he may feel passive and helpless. The female abused at this age risks premature excessive sexual stimulation, as well as increased oedipal strivings and, in turn, guilt. Both male and female children are at risk for becoming eroticized and sexualizing subsequent relationships (Yates, 1982).

A second issue at this stage concerns the acquisition of superego and the internalization of parental values. If the parent is defective in empathy and moral standards, the child is left with a faulty model with which to identify and with a mistrust of adults. This may lead to acting-out behavior in later life.

The task of the latency-age child is industry versus inferiority. Children normally put oedipal striving behind, sublimate some of their sexual and aggressive drives, and gain recognition through producing things. Sexual abuse in this period may interfere with the child's impulse control, thereby disrupting latency and leading to learning difficulties. Instead of feeling competent about herself, the child experiences a sense of inadequacy, helplessness, and inferiority due to sexual abuse, lack of protection and nurturance, and lack of academic success. The latency-age child recognizes that sexual abuse is wrong and may feel guilty and fear disclosure. Reality testing at this age remains immature, and the child may view the molestation as her fault or even a form of punishment for something she did wrong.

The task of adolescence is identity versus role confusion. Sexual abuse thwarts all of the integrative tasks of adolescence including identity formation, separating from family of origin, and establishing peer relations which are discouraged by the father when he is the abuser. The abused adolescent feels damaged, fragmented, and without control over her life, which prevents her from developing a positive sense of self and body image and competence. Brooks (1985) states that the strength of repression needed to deal with the sexual abuse may inhibit or terminate the adolescent's search for truth and lead to premature closure of identity development. The ability to establish intimate relations with the opposite sex is undermined, and normally pleasurable sexual feelings become tainted by their association with incest, guilt, and anger. Finally, incest undermines the victim's perceptions if they are denied by the rest of the family. One teenage girl continued to doubt herself years after an incestuous experience with her uncle and kept saying, "I shouldn't have believed him. I was stupid. I should have known better."

Other factors to consider are the child's relationship to the offender, age differences, and duration of sexual abuse. Generally, the closer the blood ties and the greater the age discrepancy, the more traumatic the sexual abuse. Thus, a teenager is better able to extricate herself from an incestuous relationship with her brother than with her father as there is less abuse of power involved in the former relationship. How invasive or painful the abuse has been will affect the outcome, as will whether or not the victim was a participant or an accidental victim. Where force is involved and the abuse is isolated, the victim is less likely to blame herself than when the abuse is part of an ongoing relationship. For similar reasons, families are more likely to lend support to the rape victim than to the incest victim (Rosenfeld, 1979).

The male victim of sexual abuse often suffers the double stigma of victimization and homosexuality. His concerns about becoming homosexual are likely to be more pronounced as he enters adolescence.

Finally, one needs to assess level of ego functioning and try to differentiate problems that may have preceded the abuse from those directly related to it. Several authors have noted ego impairment in many incest victims which they felt may have predisposed them to incest (Browning & Boatman, 1977; Gomes-Schwartz, Horowitz, & Sauzier, 1985).

4. Diagnosis

For lack of a better diagnostic category at this time, many sexually abused children fall under the various Adjustment Disorders or Post-Traumatic Stress Disorder. At present, there is no specific category in DSM-III-R to designate child sexual abuse, although it may be indicated under Axis III when appropriate. Several proposals were put forth at the 1985 Summit Conference on Diagnosing Child Sexual Abuse in Los Angeles for new diagnostic categories. These included a category of Sexually Abused Child Disorder, Sexualized Disorder of Childhood, which would include the eroticized child, and a Post-Traumatic Stress

Disorder that was specific for children. Concerns regarding a Sexually Abused Child Disorder were the labeling effects such a category might have on the child and the fact that if the child did not fit the syndrome some might try to use this to exclude child sexual abuse.

Clinicians should be aware of the strong correlation between child sexual abuse and multiple personality disorder (MPD) (Wilbur, 1984). Although not often diagnosed in childhood, this may in part be due to lack of familiarity with the disorder and failure to inquire about it. It may also be more difficult to diagnose in younger children because of the shifts in personality that occur in childhood and adolescence (Bowman, Blix, & Coons, 1985). Kluft (1984) notes that MPD is assumed to develop as a consequence of early childhood traumas and is thought to exist in some form in childhood. Kluft (1985) believes that dissociative defenses are commonly used among youngsters with dissociative potential. However, when dissociation becomes the predominant mode for dealing with traumas, it may become fixated and pathological.

Dissociative disorders involve: 1) disturbance in memory such as amnesia, time loss, or intrusive recall; 2) disturbance in sense of identity involving fragmented sense of self and depersonalization; and 3) linkage of these events to a trauma. Common symptoms in adults with multiple personalities include amnesia, depression, suicide attempts, panic attacks, sexual dysfunction, conversion symptoms, phobias, substance abuse, self-mutilation, compulsive rituals, gastrointestinal symptoms, migraine, and auditory or visual hallucinations. These patients with their panoply of symptoms may often be misdiagnosed as borderline personalities, depressed or schizophrenic. Kluft (1985) stresses that incipient cases of MPD diagnosed in childhood are much more readily treated, hence the importance of early identification.

Goodwin (1987) outlines four categories of indicators that should prompt more extensive screening for dissociative disorders in children. These include:

1. Familial and constitutional factors such as MPD or other severe psychopathology in a parent, or conditions that place the child at risk.
2. Medical indicators such as loss of a parent through violence, hospitalization of child or sibling for nonaccidental injuries, presence of severe physical sequelae of sexual abuse, intrusive or bizarre health care, evidence of distorted body image, conversion disorder, or pseudoseizures.
3. Family or environmental indicators such as extreme physical, sexual, or psychological abuse, excessive isolation or secrecy,

excessive blaming and humiliation, extreme denial of documented abuse, and lack of a close, nurturing, and protective relationship.

4. Dissociative symptoms in a child or adolescent including forgetfulness, imaginary companions, active fantasy world, trance-like states, multiple ego states, stereotypic behaviors, extreme depression, self-mutilation or accident proneness or other self-destructive behavior, the presence of multiple diagnoses that are difficult to integrate, and finally, severe Post-Traumatic Stress Disorder.

As noted in Chapter 3, Post-Traumatic Stress Disorder is another common sequelae of childhood sexual abuse and this should be ruled out before making a diagnosis of personality disorder.

5. Competency to Testify

Competency to testify in criminal proceedings is a legal issue which the clinician may or may not be asked to address in doing a psychiatric evaluation. It is a critical issue in the decision to go forth with criminal charges when the witness is a child, as the case often hinges on the child's ability to give credible testimony. Findings that may preclude the child's participation, such as impaired reality testing, cognitive immaturity, inability to cooperate or withstand the rigors of cross-examination, or fear of confronting the offender, should be noted. Measures that might facilitate the child's testimony such as adequate preparation should also be mentioned. (For a more detailed discussion of the problems of the child as a witness, the reader is referred to Chapter 10.)

6. Preparation for the Physical Exam

Every child who has been sexually abused deserves a thorough physical exam not just for purposes of gathering evidence or ruling out injury but also to reassure her that she is physically all right. Because the physical exam is associated with the sexual abuse, some victims may interpret it as yet another form of abuse or even punishment. The clinician can allay some of these anxieties through careful preparation and use it as an opportunity to allow the child to discuss some of her concerns, e.g., Will I still be able to have children? Am I still a virgin?

7. Disposition

The immediate decision to be made (usually by protective services with input from the clinician) is whether or not it is safe to allow the child to return home. This decision rests on several factors including: 1) whether the offender, if a family member, admits his guilt and is ready to accept responsibility for his actions and treatment; 2) whether the mother can offer the child support and protection; 3) the availability of services; and 4) the child's wishes. Interestingly, the National Center for Child Abuse and Neglect Demonstration Project (Finkelhor, 1983) found that children tended to receive placement in or out of their home usually in accord with their wishes. Foster care was found to be more likely when the abuser was in the family. Those factors associated with foster care placement included very large and multiproblem families and the presence of other kinds of abuse or neglect as well. Regional differences also enter into the decision to place, with, for example, 37% of sexual abuse cases in the Rocky Mountain region going into foster care and only 13% in New England (Finkelhor, 1983).

The diagnostic assessment of the family will have important bearing on the disposition. It is important to understand the family's strengths, vulnerabilities, and available support systems. The potential for acting out in these families is high. Goodwin (1981) notes suicide attempts occurred in 5.4% of 201 families in which sexual abuse had been substantiated. Browning and Boatman (1977) also found a high incidence of violent sequelae after revelation of sexual abuse. The violent, vindictive, or paranoid parent obviously is not a good candidate for family therapy. As noted by Anderson and Shafer (1979), many of these families are character-disordered, have conflicts about dependency, and do not tolerate intimacy, which affects their willingness and ability to stay in treatment. In spite of the emphasis given to family reconstruction in many treatment programs, some authors caution that it may not be desirable in all instances (Server & Janzen, 1982).

Decisions need to be made about the need for treatment, what kind, and for which family members. Recommendations must be tailored to the age and sex of the victim, family needs, willingness to accept treatment, and the availability of services. Resistance to recommendations for treatment is likely to be high from families and sometimes even professionals. Byrnes and Valdiserri (1982) studied 79 patients seen for sexual abuse in a Philadelphia emergency ward and found that 43% failed to keep appointments for follow-up. The mean age of the children seen was 7.7, 18% were male, and all were symptomatic. Children who had been abused within the family were twice as likely not to return as those abused outside of the family. Reasons offered by families for not keeping appointments included temporary foster care, illness, and language barriers. The authors note that these families were characterized by a high degree of chaos, unwillingness to recognize psychic trauma, and extensive use of denial.

Adams-Tucker (1984) compared sexually abused children who received psychiatric evaluation with those who were merely reported. She found that those most likely to be referred were younger, white, and from two-parent homes or father-headed families. Also, children who had been molested by a relative were more likely to be referred than those molested by a stranger or neighbor. The average duration of agency evaluation was three months and only 22% of valid cases were referred on for psychiatric help. Adams-Tucker noted 13% of cases were closed because the perpetrator stopped living in the home, which suggests that many agencies view their role as one of merely protecting children rather than attempting to undo psychic trauma.

INTERVIEWING THE SEXUALLY ABUSED CHILD

Kreiger and colleagues (1980) caution on the need to be consistent, predictable, and safe when working with a sexually abused child, given the fact that she has been repeatedly deceived or used in her dealings with adults. The skillful interviewer should be able to establish rapport with the child and proceed with an interview that is both diagnostic and therapeutic in the sense that it allows the child to unburden her secret, be believed, and feel that she will be protected.

In interviewing the young child it is important to attend carefully to the child's affect, play, behavior, and fantasy life, as well as her verbal productions. When eliciting information, it is important to avoid pressuring the child or conveying impatience or frustration and to allow her to tell the story at her own pace and in her own words with her own emphasis. The child's subjective experiences need to be dealt with and should not be cut off in eagerness to get to the facts. The child's fantasy life may reveal a great deal about her fears, perception of events, and reality testing. However, for purposes of gathering evidence, it is also necessary to cover certain factual material such as, How did it begin? What happened next? Where did it happen? How many times? When? Was anyone else there? What did he say to you? What did you say? Were you threatened in any way? Adams-Tucker (1984) recommends exploring various sensory modalities such as taste, smell, noises, and how it felt. She also stresses the need to explore affective responses and react to them, rather than assuming "a passive analytic posture."

Given the tendency of young children to answer questions either quite literally or according to their own unique interpretations, it is useful to repeat questions using different phrasing. For instance, a 4-year-old girl was asked if she had ever seen her grandfather hurt animals. She denied this but several minutes later, when asked if he had ever been mean to an animal, she described him killing a bird in front of her.

Children rarely use technical terms to describe sexual acts, and if they do, this should raise suspicion of coaching. In contrast, a child's graphic statement, such as "sticky white cotton candy comes out of grandpa's pee pee" or her father's "pickle tickled when he put it in (her mouth)" will carry a lot more weight in court.

The preschooler may not be able to quantify the number of incidents of abuse but is often able to relate them temporally to important events in her life such as a parent going to work, TV shows, being home sick, or a birthday or special time of year. The young child is not likely to know the months of the year but should understand the seasons if asked about the weather outside.

INTERVIEWING ADOLESCENTS

Adolescents who have been sexually abused may have difficulty talking about it because of embarrassment or fear of exposure. It is useful for the clinician to reassure them that he is comfortable discussing it and has seen many similar cases. Often adolescents will feel that they are the only ones who have ever gone through anything like this. Some may be better able to discuss sexual abuse in the third person in terms of a friend with a problem, and the interviewer can use this avenue to help them open up. If they respond to specific questions with "I can't remember" or denial, it may be helpful to interpret this as their wish not to have to deal with the sexual abuse. For nonverbal teenagers, drawing may be offered as an option. Confidentiality is always an issue with teens, and the need and rationale for reporting the abuse should be discussed with the patient.

SPECIFIC TECHNIQUES FOR INTERVIEWING

Drawings

The school-age child may be more comfortable with verbal interchanges than the younger child but should also be given the option of showing what happened with dolls or drawings. Sgroi (1984) recommends having the child draw a picture of where the abuse occurred by way of helping the child focus on the incident and facilitating recall. This technique was used with 10-year-old Will who four years earlier had resisted sexual abuse by a male babysitter. He drew himself lying on the floor of the hall with the sitter standing over him with an exposed erect penis threatening to "shoot" him (Drawing 1a). With vivid recall Will described how he had run to the kitchen and gotten out his mother's butcher knife, telling his sitter that if he did not stop he would use the knife on him and he did not think he would want to go through life being called "stumpy" (Drawing 1b).

The child may be asked to draw herself, family members, the perpetrator, and her thoughts about what she looks like inside. Drawings may reveal more about the child's feelings about the offender than does her affect. One little girl who was loath to talk about her abuser drew him in jail clothes. Another child spoke matter-of-factly about the sitter who abused her but then depicted him falling off a cliff.

Children do not ordinarily draw nude figures or genitalia (DiLeo, 1973) and if they do, this should be cause for suspicion of abuse or problems with aggression or emotional disturbance (Koppitz, 1968). Hibbard, Roghmann, and Hoekelman (1987) compared drawings of sexually abused children with those of nonabused children and found that children known to have been sexually abused were 6.8 times more likely to draw genitalia than were comparison nonabused children. They urge that drawing of genitalia by children should sensitize examiners to exploring the possibility of sexual abuse. Satterfield (personal communication, 1986) cautions that one may get false positives in this regard from children from medical families and those who have been exposed to anatomically correct dolls. Yates, Beutler, and Crago (1985) compared drawings done by child victims of incest with those done by psychiatric patients who had not been sexually abused. They found that child incest victims had more poorly developed impulse controls and a defensive structure that emphasized repression. Victims tended to either exaggerate or minimize sexual features, suggesting they either highly cathected sexual aspects of the abuser or felt a need to defend against sexual interest and impulses.

Depending on the nature of the abuse, the child may sexualize other parts of the body. The 5-year-old girl who produced Drawing 2 used to play a game called rhinocerous with her father in which he would butt her pubic area with his head. When examined by her pediatrician she told him he might find her Daddy's hair in her vagina. Her drawing of a robot shows undue emphasis on hair and also delineates the vaginal area. Depersonalization is also suggested by her insistence that the

Drawing 1a

Drawing 1b

figure was a robot and by the way in which it seems to be floating in space.

Use of Anatomically Correct Dolls

The use of anatomically correct dolls has become a popular means of evaluating sexually abused children. Renshaw (1985) cautions, "Explicit dolls or cartoons do not make an instant expert of a caseworker, police officer, or state's attorney" (p. 49). These dolls are useful for clarifying the child's understanding of anatomy and allowing the child to demonstrate what happened. They should not, however, be used to teach, coach, or suggest to the child what might have happened, as this contaminates the interview. Further, the dolls should never be forced upon the child. Unfortunately, many of them are quite unappealing (one critic referred to them as "anatomically grotesque dolls") and it may be difficult to interest the child in them.

White and colleagues (1986), who have developed a protocol for the use of the dolls, stress objectivity and the need to maintain control over the child and not allow her to be distracted by too many toys in

Drawing 2

the room. White et al. are among the few professionals who have studied
how normal children play with these dolls but point out that one can
never be sure that one's controls have not been abused. These researchers
found that sexually abused children demonstrated more sexually related
behaviors when presented with the dolls than did controls. Three-year-
olds were found to be most responsive to the dolls, whereas older
children tended to either reveal their experiences or become non-
responsive (White et al., 1986). Jampole and Weber (1987) also concluded
that sexually abused children demonstrated more sexual behavior with
anatomically correct dolls than did nonsexually abused children. However, their study included only 10 abused children and failed to control
for numerous variables.

In contrast to the above findings, Jensen and colleagues (1986), in a
small study of 15 children who were videotaped while playing with the
dolls, found that children with a history of sexual abuse could not be
discriminated from psychiatric or normal controls by a panel of blind
evaluators. Gabriel (1985) observed 16 nonabused preschoolers playing
with anatomically correct dolls and found that the dolls elicited a wide
variety of sexual behaviors. She cautioned that the dolls not be used
as part of a "fishing expedition." A final commentary on the state of
the art comes from the California Court which has disallowed evidence
obtained from using dolls until the technique "has been generally accepted as reliable in the scientific community in which it was developed"
(In re Amber B. & Tella B. 1987 191 Calif 3rd 682; In re Christine C.
& Michael C. 1987 191 Calif App 3rd 676).

Videotapes

Videotaping the initial evaluation of the child is useful for preserving
accuracy of what is said and as a teaching tool and means of improving
interviewing skills. It may also be used to spare the child additional
interrogations, to refresh her memory prior to trial, and as a means of
decreasing possible recantation. In some states the videotape may be
presented to the jury in lieu of the child. Another very effective use of
the videotape when it confirms child sexual abuse is to share it with
the defense attorney, who may then try to persuade her client to enter
a guilty plea, thereby sparing the child the ordeal of testifying in court.
Sharing the videotape with nonabusing parents may help them believe
the child's allegations. Videotapes are not without risk, however, as
parts of them may be shown out of context and they may be shown
to juries without benefit of interpretation by a child mental health

expert. Finally, it is not clear whether videotapes have as much impact on juries as does live testimony.

Hypnosis

A few clinicians such as Kliman (1985) have used hypnosis to help verify allegations of child sexual abuse. However, as a tool for use in court it has come under much criticism from Orne (1985), who believes that hypnosis introduces contamination and an element of suggestion from the hypnotist. Orne maintains that anyone who has been hypnotized should be excluded as a witness.

Psychological Testing

Testing may be relevant, as when questions are raised about the child's reality testing, IQ, or the extent of emotional disturbance. However, as a diagnostic tool per se to determine whether or not sexual abuse has occurred it is not that useful.

COMMON SOURCES OF ERROR IN SEXUAL ABUSE EVALUATIONS

Some common sources of error in performing evaluations on sexually abused children include interviewer bias (e.g., referring to the offender and victim prior to any finding of fact), leading, coercive or threatening questions, reinforcing or rewarding the child for certain responses, misuse of the anatomical dolls (e.g., "Did he do it this way or that way?"), and neglect of family dynamics. Further, the interviewer may fail to consider possible prior sexual abuse, may fail to deal with the child's subjective experience in his eagerness to get the facts, and may not adequately follow up on the child's statements. Some who are inexperienced in talking with young children may ask age-inappropriate questions (e.g., asking a 3-year-old what time something happened) or they may fail to scale down their language to the child's developmental level, leaving the child confused and guessing about what answers the interviewer wants. A faulty assessment may invalidate the entire case and result in it being dropped or an acquittal. In some instances, convictions have ensued in spite of evidence obtained through deplorable, unacceptable techniques. Of particular concern to the clinician should be the number of countersuits being brought about against therapists and agencies by parents whose children have been removed because of suspected sexual abuse without proper evaluation.

SUMMARY

In closing, there are no easy shortcuts to evaluating child sexual abuse. Clinicians should not attempt to evaluate allegations of child sexual abuse unless willing to do a thorough evaluation and see the case through to the end. It is hoped that this chapter has familiarized the reader with what the issues are and rendered these evaluations less formidable. If those qualified shirk from doing these evaluations, important decisions will be left to persons less well trained. These cases are always challenging and can be rewarding if properly handled.

REFERENCES

Adams-Tucker, C. (1974). The early treatment of child incest victims. *Am. J. Psychother.*, 38(4):505–516.

Adams-Tucker, C. (1984). The unmet needs of sexually abused youths: Referrals from a child protection agency and clinical evaluation. *J. Am. Acad. Child Psych.*, 23(6):659–667.

Anderson, L., & Shafer, G. (1979). The character disordered family: A community treatment mode for family sexual abuse. *Amer. J. Orthopsychiat.*, 49(3):436–445.

Bowman, E., Blix, S. & Coons, P. (1985). Multiple personality in adolescence: Relationship to incestuous experiences. *J. Am. Acad. Child Psych.*, 24(1):109–114.

Brant, R., & Sink, F. (1984). Dilemmas in court-ordered evaluation of sexual abuse charges during custody and visitation proceedings. Presented at the 31st Annual Meeting of the American Academy of Child Psychiatry, Toronto, Canada, October 12, 1984.

Brooks, B. (1985). Sexually abused children and adolescent identity development. *Amer. J. Psychother.*, 39(3):401–410.

Browning, D., & Boatman, B. (1977). Incest: Children at risk. *Amer. J. Psychiat.*, 134:69–72.

Byrnes, J., & Valdiserri, E.V. (1982). Sexual abuse: A follow-up of a non-compliant population. *Hosp. & Comm. Psychiatry*, 33(11):936–40.

Conte, J. (1985). Report on NIMH funded Research Project on effects of sexual abuse on children. Presented at National Summit Conference on Diagnosing Child Sexual Abuse, Los Angeles, October 18, 1985.

DiLeo, J. (1973). *Children's Drawings as Diagnostic Aids.* New York: Brunner/Mazel.

Erikson, E. (1950). *Childhood and Society.* New York: W.W. Norton.

Finkelhor, D. (1980). Risk factors in the sexual victimization of children. *Child Abuse and Neglect*, 4:265–273.

Finkelhor, D. (1983). Removing the child—prosecuting the offender in cases of child sexual abuse: Evidence from the National Reporting System for Child Abuse and Neglect. *Child Abuse and Neglect*, 7:195–205.

Gabriel, R.M. (1985). Anatomically correct dolls in the diagnosis of sexual abuse of children. *J. of the Melanie Klein Society*, 3(2):41–49.

Gomes-Schwartz, B., Horowitz, J.M., & Sauzier, M. (1985). Severity of emotional disorders among sexually abused preschoolers, school age and adolescent children. *Hosp. & Comm. Psychiatry,* 36:503-508.

Goodwin, J. (1981). Suicide attempts in sexual abuse victims and their mothers. *Child Abuse and Neglect,* 5:217-221.

Goodwin, J. (1985). Post-traumatic stress symptoms in incest victims. In S. Eth, & R. Pynoos (Eds.), *Post-Traumatic Stress Disorder in Children.* Washington, DC: APA Press.

Goodwin, J. (1987). Dissociative reactions in abused children. In J. Goodwin, *Incest Victims and Their Families* (2nd ed.). Boston: John Wright PSC.

Goodwin, J., McCarthy, T., & DiCasto, P. (1981). Physical and sexual abuse of the children of adult incest victims. *Child Abuse and Neglect,* 5:87-96.

Hibbard, R.A., Roghmann, K., & Hoekelman, R.A. (1987). Genitalia in children's drawings: An association with sexual abuse. *Pediatrics,* 79(1):129-137.

Jampole, L., & Weber, M.K. (1987). An assessment of the behavior of sexually abused children with anatomically correct dolls. *Child Abuse and Neglect,* 11:187-192.

Jensen, J.B., Realmuto, G.M., Wescoe, M.D., & Garfinkel, B.D. (1986). Are there differences in the play with anatomically complete dolls: Abused versus non-abused children. Presented at the Annual Meeting of the American Academy of Child and Adolescent Psychiatry, Los Angeles, October 17, 1986.

Kliman, G. (1985). New areas in litigation for children. In D. Schetky & E. Benedek (Eds.), *Emerging Issues in Child Psychiatry and the Law.* New York: Brunner/Mazel.

Kluft, R. (1984). Multiple personality in childhood. *Psychiat. Clin. North America,* 7(1):121-134.

Kluft, R. (1985). *Childhood Antecedents of Multiple Personality.* Washington, D.C.: APA Press.

Koppitz, E.M. (1968). *Psychological Evaluation of Children's Human Figure Drawings.* New York: Grune & Stratton.

Kreiger, J.J., Rosenfeld, A., Gordon, A., & Bennett, M. (1980). Problems in psychotherapy of children with histories of incest. *Am. J. Psychother.,* 24(1):81-88.

MacFarlane, K. (1986). *Response to Child Sexual Abuse: The Clinical Interview* (videotape). Los Angeles: United Way.

Orne, M. (1985). Forensic Hypnosis. Annual Meeting of the American Academy of Psychiatry and the Law, Albuquerque, N.M., October 11, 1985.

Racusin, R., & Felsman, K. (1986). Reporting child abuse: The ethical obligation to inform parents. *J. Am. Acad. Ch. Psych.,* 25(4):485-489.

Renshaw, D. (1985). When sex abuse is falsely charged. *Medical Aspects of Human Sexuality,* 19(7):44-52.

Rosenfeld, A. (1979). The clinical management of incest and sexual abuse in children. *J.A.M.A.,* 242(16):1761-1764.

Russell, D. (1984). The prevalence and seriousness of incestuous abuse: Step-fathers v. biological fathers. *Child Abuse and Neglect,* 8:12-22.

Sauzier, M. (1986). Panel on Implication of New Research and Theory. Fourth National Conference on Sexual Victimization of Children, New Orleans, May 15, 1986.

Server, J., & Janzen, C. (1982). Contraindications to reconstitution of sexually abusive families. *Child Welfare,* 51(5):268-279.

Sgroi, S. (1975). Sexual molestation of children. The last frontier in child abuse. *Children Today,* 4:18-21.

Sgroi, S. (1977). Kids with clap. Gonorrhea as an indicator of child sexual assault. *Victimology*, 2:251-267.
Sgroi, S. (1984). Validation of sexual abuse. In S. Sgroi (Ed.), *Handbook of Clinical Intervention in Child Sexual Abuse.* Lexington, MA: Lexington Books.
Terr, L. (1980). The child as a witness. In D. Schetky & E. Benedek (Eds.), *Child Psychiatry and the Law.* New York: Brunner/Mazel.
Tilelli, J., Turek, D., & Jaffe, A. (1980). Sexual abuse of children: Clinical findings and implications for management. *N. Eng. J. Med.*, 302:319-323.
Wilbur, C. (1984). Multiple personality and child abuse: An overview. *Psychiat. Clin. North America*, 7(1):3-7.
White, S., Strom, G., Santilli, G., & Halpin, B. (1986). Interviewing young sexual abuse victims with anatomically correct dolls. *Child Abuse and Neglect*, 10:519-529.
Yates, A. (1982). Children eroticized by incest. *Amer. J. Psychiat.*, 139(4):482-485.
Yates, A., Beutler, L., & Crago, M. (1985). Drawings by child victims of incest. *Child Abuse and Neglect*, 9:183-189.

5

The Medical Evaluation of Child Sexual Abuse

Martin A. Finkel

The purpose of the medical evaluation of the child who has been sexually abused is threefold: 1) to evaluate medical problems related to the abuse, e.g., venereal disease, physical trauma, and pregnancy; 2) to gather medico-legal evidence of sexual abuse; and 3) to provide a protective and supportive environment enabling the child to deal with the issues surrounding victimization.

The physician plays an extremely important role in the evaluation of a child who is suspected of being sexually abused. He/she is frequently pivotal in validating he suspected abuse. The process of validation begins when a case is referred for evaluation or when a case is identified within clinical practice. A complaint can be validated with historical and/or physical indicators. The history is best obtained by a physician who understands the process by which children are victimized. The history should reflect information about engagement, progressive sexual interaction, secrecy, and the circumstances surrounding disclosure (Sgroi, 1982a).

The information obtained by the physician is used by the investigative team to determine the validity of the child's statements and the probability that the child has been abused. The history takes on great importance because so few children who are abused have definitive findings on examination. The history and physical examination are considered together when the physician makes a case assessment. Since sexual abuse of children is rarely corroborated by a third party, examining physicians have responsibility to make an informed diagnosis as they do in noncorroborated trauma, such as in physical abuse.

Martin A. Finkel, D.O., is Associate Professor of Clinical Pediatrics, University of Medicine and Dentistry of New Jersey, School of Osteopathic Medicine, Stratford, N.J.

WHEN TO EXAMINE

Although the timing of the physical examination is not always at the discretion of the examining physician, he can help determine the relative urgency of an examination. Criteria that necessitate an immediate examination are: (a) history of genital or extragenital trauma within 72 hours; (b) history of sexual assault within 72 hours; (c) postmenarchal female, which suggests the possibility of pregnancy and the need for therapeutic intervention. A relative indication for immediate examination is a history suggestive of a sexually transmitted disease. If a vaginal discharge has been present for several weeks prior to disclosure, it serves little purpose to rush a child to the emergency room to be examined by a physician, who in all probability cannot provide the necessary time to develop rapport, interview, and examine the child. When disclosure occurs more than 72 hours after the alleged incident, child protective services is afforded the opportunity to schedule the examination. The unanticipated presentation of a sexual abuse case can be disruptive and could result in an inadequate assessment. If the physician is aware that a sexual abuse evaluation is being scheduled, he or she can elect to participate in the evaluation or refer to a colleague who may have more expertise, interest, and/or time.

When cases of suspected sexual abuse present themselves, they do so because of accidental or purposeful disclosure. If the disclosure is purposeful, the reason for disclosure must be assessed. Purposeful disclosures afford the opportunity to interview and examine the child in an environment which is not under crisis pressure. If the disclosure is accidental, which implies that neither the victim nor the offender were prepared to disclose the activity, timing of the examination is more critical (Sgroi, 1982b). Unless there is a medical urgency for the examination in accidental disclosure, the examination should be delayed until the investigative interview can be completed and the stabilization of the family initiated.

PREPARATION FOR THE EXAMINATION

The examining physician is one of many professionals involved in the investigation of cases of sexual abuse. All professionals must complete their component of the investigation with an approach that will not victimize the child. That process begins with obtaining the skills necessary to do a sensitive and thorough history and examination of the victim, which includes a review of normal ano-genital anatomy and appropriate descriptive terminology. The infrequent inclusion of the ano-genital examination as part of the routine health maintenance assessment has resulted in many physicians having limited experience in this area. A careful, knowledgeable, and unhurried examination is essential if an appropriate assessment is to emerge.

Physicians have developed experience in the recognition, treatment, and overall management in cases of physical abuse. A physician's comfort with these cases evolves from an increased sense of mastery of the cognitive and technical skills necessary to examine these children. The examining physician must maintain affective neutrality, setting aside personal attitudes which could interfere with an objective assessment. Rosenfeld (1982) notes that "attitudes often determine what we are emotionally able to perceive and what we perceive molds our actions and reactions" (p. 57). Anglin (1984) suggests that recognition of any personal limitations, e.g., previous experience with sexual abuse, level of comfort with human sexuality issues, and level of knowledge concerning sexual abuse, prior to assuming the responsibility for examining these children is essential. Many physicians do not have the same sense of mastery in the evaluation of sexual abuse as they have with physical abuse, leading to considerable discomfort when called upon to examine these children.

The history-obtaining component of the evaluation facilitates the development of rapport with the child. It may be helpful to have as much background information as possible concerning the family structure, suspected offender, and the child's names for his or her body parts before proceeding, although some authorities believe that entering an interview with a minimal amount of information affords greater objectivity (White, 1986).

During the examination a parent, adult ally, or caseworker should be present along with a nurse. Every effort should be made to anticipate and decrease the child's anxiety concerning the examination. Prior to doing the examination, the child and the parent should be assured that the examination will not hurt. The physician should tell the child that she will be looked at from head to toe to deemphasize the genitalia which have been focused upon. One of the messages the child should clearly receive is that all parts of her body are important and the child should be examined within that context. The child should be told the purpose of the examination and encouraged to ask questions during it.

It is sometimes useful to allow the child to participate in the process of the examination. For example, have the child hold culturettes or instruments that will be utilized. If the child has a desire to observe the examination of the genitalia, the use of a mirror or having the child in the sitting position while examining the genitalia will also allow the child a sense of participation, observation, and control.

THE EXAMINATION

Positioning the child for examination is quite variable. Selection of
the optimal position will depend upon the child's age, the degree of
comfort, and his/her ability to detach from an adult ally. The position
in which the child is most cooperative is the best position. In males,
a lateral recumbent position is preferable to the knee-chest position if
they have been anally penetrated. In females, generally the most satisfactory position is the supine frog-leg position. In the alternative the
knee-chest position may provide good visualization of the genitalia and
anus (Emans & Goldstein, 1980). The child should feel comfortable and
secure whether examined on the table or on the adult ally's lap. No
child should be forced if he or she is uncooperative; however, if the
examination is absolutely essential because serious trauma cannot be
adequately assessed, then the child will need to be examined under
general anesthesia. If the child is uncooperative and does not need an
immediate examination, the physician can use that time to develop
rapport to facilitate a future encounter that could allow the examination.

The examination documents not only abnormality, but also normality.
Both acute and chronic signs of sexual assault may be noted on physical
examination, but the examiner must keep in mind that if only signs
of acute trauma are looked for much will be missed. The easiest findings
to observe are those of acute trauma, i.e., lacerations, abrasions, hematomas, petechiae, edema, and contusions. Regardless of the findings,
the medical record must be explicit in details concerning the description
of the external genitalia, hymenal and peri-hymenal tissues, anus, rectum
and/or, in the case of a male, penis and scrotum.

Since most offenders have a desire to repeat the sexual activity with
the child over time, they may go to great lengths to be gentle and not
make the activity uncomfortable for the child (Groth, 1984). When
acute signs are absent or healed, the examiner will need to look for
the more chronic, and possibly more subtle, signs. Woodling and Heger
(1986) have utilized effectively the colposcope as an aid in the observation of the subtle signs of trauma to the hymenal and peri-hymenal
tissues and anus.

The colposcope is a gynecologic tool used primarily in adults and
first applied by Dr. Wilmes Teixara (1981) for the assessment of sexual
assault. The colposcope is essentially a binocular microscope with the
capability of 5 to 30 magnification. The most useful magnification is
in the 5x, 7½x, and 10x range. With magnification and the use of a
green light, the observation of scar tissue and changes in vascular
pattern of the hymenal and peri-hymenal tissues and anus is made
easier because they appear more prominent. A colposcope is not however

required to do an adequate examination. An alternative aid is a good light and a handheld magnifying glass.

In those cases in which sexual assault has occurred within 72 hours, the collection of evidence differs from cases in which the assault has been greater than 72 hours. In a recent assault case, it will be necessary to save clothing, hair, debris, etc., as is done in the approach to the adult rape victim. The record should also reflect whether or not the child has been bathed prior to the examination. Dried secretions, saliva, and semen can be noted by a glistening appearance and can be lifted with the careful use of a distilled water-moistened cotton swab. The use of a long-wave ultraviolet light (Woods) to scan the body and clothing may help detect semen as it fluoresces blue–white. Semen stains are stable for years on clothing, even if the garment has been washed. Forensic specimens which would allow blood typing from stains or saliva and identification of semen-specific P-30 protein are invaluable (Sensabaugh, 1978).

When specimens are collected from a specific area of the body, careful attention should be paid not to contaminate an adjacent area. For example, if seminal fluid appears on the buttocks and anus, collect those specimens first, then clean the area and obtain rectal cultures and rectal swabs for semen. This will help assure that semen from ejaculation onto the child's body would not be inappropriately identified on the rectal smear due to passage over skin secretions and into the rectum, falsely suggesting anal penetration. The technique by which specimens are obtained and how the chain of custody of evidence is maintained should be documented. Several excellent sources for explicit details concerning the collection of forensic specimens are available. (Paul, 1975, 1977; Pole, 1976; Woodling & Kossofis, 1981).

When findings are recorded, specific reference to the position in which the child was examined should be noted. For example, "The child was examined supine with the legs in the frog-leg position." The findings might be described as if the examiner were standing at the child's feet looking toward the head and noting findings as a clock face, 12 o'clock being the abdomen and 6 o'clock being the back. A clear description as given above in lay terms is also helpful when describing findings during court testimony.

Photography may be necessary as part of the process of documentation of findings that could have evidentiary value. The appropriate consent forms must be obtained prior to photographing. Photographing the child clothed prior to photographing portions of the unclothed body tends to make the introduction of the camera easier. Ask the child if he/she has ever been photographed with his/her clothing off before. This question may uncover unsuspected child pornography. If the camera is not introduced in an appropriate fashion, it may be perceived as an invasion of privacy. It might be explained to the child that a doctor needs to gather information from his/her patients by asking questions and sometimes by taking pictures. The child's desire not to be photographed should be respected.

The camera held freehand is utilized in photographing the child clothed and unclothed when extragenital signs of trauma are present. A colposcope outfitted with a 35 mm, Polaroid, or stereoscopic camera affords a photographic record and documents clearcut alterations in genital and/or anal anatomy secondary to trauma and establishes a baseline record for reference if the child continues in a high-risk environment. In those cases in which the examiner is unsure of the interpretation of a particular finding, a colposcopic photograph can be reviewed by others for another opinion. A camera equipped with a data back will permanently identify the photograph.

EXAMINATION OF THE FEMALE GENITALIA

Adequate examination of the genitalia requires complete observation of the labia majora, labia minora, and vaginal vestibule with its six component parts. Visualization of the vestibule is simplified when the child is examined in the supine frog-leg position and gentle downward and lateral pressure is exerted posterior and lateral to the fourchette on the buttocks (Cowell, 1981). The vaginal vestibule encompasses the area between the clitoris anteriorly, the fourchette posteriorly, and the labia minora laterally. Involved in the structures of the vestibule are the urethra, peri-urethral glands (Skenes glands), hymenal membrane, hymenal orifice, Bartholin's glands, and the fossa navicularis (Figure 1). Most of the attention should be focused on the hymenal membrane, which is a double plate of mucosa lined by stratified epithelium. Between the two mucosal surfaces there is well-developed, rather firm connective tissue, which is well supplied with blood vessels (Monie, 1976). This firm connective tissue provides elasticity to the hymenal membrane.

Because of the nature of the embryologic formation of the hymenal membrane, a considerable number of normal anatomic variations occur. These variations are revealed both in the character of the hymenal orifice and the membrane itself. The hymenal orifice may be annular, crescent-shaped, cribriform, septate, fimbriated, or imperforate (Pritchard & MacDonald, 1985). The membrane itself may vary considerably

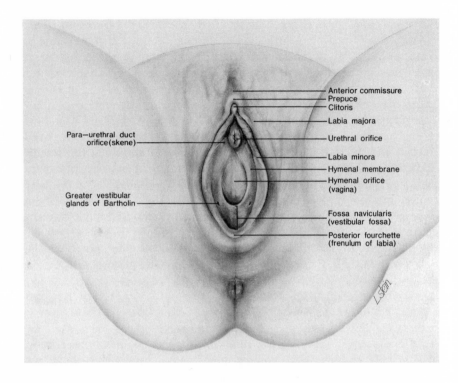

Figure 1

in thickness. It may have a very thin, translucent edge, which is described as velamentous, or a quite thickened and redundant edge. Although many variables of the genital anatomy exist, the author was unable to find any supportive documentation for what some clinicians label congenital absence of the hymen. Congenital absence of the hymen cannot exist as a sole entity on an embryologic basis.

The normal membrane will demonstrate variations in its surface vascular pattern. The vascular pattern is commonly described as fine and lacy. Interruptions in the vascular pattern of the hymenal membrane and peri-hymenal tissue may be secondary to deep or superficial trauma to the membrane surface with subsequent scar tissue formation (Norvell & Benrubi, 1984). Naturally occurring interruptions in the vascular pattern are usually midline and appear as fusions.

The transverse diameter of the hymenal orifice can also be quite variable. The examiner should record the transverse diameter and vertical measurements in millimeters but should be cautious not to overinterpret small, average, or large hymenal orifices without other corroborative findings. The normal membrane orifice may vary several millimeters depending upon the state of relaxation at the time of the examination. Some literature notes the significance of specific hymenal diameters as having a correlation with sexual abuse (Cantwell, 1981). However, until more normative studies have been completed, the physician should not rely solely on measurements.

The youngest children are likely to have the most significant findings as a result of attempted or completed introduction of a foreign body into the vagina. The classic signs of penile penetration as described by Snyder (1967) and Paul (1977) are "circumferential superficial tears of the vestibular mucosa; posterior linear tears of the hymen extending upwards into the posterior vaginal wall and downwards to involve the skin of the perineum and the perineal body" (p. 253). These classic findings are seen with attempted penetration of an erect adult penis. If penetration was attempted by a smaller diameter object, such as a finger, then less tissue damage will occur. In these cases, no shearing force produces the circumferential vestibular surface tears, and the findings may be restricted to discrete linear tears of the hymen in the posterior or posterior-lateral aspects of the membrane.

When trauma to the hymenal membrane is sufficient to produce scar tissue, the adhesions (synechiae) that form in the reparative process distort the shape of the membrane and adjacent tissues. Adhesions must be differentiated from congenital supporting fibers (trabeculae) transversing the anterior superior quadrants of the hymenal membrane. Paul's (1977) descriptions of the effect of blunt trauma to the anogenital tissues is helpful in understanding the nature of penetration injuries.

Emans (1985) recommends when examining the hymen and perihymenal tissues that the examiner notes the presence or absence of the following: 1) clefts or bumps of the hymenal membrane; 2) synechiae and its alteration of hymenal structure; 3) labial adhesions; 4) alteration of the hymenal orifice; 5) friability of the tissue during examination (post-traumatic fusion); 6) rounding of the hymenal edges and particular attention to the examination of the fossa navicularis and posterior fourchette for: (a) increased vascularity and alterations of vascular pattern; (b) scarring, circumferential or perpendicular to the orifice; and (c) erythema. When a standardized approach to observation is utilized, consistency and thoroughness of the examination is more likely to occur.

Most observations in prepubertal female children can be made without the use of a vaginal speculum. Specialized pediatric instruments are available to look into the vagina if deemed necessary. In small children, the use of a child's otoscopic or veterinary speculum can allow visualization of the cervix. A vaginoscope or Huffman pediatric speculum are available for older children (Huffman, 1977). Placing a digit through the hymenal orifice in prepubertal children is unnecessary and may traumatize the tissues. A recto-vaginal examination is most appropriate when indicated in prepubertal girls.

ANAL-RECTAL EXAMINATION

The findings of anal-rectal penetration can be quite variable, depending upon the child's cooperativeness, the position, the use of force, the size of the object, and the use of lubricant. Acute anal penetration is most likely to demonstrate the classic signs of trauma. Particular attention is to be paid to the presence of anal verge hematomas which result in prolapse of anal tissue. With the resorption of blood, a loose skin tag is formed (Paul, 1977). This skin tag may persist for several weeks and must be differentiated from congenital skin tags which lack the stigmata of a traumatic etiology.

Chronic anal penetration findings may be quite variable. The examiner observes for symmetry of the circumferential parallel folds (rugae) of the anal sphincter. The sphincter tone is noted along with the presence or absence of scar tissue. Two helpful signs are the buttocks separation sign and the anal wink (Paul, 1977). In children who have been repeatedly sodomized, traction applied to the buttocks laterally may result in dilatation of the anal sphincter. When the anal sphincter is touched with a Q-tip or examining finger, there may be slight constriction, but then there is usually dilation allowing the intromission of a foreign body. When the anus has received repeated blunt trauma there may be: 1) loss of the fine circumferential puckered pattern of the anal sphincter folds with formation of a few large rugae; 2) loss of subcutaneous tissue with cupping or coving between the rugae; and 3) perianal pigmentary changes (hypo or hyper). Scar tissue, if noted around the anus, will generally have the apex directed internally, whereas tears to the sphincter from the passage of a hard stool will have the apex of the tear directed externally (Paul, 1977). In most children, the use of a water-lubricated test tube will afford adequate proctoscopic examination.

EXTRAGENITAL SIGNS OF TRAUMA

Extragenital signs of trauma are more likely to be found when the assault has been forceful. Depending upon the degree of resistance, few or many findings may be apparent. The younger child is unlikely to struggle and is usually coerced into age-inappropriate sexual activity rather than physically forced. Older children may be attacked more violently and demonstrate findings consistent with such. In forced fellatio, tears of the lingular and labial frenulum, mucosal abrasions, and loose teeth may be noted. Semen can be collected from the oral pharynx. Attempts to silence a resisting, screaming child may appear as grasp marks or signs of attempted suffocation. Additional findings of trauma to the buttocks, thighs, and breasts may be found (Wynne, 1980).

The responsibility of the examining physician will be to help differentiate whether or not the extragenital and/or genital signs of trauma may have occurred in an accidental fashion or were inflicted. Intrafamilial perpetrators frequently provide some of the most extraordinary explanations for how the injuries occurred. The allegation of sexual abuse is very serious and sifting through all of the information in formulating an opinion is a difficult task.*

SEXUALLY TRANSMITTED DISEASES

Many researchers have noted an association between child sexual abuse and the major sexually transmitted diseases: gonorrhea, trichomonas vaginalis, syphillis, chlamydia trachomatis, herpes simplex, condyloma acuminata, and gardnerella vaginalis (Bell, 1983). Sexually transmitted diseases in prepubertal children, other than newborn, should be taken as presumptive evidence of sexual abuse until proven otherwise.

---

* Many of the classic signs of anogenital trauma have been outlined in the preceding section. However, considerable controversy continues to exist over the interpretation of the often subtle chronic findings of trauma to the genitalia and anus. The examining physician is called upon to interpret what may be residual of trauma in a child long after the obvious signs of acute lacerations, contusions, and abrasions have healed. It is only recently that the genitalia and anus of children are being scutinized with both gross macroscopic and colposcopic visualization. We need more studies that look at normal preadolescent and adolescent genitalia. There is paucity of documentation on the healing chronology of anogenital trauma. For example, examiners must begin to follow children with healing acute trauma as closely as possible and begin to correlate the historical details, when available, with the physical findings. Studies looking at the anus of non-traumatized as well as constipated and encopretic children of all age groups need to be done to provide comparative and normative data. These studies must document variations in anal verge tissue, sphincter tone, pigmentation, venous patterns and responses to two commonly used tests, the buttocks separation and anal wink. Studies looking at the incidents of rectal tags, hemorrhoids, and fissures in the pediatric age group are also important to our understanding of anal genital development and its disorders. For example, what is the effect of encopresis on anal anatomy? Is the healing chronology of anal trauma different than trauma to other body tissues? Research in these areas will help to provide a more scientific and objective approach to the evaluation of the sexually abused child.

Physicians at times have gone to great lengths to contrive alternative explanations for the acquiring of a sexually transmitted disease which would be considered preposterous if used as an explanation for transmission among adults. The American Academy of Pediatrics (1983) states: "Physicians should assume that children with gonorrhea acquired it by sexual contact and that most such contacts are abusive" (p. 553). In spite of the common viewpoint that nonsexual transmission of venereal disease occurs, the bulk of evidence is to the contrary.

Of the sexually transmitted diseases in children, gonorrhea is the most widespread (Nazarean, 1967). The prepubertal female is particularly susceptible to it because of her thin vaginal wall and its alkaline pH, as a result of which she may develop a diffuse vaginitis (Huffman, 1981). The human is the only reservoir of gonococcal infections, and the organism can only enter at mucosal surfaces. Its usual incubation period is two-to-five days (Litt, Edber, & Finberg, 1974).

Infection in the prepubertal child seldom has the classic clinical findings as would be seen in adolescents and adults. In the prepubertal child the clinical picture most commonly includes peri-anal pruritus, vaginitis, and dysuria. The adolescent is more likely to present with the classical signs and symptoms of pelvic inflammatory disease, cervicitis, urethritis, or epididymitis in males (Kramer & Jason, 1982). Although some infections may be asymptomatic (in the range of 10% males), complicated gonococcal infections such as septic arthritis or acute perihepatitis (Fitz-Hugh Curtis syndrome) can be observed in the pediatric age group (Kramer & Jason, 1982). In 1927, Cooperman (1927) described a gonorrhea epidemic in a newborn nursery in Philadelphia. He believed the route of transmission to be contaminated rectal thermometers. Unfortunately, this paper provided some of the early support to the belief that most gonorrhea was transmitted nonsexually.

Many clinicians have looked at the venereal versus nonvenereal transmission of sexually transmitted diseases. Branch and Paxton (1965) elaborated on transmission of gonorrhea in their study of 180 infected children. All of the children under 11 months of age contracted it from infected mothers at birth. In the age group of 1 to 9 years transmission was via sexual contact with infected relatives in the household with one exception, and in the 10- to 14-year-old groups, seven were molested and the remainder had contracted it through sexual activities with peers.

Most authors note the fragility of the organism and Sgroi (1977) contends it cannot live outside the human body, whereas DeJong (1985) states it can be viable for up to two or three hours on subjects covered with purulent discharge; hence, he believes it is possible to contract gonorrhea from contaminated objects. The debate continues and is of importance because of the legal implications. It is safe to say that generally the more thorough the evaluation, the more likely it is to turn up sexual abuse as the mode of transmission of gonorrhea. Shore and Winkelstein (1971) describe seven Alaskan native children whom they believe contracted gonorrhea indirectly by sharing beds with infected parents or siblings. Their study, however, did not always include contact with or culture of parents and failed to rule out the possibility of sexual abuse occurring amidst the crowded sleeping arrangements.

Neinstein and Goldenring's (1984) review of the nonsexual transmission of sexually transmitted diseases also suggested this mode of transmission is infrequent. The random culturing of community toilets and venereal disease clinic bathrooms has failed to yield positive cultures in Gilbaugh and Fuchs' study (1972). In an experimental setting, gonorrhea has been demonstrated to survive on a toilet seat and towels, but no study reviewed by the author has demonstrated the transmission of the disease.

Many clinicians have seen children where after thorough and competent investigation there did not appear a likely explanation for sexual transmission. In these cases, a nonvenereal transmission mode seemed more plausible. It is the author's opinion that these children should still be considered at high risk and monitored until child protective services can be as assured as possible that these children are not at risk for sexual abuse.

Even more controversy arises in assessing the venereal versus nonvenereal transmission of condyloma acuminatum, herpes simplex, and chlamydia trachomatis. The American Academy of Dermatology (1984) task force on pediatric dermatology looked at the association of genital warts and sexual abuse. Their review of the literature indicated that the association was significant in that in at least 50% of the cases there was documentation of a sexual mode of transmission. The Academy states that "genital warts in children indicate the possibility of sexual abuse" (p. 529).

The investigation of venereal warts is also complicated by a long and variable incubation period, making it difficult to trace possible contacts (Clark, 1986). Causative agent of the ano-genital wart is the human papilloma virus. Viral typing to date has not been helpful in clarifying transmission (Dunn & Weinstein, 1981). A child with ano-genital warts should be evaluated for other sexually transmitted diseases (Seidel & Zonana, 1979).

Herpes simplex virus (HSV) I, II can be acquired sexually or, in the case of the newborn, via the maternal route. All children with signs and symptoms of herpes infection should be evaluated from the perspective that they have acquired the disease through sexually inappropriate contact. Transmission can occur through oral-genital contact, genital-genital contact, or contact with infected genital secretions during fondling. The viability of virus on inanimate objects for up to 72 hours has been documented but transmission from such has not.

The clinical investigation of a child suspected to have a genital herpes infection should include a Tzanck smear, culture, and serologic tests. The serologic tests may include acute and convolescent compliment fixing antibody to HSV and neutralizing antibody to HSV I and HSV II.

Although HSV I infections are generally considered to involve the oral pharynx they account for 15% of primary genital herpes and 3% of nonprimary genital infections in adults (Reeves & Corey, 1981). No similar studies have been completed in the pediatric population. Differentiating type I from type II infections may provide prognostic information. Type II infections have a recurrence rate of 60%, while Type I recurrence rate is 14%. The presence or absence of circulating antibody to HSV Type I-II with clinical disease will help differentiate whether or not the infection is a primary or nonprimary genital infection.

Chlamydia trachomatis infections of the genital tract of children are being reported with increasing frequency in the literature. Chlamydia is considered to be a sexually transmitted disease in adults. The sexual mode of transmission has been documented in case reports of sexually abused children, but the asexual transmission has not. Neonates and infants manifest chlamydia infections as conjunctivitis or pneumonia. They are considered to have acquired these infections through the vaginal route. Reports by Hammerschlag & Doraiswamy (1984), Ingram & Runyan (1984), and Rettig (1984) raise many of the same questions concerning chlamydia as a marker for sexual abuse.

Chlamydia is difficult to culture and calcium alginate swabs and appropriate media are essential. Serologic antibody detection is rapid and relatively inexpensive (Murphy, 1983). Because infections may be asymptomatic, the differentiation between recent and older infections complicates the investigation of contacts. A careful investigation assessing the possibility of sexual contact is essential. Controversy continues as to whether all children when evaluated for sexual abuse should be cultured for chlamydia.

Specific guidelines for detection of sexually transmitted diseases in children are provided in Tables 1 through 3 from the Centers for Disease Control (Kramer & Jason, 1982). Guidelines for the office laboratory diagnosis of sexually transmitted diseases are reviewed by Murphy (1983). Table 4 outlines the Centers' guidelines for the treatment of vulvovaginitis and sexually transmitted diseases in children. Kramer and Jason (1982) from the Centers recommend against prophylactic treatment of gonorrhea noting the infection rate is only about 4% of sexually abused children. When cultures and Gram stains are positive, they recommend treatment with weight-appropriate dosages of antibiotics and preferably in oral form, as shots may be perceived as punitive.

Table 1

Management of Child Victims with History of Sexual Assault: Guidelines for Detection of Sexually Transmitted Diseases (STDs)*

Laboratory tests
  A. Mandatory immediate tests
    1. Gram stain of any discharge from genitals, urethra, or anus for intracellular gram-negative diplococci
    2. *Neisseria gonorrhoeae* cultures from cervix/vagina, urethra, anus, and throat, as indicated by history; confirm positive cultures with sugar utilization tests
    3. Syphilis serology
    4. Pregnancy test in postmenarcheal girls
    5. Wet preparation for trichomonads
    6. Test for presence of semen
  B. Recommended immediate tests (if available)
    1. *Chlamydia trachomatis* cultures
    2. *Ureaplasma urealyticum* cultures
  C. Recommended follow-up tests
    1. *N. gonorrhoeae* cultures
    2. Syphilis serology
    3. *C. trachomatis* cultures (if available)
    4. *U. urealyticum* cultures (if available)
    5. Herpes simplex virus cultures, if suspicious lesion appears
    6. Repeat pregnancy test, if appropriate
  D. Mandatory follow-up tests
    1. Test of cure 3-7 days after treatment of proved *N. gonorrhoeae* infection
    2. Repeat syphilis serology
    3. Follow-up culture of any previously cultured pathogen
Treatment of STDs
  A. Treat gonorrhea on the basis of positive gram stain
  B. No prophylaxis when assailant unknown
  C. Epidemiologic treatment indicated if assailant known to have disease
General management
  A. Report to appropriate legal and child protective services
  B. Follow-up by social worker, psychologist, etc.
  C. Interview for abuser and contact tracing

*From Kramer, D.J. & Jason, J. Sexually abused children and sexually transmitted diseases. *Reviews of Infectious Diseases*, Vol. 4 (Supplement), 1982, p. 886. Reprinted with permission from the Centers for Disease Control.

Table 2
Management of Children with Genital Symptoms: Guidelines for Detection of Sexually Transmitted Diseases (STDs) and Possible Child Abuse*

Laboratory tests for children with discharge
A. Mandatory immediate tests
1. Gram stain of discharge for intracellular gram-negative diplococci
1. *Neisseria gonorrhoeae* cultures from cervix/vagina, urethra, anus, and throat, as indicated by history; confirm positive cultures with sugar utilization tests
3. Syphilis serology
4. Pregnancy test in postmenarcheal girls
5. Wet preparation for trichomonads
B. Recommended immediate tests (if available)
1. *Chlamydia trachomatis* cultures
2. *Ureaplasma urealyticum* cultures
C. Follow-up tests
1. *N. gonorrhoeae* cultures
2. Syphilis serology
3. *C. trachomatis* cultures (if available)
4. *U. urealyticum* cultures (if available)
5. Herpes simplex virus cultures, if suspicious lesion appears
6. Repeat pregnancy test, if appropriate
D. Mandatory follow-up tests
1. Test of cure 3-7 days after treatment of proved *N. gonorrhoeae* infection
2. Repeat syphilis serology if another STD confirmed
3. Follow-up culture of any previously cultured pathogen
Laboratory tests for children with no discharge
A. Mandatory immediate tests
1. *N. gonorrhoeae* cultures from cervix/vagina, urethra, anus, and throat, as indicated by history; confirm positive cultures with sugar utilization tests
2. Syphilis serology
3. Pregnancy test in postmenarcheal girls
4. Wet preparation for trichomonads
B. Recommended immediate tests (if available)
1. *C. trachomatis* cultures
2. *U. urealyticum* cultures
C. Follow-up tests
1. *N. gonorrhoeae* cultures
2. Syphilis serology
3. *C. trachomatis* cultures (if available)
4. *U. urealyticum* cultures (if available)
5. Herpes simplex virus cultures, if suspicious lesion appears
6. Repeat pregnancy test, if appropriate
D. Mandatory follow-up tests
1. Test of cure 3-7 days after treatment of proved *N. gonorrhoeae* infection
2. Repeat syphilis serology if another STD confirmed
3. Follow-up culture of any previously cultured pathogen
Treatment of STDs
A. Treat gonorrhea on the basis of positive gram stain
B. If gram stain negative, await culture results before treating
General management
A. Report to appropriate legal and child protection services
B. Follow-up by social worker, psychologist, etc.
C. Interview for abuser and contact tracing

* From Kramer, D.J. & Jason, J. Sexually abused children and sexually transmitted diseases. *Reviews of Infectious Diseases*, Vol. 4 (Supplement), 1982, p. 887. Reprinted with permission from the Centers for Disease Control.

Table 3
Management of Children with Suspected Abuse Because of Behavioral Symptoms: Guidelines for Medical and Social Evaluation*

Initial visit
   A. Complete history and physical should include vaginal/cervical and anal cultures in girls or penile and anal cultures in boys for *Neisseria gonorrhoeae*
   B. Consider other nontraumatic tests for STD
      1. Syphilis serology (?)
      2. Wet preparation for trichomonads
      3. Others as appropriate and available
   C. Consider pregnancy test
General management
   A. Careful interviewing for history of sexual abuse
   B. Consider social or psychological evaluation
   C. Consider reporting to legal authorities if abuse suspected

* From Kramer, D.J. & Jason, J. Sexually abused children and sexually transmitted diseases. *Reviews of Infectious Diseases*, Vol. 4 (Supplement), 1982, p. 888. Reprinted with permission from the Centers for Disease Control.

FORMULATING A CONCLUSION

After the physician has obtained a history, completed an examination, and reviewed all laboratory tests, the final conclusion and case disposition recommendations must be made. The clinician's responsibility does not involve determining who the perpetrator is or determining guilt or innocence. The clinician's responsibility does include formulating an opinion. Heger (1985) suggests phrasing the diagnostic impressions as follows:

1. When historical information and physical evidence of sexual abuse are present, one may conclude that "the clinical evaluation is consistent with sexual abuse" (p. 23). The physician may continue to outline the specific inappropriate acts and the supportive historical physical findings for each in lay terms.
2. When the historical information is clear and convincing but the physical examination fails to reveal signs of acute or chronic trauma, venereal disease, or seminal products, the physician may conclude that "the physical examination neither confirms nor denies a history of sexual abuse" (p. 23). This is the most common conclusion in cases of sexual abuse.

Most children will not have lacerations, abrasions, or contusions, which readily heal in a short period of time. But most children who

Table 4

Vulvovaginitis—Treatment Guidelines

Etiologic Agent	Treatment	Alternative Therapy Comments
Beta-streptococcus-Group A	Penicillin V Potassium 125 mg. to 250 mg. q.i.d. for 10 days	Erythromycin in penicillin-allergic patient at 40 mg/kg/day in 4 divided doses for 10 days
Candida albicans	Nystatin, miconazole or clotrimazole topically for 7 days	In small children oral nystatin may be necessary in resistant cases
Chlamydia trachomatis	Erythromycin ethylsuccinate (ESS) 50 mg/kg/day in 4 divided doses for 7 days	If > 45 kg and/or > 8 y.o. tetracycline hydrochloride 500 mg. p.o. q.i.d. for 7 days or doxycycline 100 mg. b.i.d. for 7 days
Condylomata acuminata	10-25% podophyllin topically followed by thorough bathing 1–4 hours later. Apply podophyllin weekly for 4 weeks	If extensive lesions or in difficult location consider the use of laser surgery in preference to topical therapy.
Herpes genitalis (Type II)	5% Acyclovir ointment q. 4 hrs. for 7 days	In initial infection oral acyclovir may be indicated
Heamophilus Influenza	Amoxicillin 20 mg. to 50 mg./kg/day p.o. t.i.d. for 7 days	
Neisseria gonorrhea	<45 kg. child Amoxicillin 50 mg./kg and probenecid 25 mg/kg as a single dose p.o.	> 45 kg. child Amoxicillin 3 gm p.o. and probenecid 1 gm p.o. as a single dose

Table 4 *(continued)*

Etiologic Agent	Treatment	Alternative Therapy Comments
	Procaine penicillin G IM 100,000 U/kg and probenecid 25 mg/kg	Procaine penicillin G 4.8 million U IM and probenecid 1 gm. p.o.
	Erythromycin 40 mg/kg/day in 4 divided doses p.o. for 7 days	Use if less than 8 y.o., and/or allergic to penicillin
	Spectinomycin 40 mg/kg IM as a single dose	Spectinomycin 2 gm use only if penicillin resistant organism or allergy to penicillin
	Tetracycline 40 mg/kg in 4 divided doses for 7 days if less than 45 kg but older than 8 years	Tetracycline 500 mg. q.i.d. p.o. for 7 days also effective for chlamydia
Nonspecific Vaginitis NSV (Gardnerella Vaginalis)	Metronidazole 15 mg. kg/day in three divided doses for 7–10 days	In adolescent use Metronidazole 500 mg. b.i.d. p.o. for 7 days
Treponema pallidum	Benzathine penicillin G 2.4 million UIM once per week for 3 weeks if greater than 1 year old	In penicillin allergic patient erythromycin or tetracycline dose depending upon age and weight
Trichomonas vaginalis	Metronidazole 15 mg/kg/day in three divided p.o. doses for 7–10 days	In adolescent Metronidazole 2 gm. p.o. as single dose

Sources:
-*CDC MMWR Treatment Guidelines* (supplement), October 18, 1985, Vol. 34, p. 45.
-Emans, S.J. Vulvovaginitis in the child and adolescent. *Pediatrics in Review*, Vol. 8 (1), July 1986, pp. 12-19.

have been victims of sexual abuse will have very difficult emotional issues that may be long-standing if not dealt with in a timely and appropriate fashion.

Physicians become most effective when they extend themselves beyond their traditional role and look at victims of abuse as more than children with healing wounds.

Finkelhor and Browne (1985) conceptualize the impact of sexual abuse as including traumagenic sexualization, betrayal, powerlessness, and stigmatization. These issues in the long run have greater significance than the healing laceration. It is just as important to outline a plan of action to deal with these problems in a timely and appropriate fashion as it is for the medical problems. If these problems are ignored and only the laceration or sexually transmitted disease resolves, then the profession has fallen far short of what these children deserve.

INTERAGENCY COORDINATION

The physician is not ipso facto the expert in the evaluation of suspected sexual abuse. The physician must appreciate that many systems are involved in the detection, treatment, and prosecution of child sexual abuse. The physician has an important leadership role in minimizing problems in coordination of efforts. The legal system emphasizes punishment and social services protection, whereas the medical profession emphasizes diagnosis and treatment. Each system has its own language and protocol and would like to be "in charge" of the case. It is therefore not surprising that families feel overwhelmed by the barrage of interrogations and mixed messages that can result in fragmented case management. Bander, Fein, and Bishop (1982) feel the key to relationships between agencies involves mutual understanding of the operating procedures and constraints of each system. Further, it is necessary to appreciate the different timetables under which personnel must operate, e.g., the police officer is under pressure to get a restraining order or the court to obtain hospital records. Communication and follow-up of cases are an important component of overall case management, but unfortunately interagency cooperation is generally suboptimal.

Finally, interdisciplinary workshops would help to bridge the gaps between the professions and lead to better understanding of one another's roles and perspectives.

SUMMARY

This chapter has presented a practical perspective on the medical approach to and evaluation of the sexually abused child. The physician has an important role in the validation of an allegation of sexual abuse. It is often the physician's opinion that gives credibility to a child's statements. Validation facilitates protection. An examination completed with sensitivity and empathy has considerable therapeutic value for the child.

Anticipatory guidance concerning private parts offers valuable preventive information. Talking about private parts can serve as a natural transition to begin the genital examination. The genital examination should be a part of every health maintenance assessment. Examination of nonsexually abused children's genitals will also result in the physicians having: 1) improved expertise in doing an examination; 2) increased awareness of the spectrum of normal; and 3) better recognition of the sexually abused child.

REFERENCES

American Academy of Dermatology (1984). Task Force on Pediatric Dermatology. Genital warts and sexual abuse in children. *J.A.M. Acad. Dermatology,* 11:529-530.

American Academy of Pediatrics (1983). Committee on early childhood, adoption and dependent care: Gonorrhea in prepubital children. *Pediatrics,* 71:553.

Anglin, T.M. (1984). Physician management of sexually abused children and adolescent. *Current Problems in Pediatrics,* 14(7):13-15.

Bander, K., Fein, E., & Bishop, G. (1982). Child sex abuse treatment: Some barriers to program operation. *Child Abuse and Neglect,* 6:185-190.

Bell, T.A. (1983). Major sexually transmitted diseases of children and adolescents. *Ped. Inf. Disease,* 2(2):153-161.

Branch, G., & Paxton, R. (1965). A study of gonococcal infections among infants and children. *Public Health Reports,* 80:347-352.

Cantwell, H. (1981). Vaginal inspection as it relates to child sexual abuse in girls under thirteen. *Child Abuse and Neglect,* 7:171-176.

Clark, D.P. (1986). Condylomata acuminata in children. *Current Concepts in Skin Disorders,* 17(2):10-17.

Cooperman, M. (1927). Gonococcal arthritis in infancy. *Amer. J. Dis. Child,* 33:932-948.

Cowell, C.A. (1981). The gynecologic examination of infants, children and young adolescents. *Pediat. Clin. North America,* 28:247-266.

DeJong, A.R. (1985). The medical evaluation of sexual abuse in children. *Hosp. & Comm. Psychiatry,* 36(5):509-512.

Dunn, J., & Weinstein, L. (1981). Immunologic detection of condylomata acuminata-specific antigens. *Obstet. Gynecol.,* 57:351-356.

Emans, S.J. (1985). Personal communication concerning standardizing the genital examination in the collection of normative data.

Emans, S.J., & Goldstein, D.P. (1980). The gynecologic examination of the prepubertal child with vulva vaginitis: Use of the knee-chest position. *Pediatrics,* 65(4):758-60.

Finkelhor, D., & Browne, A. (1985). The traumatic impact of child sexual abuse: A conceptualization. *Amer. J. Orthopsychiat.*, 55(4):530-541.

Gilbaugh, J.H., & Fuchs, P.C. (1972). The gonococcus and the toilet seat. *N. Eng. J. Med.*, 301(2):91-93.

Groth, A.N. (1984). *Men Who Rape.* New York: Plenum Press, pp. 141-150.

Hammerschlag, M.R., & Doraiswamy, B. (1984). Are rectogenital chlamydial infections a marker of sexual abuse in children. *Ped. Inf. Dis.*, 3(2):100-104.

Heger, A. (1985). *Response: Child Sexual Abuse, A Medical View.* Los Angeles: United Way and Children's Institute International, pp. 23-24.

Huffman, J.W. (1977). Premenarchal vulvovaginitis. *Clinical Obstetrics and Gynecology*, 20(3):581-593.

Huffman, J.W. (1981). Anatomy and physiology. In J.W. Huffman (Ed.), *The Gynecology of Childhood and Adolescents* (2nd ed.). Philadelphia: W.B. Saunders, pp. 24-28.

Ingram, D.C., & Runyan, D.K. (1984). Vaginal chlamydia trachomatis infection in children with sexual contact. *Ped. Inf. Dis.*, 3(2):97-99.

Kramer, D.G., & Jason, J. (1982). Sexually abused children and sexually transmitted diseases. *Reviews of Infectious Diseases* (Suppl.), 4:883-890.

Litt, I.F., Edber, S.C., & Finberg, C. (1974). Gonorrhea in children and adolescents: A current review. *Journal of Pediatrics*, 85(5):595-606.

Monie, J.W. (1976). Embryology of the female genitalia. *Obstetrics and Gynecology Annual*, 5:1-20.

Murphy, D.M. (1983). Office laboratory diagnosis of sexually transmitted disease. *Ped. Inf. Dis.*, 2(2):146-152.

Nazarean, L.F. (1967). The current prevalence of gonococcal infection in children. *Pediatrics*, 39(3):372.

Neinstein, L.S., & Goldenring, J. (1984). Nonsexual transmission of sexually transmitted diseases: An infrequent occurrence. *Pediatrics*, 74(1):64-75.

Norvell, M.K., & Benrubi, G.I. (1984). Investigation of microtrauma after sexual intercourse. *Journal of Reproductive Medicine*, 29(4):269-271.

Paul, D.M. (1975). Medical examination in sexual offenses. *Med., Sci., Law*, 15(3):154-162.

Paul, D.M. (1977). The medical examination in sexual offenses against children. *Med., Sci., Law*, 17(4):251-258.

Pole, K. (1976). The medical examination in sexual offenses. *Med., Sci., Law*, 16:73.

Pritchard, N.A., & MacDonald, P.C. (1985). The anatomy of the reproductive tract of women. In J.W. Williams (Ed.), *Obstetrics* (17th ed.). New York: Appleton-Century-Crofts, pp. 7-11.

Reeves, W.C., & Corey, L. (1981). Risk of recurrence after first episodes of genital herpes. *New Eng. J. Med.*, 305(6):315-319.

Rettig, P.J. (1984). Pediatric genital infection with chlamydia trachomatis: Statistically nonsignificant, but clinically important. *Ped. Inf. Dis.*, 3(2):95-96.

Rosenfeld, A.A. (1982). Sexual abuse of children: Personal and professional responses. In E.H. Newberger (Ed.), *Child Abuse.* Boston: Little, Brown, pp. 57-58.

Seidel, J., & Zonana, J. (1979). Condylomata acuminata as a sign of sexual abuse in children. *Journal of Pediatrics*, 95:553-554.

Sensabaugh, G.F. (1978). Isolation and characterization of a semen-specific protein from human seminal plasma: A potential new maker for semen identification. *Journal of Forensic Sciences*, 23:106.

Sgroi, S.M. (1977). Kids with clap: Gonorrhea as an indicator of child sexual assault. *Victimology,* 2:251-267.

Sgroi, S.M. (1982a). Child sexual assault: Some guidelines for intervention assessment. In A. Burgess & A.N. Groth (Eds.), *Sexual Assault of Children and Adolescents.* Lexington, MA: Lexington Books, pp. 129-142.

Sgroi, S.M. (1982b). *Handbook of Clinical Intervention in Child Sexual Abuse.* Lexington, MA: Lexington Books, p. 17.

Sgroi, S.M., & Porter, K.S. (1982). Validation of child sexual abuse. In S.M. Sgroi (Ed.), *Handbook of Clinical Intervention in Child Sexual Abuse.* Lexington, MA: Lexington Books, pp. 12-27.

Shore, W.B., & Winkelstein, J.A. (1971). Nonvenereal transmission of gonococcal infections to children. *Journal of Pediatrics,* 79(4):661-663.

Snyder, L. (1967). *Suspected Sexual Assault, Homicide Investigation* (2nd ed.). Springfield, IL: Charles C. Thomas, pp. 354-358.

Steele, B., & Alexander, H. (1981). Long-term effects of sexual abuse in childhood. In P. Mrazek & C. Kempe (Eds.), *Sexually Abused Children and Their Families.* New York: Pergamon Press.

Teixara, W.R. (1981). Hymenal colposcopic examination in sexual offenses. *Amer. J. Forensic Med. & Pathol.,* 2(3):209-214.

White, S. (1986). Interviewing young sexual abuse victims with anatomically correct dolls. *Child Abuse and Neglect,* 10:519-529.

Woodling, B.A., & Heger, A. (1986). The use of the colposcope in the diagnosis of sexual abuse in the pediatric age group. *Child Abuse and Neglect,* 10(1):111-114.

Woodling, B.A., & Kossofis, P. (1981). Sexual misuse: Rape, molestation and incest. *Pediat. Clin. North America,* 28(2):493-499.

Wynne, J.M. (1980). Injuries to the genitalia in female children. *S.A. Medical Journal,* 57:47-50.

6

True and False Allegations of Child Sexual Abuse

Arthur H. Green and Diane H. Schetky

As reports of child sexual abuse have increased dramatically over the past few years, so have unfounded and false reports of sexual abuse. Professionals, aware of their duty to report suspected sexual abuse and fearful of possible malpractice suits if they fail to, are filing more reports. Extensive media attention to child sexual abuse has made the public aware of the problem and more likely to take action if it is suspected. Complicating the issue of sifting out these complex cases is the fact that children are exposed to much more sexuality in today's more permissive society. Thus, excessive sexual stimulation may come from sources such as cable TV, home videos, TV, movies, and explicit sex in the home, as well as from being a victim of sexual abuse.

A small number of parents caught up in custody battles or visitation disputes have exploited the epidemic of sexual abuse by using such allegations to promote their own interests at the expense of their child and their former spouse. Allegations have become a surefire way of getting a judge's attention and cutting off visitations. They have the same emotional impact that issues of adultery once had in custody battles a decade or more ago.

If allegations of sexual abuse are proven, the perpetrator (usually the husband/father) is excluded from contact with his children. Visitation is suspended and the plaintiff is awarded full custody of the children. These cases comprise a continuum, ranging from obvious cases of sexual molestation corroborated by the child, testimony of witnesses, and physical evidence of sexual contact, to situations in which the allegations

This chapter is an expanded version of an article by Arthur H. Green entitled "True and False Allegations of Sexual Abuse in Child Custody Disputes," which appeared in the *Journal of the American Academy of Child Psychiatry, 25*, 449–456, copyright © by the American Academy of Child and Adolescent Psychiatry, 1986. Reprinted with permission.

are firmly denied by the child and are held to be unlikely by all except the plaintiff and her counsel. Child psychiatrists are frequently used by both sides to evaluate the child and make a determination about the authenticity of the charges. The drama often unfolds in the following manner: The irate wife describes how she discovered the sexual abuse and brings in audiocasettes of the child's confession. The husband is outraged and indignant, and vehemently denies such perverse behavior. The key to the solution usually lies within the child and can be tapped by a sensitive psychiatric evaluation of the child and the parents, which should include observation of the child interacting with each parent. The child psychiatrist must try to provide the correct answer, which will be conveyed to the court. A mistake might jeopardize a child's future or destroy a man's family life and career, and the parent-child relationship.

This chapter is devoted to preparing the child psychiatrist for this awesome task by reviewing the expanding data base concerning child sexual abuse and suggesting a modification of the traditional child psychiatric evaluation designed to differentiate true victims of child sexual abuse from those falsely implicated in sexual activity with adults.

REVIEW OF THE LITERATURE

Despite the increasing numbers of sexually abused children referred to child psychiatrists for psychiatric evaluations, there have been very few publications dealing with the phenomenon of false allegations of sexual molestation. Peters (1976) reported four false accusations in a total of 64 children brought to a hospital emergency room for suspected sexual abuse. Goodwin, Sahd, and Rada (1978) discovered that three of 46 sexual abuse cases reported to a child abuse agency were based upon false allegations. Thus, 6% of reported cases of child sexual abuse could not be substantiated. Child psychiatrists who evaluate sexually abused children must be aware of this small but significant number of "false positives."

More frequent false allegations of sexual abuse are made by parents during court litigation involving custody and/or visitation. Benedek and Schetky (1985) failed to document charges of sexual abuse in 10 of 18 children evaluated during disputes over custody and visitation. This strikingly high (55%) incidence of unfounded allegations is somewhat comparable to Green's (1986) documentation of four false allegations in 11 children reported to be sexually abused by the noncustodial parent in the context of child custody and visitation disputes (36%). Brant and Sink (1984) reported that the noncustodial parent accused the custodial parent of brainwashing the child to make a false allegation of sexual abuse in three of four sexual abuse evaluations during custody disputes. Kaplan and Kaplan (1981) cited one case report of two children who falsely accused their father and paternal grandparents of sexual assault during the time that the parents and children were living together, and attributed the false allegations to brainwashing and the phenomenon of folie-à-deux.

Guyer and Ash (1986) noted a marked increase in the number of allegations of sexual abuse arising in contested custody cases, amounting to 33% of 400 court-ordered custody evaluations in the past five years. Guyer and Ash speculate whether some of these cases might actually represent a Munchausen-by-proxy syndrome (a condition in which parents get special gratification from imaginary illness in their children). They observe that whereas most parents are relieved by negative findings in a child, these parents become more distraught if their suspicions are not confirmed and obviously have much invested in clinging to their convictions.

Yates and Musty (1987) reviewed sexual abuse allegations in 19 of 80 custody and/or visitation cases involving preschool children seen at a conciliation court. Sexual abuse could only be substantiated in four of the 19 cases. In the substantiated cases, the child was directly involved in making the allegations, whereas the unsubstantiated cases were based on statements made by one parent about the other parent and not on statements made by the child. These observers suggested that the following mechanisms were involved in the fabrication of false allegations by the child: the persuasion or suggestion of a caretaker, sexualized perceptions emanating from the oedipal conflict, the emergence of primary process material, and the involvement of the child in the projective identification of a dominant caretaker.

Schuman (1986) described seven cases of unfounded sexual and/or physical abuse. These cases involved acrimonious domestic litigation usually dealing with custody and visitation disputes. Schuman posited that the psychiatric regression of adults and children involved in domestic relations litigation contributes to their projection and misperception of events, which form the basis of false allegations of sexual misconduct. According to Schuman, the child may serve as a passive screen for projectional fantasies by regression-prone adults at first, but later the child might actively furnish an ambiguous report of sexual activity that gets magnified and projected back onto the child in a "positive feedback loop," which increases the ultimate distortions. Weiss (1983) stressed the importance of appraising the child's cognitive ability and emotional development in determining his or her credibility.

Jones (1987) reviewed the 576 reports of child sexual abuse made to the Denver Department of Social Services during 1983. Seventy percent of these reports proved to be reliable, while 8% appeared to be fictitious. The fictitious reports frequently lacked detail. The children initiating false allegations demonstrated little or no accompanying emotion while describing the abuse. Descriptions of threats were absent from their accounts. Most of the mothers who made false allegations were involved in custody/visitation disputes and manifested hysterical or paranoid personality disorders. Several of them had evidence of an unresolved post-traumatic stress disorder based upon their own childhood experiences of being sexually abused.

EVALUATION OF THE CHILD

As discussed in Chapter 4, professionals need to be comfortable discussing sex with young children and aware of their own feelings and how these might affect the interview process. They must be open to the possibility that an accusation might be false and that the "alleged" perpetrator may be an innocent victim. They must be able to tolerate ambiguity and uncertainty while confronted by urgent demands for a definitive opinion. The evaluator must possess a solid understanding of the dynamics and sequelae of child sexual abuse and a thorough knowledge of child development. They must be aware of the impact of the child's cognitive limitations on his perception and recall of the events of the molestation, as well as potential distortions caused by emotional and interviewer factors.

RELIABILITY OF THE CHILD'S DISCLOSURE

The child's testimony is usually acceptable to the court if he or she is old enough to verbalize, knows what the truth is, and can distinguish right from wrong. The psychiatrist's criteria for reliability of the child's disclosure of sexual abuse are more complex. The child's verbalizations during the psychiatric evaluation cannot always be accepted at face value, because they are subjected to powerful distorting influences from within (i.e., shame and guilt) and to fear from the environment. Superego pressures result in shame regarding participation in "forbidden" sexual acts accompanied by pleasurable sensations, and guilt concerning the prosecution of a father and the subsequent breakup of a family. External threats of retaliation and punishment for betraying the perpetrator might engender fear and anxiety.

These pressures tend to inhibit disclosure of the sexual abuse, causing incest victims to deny any knowledge of the molestation. Therefore, denial of the incest allegations by the child has limited validity. On the other hand, if the child is able to describe the sexual abuse, one must give it credence. False denials, therefore, are common, but false disclosures are rare. These do occur, however, in the following seven situations:

1. *The child is "brainwashed" by a vindictive parent, usually the mother, who fabricates the incest in order to punish the spouse by excluding him from further contact with child.* The accusation might be completely without foundation, but it is usually based upon a core of reality, i.e., observations of normal, affectionate physical contact between spouse and child with seductive overtones, or the father's bathing or cleaning the genital area of the child.

2. *The child is influenced by a delusional mother who projects her own unconscious sexual fantasies onto the spouse.* The delusional mother truly misperceives the relationship between spouse and child and is usually diagnosed as a histrionic or paranoid personality disorder, or paranoid schizophrenic. There is a frequent history of previous accusations of sexual misconduct by the spouse with other family members or other women. These women bombard their children with incessant interrogations about the alleged sexual contact and pressure them to accept their delusions, creating a folie-à-deux.

   Both the vindictive and the delusional mother reinforce the child's compliance by withholding love and approval if she denies the incest or demonstrates positive feelings toward the father. Such a woman fosters abnormal dependency in the child to enhance her own narcissism and to compensate for her unsatisfactory love relationship. The vindictive or delusional mother needs to have total control over the child and may be threatened by the child's ties to the father. Such a mother may convey to the child that it is not safe to visit with father, then uses the child's anxiety about visitation as proof that something is amiss. The allegations of incest usually begin shortly after the marital separation, while the child is visiting the father. The object loss inherent in the separation and impending divorce acts as the catalyst for this pathological process.

3. *The child's allegations of sexual abuse are based upon sexual fantasies rather than reality.* This corresponds to Freud's (1917) early experiences with adult hysterics whose powerful oedipal fantasies altered their perceptions and reality testing. Fantasied incest is more common in preadolescent or adolescent girls,

who project their own sexual wishes onto the parent. They also exhibit hysterical personality traits; more rarely, they are frankly delusional and paranoid. Unless the child has experienced prior sexual activity, such allegations are usually lacking in detail. Jones (1987) reports false allegations of sexual abuse by children who were prior victims of sexual molestation. These children suffered from post-traumatic stress disorder and attached their vivid memories of traumatization to a new person. The child who has been previously sexually abused may sexualize subsequent relationships with adults and misperceive innocent situations.

4. *The child falsely accuses the father of incest for revenge or retaliation.* Careful investigation will often reveal the underlying motivation for the allegation, i.e., anger over recent punishment or deprivation, desire to remove the father or stepfather from the home, and so forth. This is more likely to occur among teenagers. Secondary gain is usually evident, i.e., a wish to alter a custody arrangement and, when confronted, the teenager usually admits to fabricating allegations.

5. *False allegations of sexual abuse may be initiated by third parties, i.e., hypervigilant parents of preschool children who have been oversensitized by sensational media coverage of sexual abuse scandals at nursery schools and day care centers.* Pediatricians and child mental health professionals may innocently institute false reports of sexual abuse based upon their misinterpretation of physical or behavioral symptoms in their patients.

6. *False allegations may be spread by contagion through exposure to the testimony of other children, in preschool and day care settings, i.e., Jordan, Minnesota (Norris & Potter, 1986) and McMartin (Summit, 1986) school cases.*

7. *Medical problems may give rise to increased sexual concerns or account for physical findings, i.e., nonspecific vulvovaginitis, anal fissures caused by constipation, and misinterpretation of medical data.* In one case, for example, a dermatologist diagnosed a skin lesion as herpes, from which a court case was built. When one of the authors later examined the records, she discovered the child's herpes antibody titer six months later was negative, precluding a herpes infection. In another case, a social worker failed to differentiate a urinary tract infection from a vaginitis and used the former as evidence of sexual abuse.

False disclosures of incest by children show the following characteristics: Details of the sexual activity are obtained rather easily during the initial interview or may even be presented spontaneously by the child; the children are outspoken and nondefensive in their descriptions of sexual activity, without significant changes in mood and affect; they often use adult terminology to describe genitals and parts of the body; their motivation for initiating or perpetuating the false allegation is discernible.

Genuine incest victims, on the other hand, are secretive about the molestation and their disclosure is delayed and conflicted, usually occurring only after weeks or months, if at all. Their allegations are often retracted and then restated. Direct questioning about the molestation usually provokes or intensifies negative affects.

Disclosure is usually accompanied by depressed mood. The children use age-appropriate sexual terminology. With younger children, the incest is usually reenacted symbolically in play or fantasy before it can be verbalized. Some severely traumatized children will avoid symbolic play with dolls or puppets, and are unable to fashion human figures out of clay or with drawings because human interaction is too closely associated with the incest experience. These children are more comfortable engaging in repetitive, concrete play.

EVALUATION OF INTERACTION BETWEEN CHILD AND PARENTS

When a clinician first sees a young, alleged victim of sexual abuse, he will usually have the mother present in order to reduce the child's anxiety and enable her to feel secure. The mother-child interaction offers the clinician a standard upon which to assess the relationship between the child and the alleged perpetrator. The sexually abused child often exhibits signs of fearfulness and inhibition with the father; at times the child might refuse to enter the office in his presence. If both parents are present, the victimized child might cling to the mother. However, if the sexual contact was gentle, gradual, and nonthreatening, the child might display seductive behavior with the father rather than a fearful response, especially if the victim is too young to appreciate the deviant nature of the molestation. The delusional and vindictive mother often controls the child by monitoring her responses through eye contact and subtle facial expressions. The "brainwashed" child responds by "checking" with her mother before proceeding. The child usually behaves in a hostile manner toward the father in the presence of the mother, but reverts to friendliness when she is no longer under her mother's scrutiny. In cases of genuine incest, the mother-child relationship might appear hostile or strained, but the child is generally more fearful with the father. The true incest victim will rarely describe the sexual activity in the father's presence, out of fear and guilt, while the "brainwashed" child will do this if the mother is also present.

Observations of the child with both parents provide the clinician with additional information which may confirm or refute original impressions derived from individual sessions with the child and her parents separately, and from the history and physical findings. If the clinician feels that the interaction between the child and the alleged perpetrator might generate undue anxiety and discomfort, such contact would not be advisable.

EVALUATION OF THE PARENTS

A separate psychiatric examination of each parent should complement the previous evaluations and provide additional clues about the reliability of the child's testimony and the family psychodynamics contributing to the incest. The evaluation should include a detailed sexual history from each parent. Both sexually abusing fathers and mothers of incest victims are more likely to have experienced physical or sexual abuse during their childhood than nonabusing fathers and their spouses. Thus, with the father, the sexual abuse of the child might represent reenactment of a passively experienced trauma during a state of helplessness. The mother might consciously or unconsciously create situations in which her child(ren) is vulnerable to molestation as a means of mastering her own incest trauma. The father should also be questioned about other forms of abnormal sexual behavior, such as exhibitionism, rape, voyeurism, and other perversions, which have often been associated with pedophilia. The father's capacity for impulse control should also be determined by inquiring about previous aggressive or antisocial behavior. A history of substance abuse should also be obtained.

Depression in the father associated with the separation or divorce might trigger the incestuous behavior. Similar depressive reactions in the mother might contribute to a withdrawal from her spouse and children, setting the stage for incest. The presence of hysterical, paranoid, or delusional psychopathology in the mother should alert one to the possibility of a false accusation, but these conditions may also coexist with actual sexual abuse.

CASE ILLUSTRATIONS

The following case histories demonstrate typical similarities and contrasts between true and false cases of sexual abuse.

A True Allegation of Sexual Abuse

Paul A. is a five-year-old youngster who was allegedly sexually molested by his father, from whom his mother had been recently divorced. Paul's mother and father were successful professionals. Mrs. A. reported that Paul informed her that his father had played with his "pee-pee-er" and put his finger in his "butty-butt" when he was two years old, just prior to the final marital separation. At the time of this disclosure, Paul acted depressed, exhibited sleep problems, and clung to his mother in bed. In retrospect, Mrs. A. recalled that Mr. A. often permitted Paul to touch his genitals when he was nude, without setting limits. She also described Paul's frequent fingering of his anus. Mrs. A. took the child for a psychiatric evaluation to see if her suspicions would be confirmed. The psychiatrist, however, could not find evidence for the molestation.

According to Mrs. A., Paul then became increasingly anxious before and during visits with his father and eventually refused to see him. After the visits had been terminated for six months, Mr. A.'s attorney filed a writ of habeas corpus and initiated a custody action. A court-appointed child psychiatrist also failed to confirm the sexual abuse, but recommended supervised visitation because Paul appeared to be so frightened. Renewal of the visits resulted in Paul's increased fearfulness with signs of regressive behavior, i.e., baby talk and rocking movements. The child was referred for evaluation at this time. During the initial interviews, Paul would not permit his mother to leave the room. Information about his feelings towards his father could not be elicited until the third session. Then he reported that his father was bad and tried to choke his mother. He was finally able to talk about how his father would touch his penis, and he fashioned a drawing of this experience. He then related a dream, "My father stabbed my mother in the nose, I killed him by cutting off his pee-pee-er." This dream followed an attempted visit by Mr. A. The major themes of the following sessions consisted of small spaceships fighting off larger ones with missiles and laser beams, and tiny animals defending against dragonlike monsters.

The mother-child relationship appeared to be warm and loving, although Mrs. A. was somewhat overprotective and overstimulating. Mr. A. completely denied the allegations and was incensed that the evaluator would be so easily misled by his "hysterical, brainwashing ex-wife." Mr. A. did admit that he had been sexually fondled by his mother during childhood. She had been frequently hospitalized for a chronic schizophrenic illness.

When Paul was evaluated with his father, the child refused to enter the office unless Mrs. A. was also present. But even with his mother close by, Paul hid behind the evaluator's chair so his father could not see him, while Mr. A. attempted to interest the child in a bag filled with Christmas presents. The evaluator recommended that Paul remain in play therapy with concomitant psychiatric treatment of each parent and that visits between Paul and his father be suspended until the child was ready for them.

This was presumed to be a genuine case of sexual abuse because the child was bright and credible, and was able to remember details of the molestation and reenact them in play and fantasy. Paul's disclosure of his victimization was delayed and conflicted, with sad and painful affect. His persistent fear of his father was intensified prior to and during their visits, which was suggestive of a post-traumatic stress disorder.

False Allegations of Sexual Abuse

Case 1. Andy B., a precocious little boy of three years 10 months, was referred for psychiatric evaluation because he had been allegedly sexually abused by his father, Mr. B. Mrs. B., Andy's mother, had charged her estranged husband with kissing the child's penis and buttocks while playing "doctor" together. She also claimed that Andy became hyperactive and enuretic after his father's visits. Mrs. B. also observed her husband kissing the child with his tongue, hired detectives to document this, and reported that Andy told her about white material coming from his daddy's penis, which he described as "penis manure."

The B.'s had been married five years previously after a whirlwind courtship which lasted for two weeks. It was the second marriage for each. Mr. B., age 59, was a successful self-made businessman who had three grown children by his first wife. Mrs. B., age 35, had been briefly married to a man she now described as a homosexual. The marital friction began shortly after Andy's birth, when Mr. B. became jealous of the baby and resented the breastfeeding, according to Mrs. B. At this time he began to get angry and assaultive with her. She said he was "oversexed" and accused him of ejaculating six times a night during lovemaking, and masturbating in front of the child in the crib. Mr. B., on the other hand, appeared to be depressed and weary from the entire litigation. He denied the allegations of sexual abuse and said that marrying Mrs. B. was the biggest mistake of his life.

The evaluation revealed that Andy was a precocious, intelligent little boy who looked like a "little old man" because of his eyeglasses and serious expression. At his mother's prompting, Andy described without

the slightest hesitation how he saw his daddy's penis and how the
"penis manure" came out of it. He said his daddy was mean and he
did not like him. He also mentioned that Betty, Mr. B.'s daughter,
tried to drown him by pushing him into a swimming pool. When the
examiner registered surprise, Mrs. B. informed him that Betty was
jealous of Andy and herself and opposed her father's marriage because
they had been previously involved in an incestuous relationship.

When Andy was seen alone with his father, he was friendly, spontaneous, and affectionate and seemed to enjoy the interaction. When
Andy was seen with both parents, he was angry and hostile toward his
father. He humiliated Mr. B. by spontaneously drawing a picture of
his father with a big erect penis and told the examiner that he and
his daddy played with each other's penises while they were naked.
During this narrative, which was presented without emotion, Andy's
gaze frequently focused on his mother's approving expression.

As the evaluation progressed, Mrs. B. presented the evaluator with
scores of taped conversations with Mr. B. in which he was either
verbally abusive or sexually excited, i.e., while arguing or engaging in
sexual talk.

Psychological testing of Mr. B. proved unremarkable, while Mrs. B.'s
revealed faulty perception and paranoid, delusional ideation.

Case 2. Betty C., a 9-year-old girl, was referred for treatment because
of alleged sexual abuse by her father, Mr. C., during weekend overnight
visits. Mrs. C., Betty's mother, became suspicious of possible incest
when the child returned from her father's house with blood-stained
panties after the weekend visitation. This event confirmed Mrs. C.'s
long-standing belief that her ex-husband had been molesting Betty since
she was an infant. Mrs. C. recalled that Betty had sucked on a toy in
a seductive manner during her baths, while saying "da-da." She concluded that Mr. C. forced the child to perform fellatio when he bathed
her as an infant. Betty appeared to be a rather shy and sensitive young
girl, who was quite resistant to questioning about the visits with her
father. She reluctantly admitted that Mr. C. had rubbed against her in
bed. Mr. C. denied these charges and claimed that Betty came into his
bed during the night while he was sleeping because she was afraid of
sleeping alone. In her psychotherapy, Betty became preoccupied with
sexual themes, so it was decided there was a real possibility of sexual
abuse by Mr. C. and the court initially recommended that the contact
between Betty and her father be limited to chaperoned, daytime visits.
Mrs. C. felt that Mr. C. might evade the chaperone and proceed to
victimize Betty, so she finally withheld Betty from the visits, which

precipitated a second court hearing. Betty denied the most recent allegations and claimed that she wanted to see her father. She finally confided in her therapist that her original disclosure of her father's "rubbing against her" was not true. She felt that she had to perpetuate the false allegations in order to please her mother and gain respite from Mrs. C.'s relentless interrogations about the suspected sexual molestation. Upon knowledge of Betty's retraction, the court ordered a gradual return to regular unsupervised visitation between Betty and her father. Mrs. C., however, remained convinced that the incest was still taking place, and she approached additional child protective agencies with the aim of initiating new investigations. She simultaneously accused the clinic staff of producing false testimony in court and conspiring with Mr. C. to cover up the sexual molestation. Mrs. C. was thought to be delusional and suffering from a circumscribed paranoid psychosis.

Case 3. Mr. E. was reported for the sexual abuse of Brenda, his five-year-old daughter, by a social worker from a child guidance center. The maternal grandparents had taken Brenda to the agency because the child protested about returning to Mr. E. after visits with them. Simultaneously, they noted that Brenda often slept in her father's bed and had recently complained of rectal and vaginal irritation. After Mr. E. ignored the social worker's request for an appointment, she filed the sexual abuse report.

Mrs. F., the maternal grandmother, had become Brenda's primary maternal caretaker after her daughter's sudden death following Brenda's birth. Mr. E. and Mrs. F. cared for Brenda jointly, the child staying with Mr. and Mrs. F. while Mr. E. was at work. Mr. E. and Mrs. F. soon began to argue over the "possession" of the child. Mr. E. resented Mrs. F. for asking Brenda to call her "mommy," while Mr. and Mrs. F. felt that Mr. E. was limiting their contact with the child. After the allegations of sexual abuse were not confirmed by the child protective services caseworker, Mr. E. became convinced that the F.'s were trying to take Brenda away from him. He then took the child to his own mother's house in another state for a month, and when he returned home he took a leave of absence from his job so that he could be Brenda's primary caretaker.

The psychiatric evaluation of Brenda and her family also failed to confirm the allegations of sexual abuse. Brenda related warmly and spontaneously with her father, although she expressed anger toward him for not letting her spend more time with her grandparents. She did not manifest any of the signs and symptoms of sexual molestation. Her preoccupation with her "bottom" was a result of a chronic rash and skin irritation, which was confirmed by the pediatrician. Brenda's reluctance to make the transition from the grandparents to her father and her insistence on sleeping with Mr. E. were a reflection of her severe separation anxiety, which was fueled by the power struggle between Mr. E. and his in-laws.

The characteristics of the children and parents involved in true and false allegations of sexual abuse are summarized in Table 1.

GRAY AREAS IN THE SPECTRUM OF CHILD SEXUAL ABUSE ALLEGATIONS

A middle range or "gray area" appears to exist in the spectrum of child sexual abuse allegations in which molestation cannot easily be proven or disproven. The young child may glibly describe a sexual contact with the alleged perpetrator, usually a father figure, with little understanding of its deviant nature. The father-child relationship is warm and affectionate, and there is evidence of strong bonding. The child seems minimally traumatized compared to victims of proven sexual abuse, except for symptoms of sexual precocity and seductive behavior which are frequently present in the child sexual abuse syndrome. The child creates an aura of secrecy and excitement, often accompanied by

Table 1
Characteristics of True and Unsubstantiated Cases
of Child Sexual Abuse

True Cases	Unsubstantiated Cases
Child initially reticent to discuss abuse with mother or others	Child discusses the abuse when prompted by mother Child checks with mother
Child rarely will confront father with the allegation, even with mother present	Child will often confront father with allegation in mother's presence, while seeking mother's approval
Child usually fearful in father's presence, congruent with affect and ideation unless molestation was gentle and nonthreatening	Discrepancy between the child's angry accusations and the apparent comfort in father's presence
Mothers often depressed; no other specific psychopathology	Prominent paranoid and hysterical psychopathology in mothers
Child usually demonstrates signs and symptoms of child sexual abuse	Child might be sexually preoccupied, but does not exhibit signs and symptoms of child sexual abuse

a plethora of sexualized fantasies. Are we dealing with an exaggerated, developmentally determined sexual responsiveness within a normal family setting, or the early onset of a pathological incestuous relationship? Can we draw the line between normal hugging, touching, and kissing occurring in healthy families and inappropriate sexual touching and fondling? We need more information about the prevalence of potentially sexually stimulating behaviors in normal families, i.e., genital touching, nudity, child sleeping in parents' bed.

Reitman and Robson (1987) described the universality of sexual arousal in parents in the context of early child rearing. Erotic parental responses towards their offspring are considered to be adaptive and a necessary component of being in love with one's child. A recent study by Rosenfeld and colleagues (1986) of childrearing practices in upper-middle-class families determined that 45% of 8-to-10-year-old boys had touched their mother's breasts or genitals, and that 30% of girls up to age 10 had touched their fathers' genitals. This behavior has often been regarded as evidence of sexual abuse. The clinician must make a thorough survey of "normal" or sexually ambiguous caretaking routines, such as touching of the child's genitals during bathing and toileting, during sexual abuse evaluations as they might be misinterpreted as evidence of molestation.

Sexual Overstimulation

Some children are exposed to chronic sexual overstimulation by one or both parents. The overstimulation may take place during routine childcare practices, such as bathing or toileting, when a parent might rub or clean the child's genital area too vigorously. It may also occur in "liberated" families in which the parents and children walk around in the nude. On other occasions, a child may be sexually stimulated by prolonged and sensual hugging and kissing, or by sleeping in the same bed with a parent. In some sexually permissive families, the parents will allow the children to touch and examine their genitals in response to questioning about sexual anatomy. Other permissive parents allow their children to enter the bathroom and observe them while urinating or defecating. These parents are usually unaware of the potential pathological impact of these practices on their children, and fail to appreciate the importance of privacy and delineating physical boundaries for the child's self-awareness and body integrity.

Children are most vulnerable to these intrusions during developmentally determined surges of sexual interest and fantasy, i.e., phallic and oedipal periods and early adolescence. These children receive conscious and unconscious gratification of voyeuristic, exhibitionistic, and incestual fantasies during these stimulating encounters, which may give rise to shame, guilt, fear of punishment or castration and may engender intrapsychic conflict. They might also exhibit seductive and sexually precocious behavior through premature eroticization and identification with the "seductive" parent. There is potential for a "snowballing" effect as the sexualized child elicits further seductive behavior from the parent. The parents usually receive unconscious sexual and incestuous gratification from these interactions, which may or may not serve as a compensation for an unsatisfactory marital relationship. These behaviors are usually ego syntonic for the parents as long as their relationship remains intact.

When a separation or divorce ensues, however, the seductive parent-child contact assumes a more threatening perspective. Typically, the seductive parent-child dyad, usually the father and daughter, become more enmeshed as a result of the anxiety generated by the separation, and the mother becomes threatened by feelings of jealousy and exclusion. In this setting, the mother can easily overreact to the sexualized father-daughter relationship and make an allegation of sexual abuse. At times, she responds to cues of increased distress by the daughter, as the latter experiences an intensification of oedipal guilt and separation anxiety following overnight and vacation visits with the oversexualized father in the mother's absence. Hysterical and paranoid mothers are more likely to misperceive this sexualized relationship as intentional sexual misuse of the child. In this highly sexualized climate, a vaginal or rectal irritation will often trigger a report of sexual abuse by a pediatrician or mental health professional, even in the absence of hard physical findings.

Cases of sexual overstimulation in children may be differentiated from actual sexual abuse in that (a) the father-child relationship is usually positive and (b) aside from signs of sexual overstimulation, there are no other symptoms of the child sexual abuse syndrome, i.e., post-traumatic stress responses, depression, regressive behavior, and social withdrawal. The allegations of sexual abuse by the father will reinforce the child's guilt, through the realization that he or she has engaged in socially unacceptable behavior. This, in turn, will make the child difficult to interview.

Case illustration. Four-year-old Mary talked with her mother and her therapist about "sucking my daddy's penis." Mary had been in play therapy because of severe separation anxiety prior to leaving her mother's home for overnight visitation with her father. Mary had been shifted back and forth between her parents since she was two, under a joint custody arrangement. The therapist made a report of child sexual abuse because of the child's preoccupation with fellatio with her father and the presence of other signs of eroticized behavior, such as open masturbation and precocious and seductive sexual talk. The therapist interpreted Mary's separation anxiety as further confirmation of the traumatic impact of her father and made no attempt to interview him prior to her report.

During their marriage, Mary's parents operated a health club together, in which the mother and father headed exercise classes and gave body massages. They both espoused a hedonistic philosophy, which included nudity in the home and extreme permissiveness concerning Mary's sex education. The family showered and bathed together with Mary, and the father continued to bathe with Mary after the marital separation. He also allowed the child to examine his penis at her request when they were in the shower in order to "satisfy her normal curiosity." This was explained as a means of instructing Mary that the genitals and sexual matters should be dealt with openly and without shame or guilt. Her father also allowed Mary to sleep in his bed whenever she was frightened or upset.

During the evaluation, Mary's father was outspoken and not at all defensive about the nature of his relationship with the child. It was difficult for him to appreciate the seductive and sexually overstimulating dimensions of his behavior. When observed together, Mary's warm and affectionate feelings toward her father were accompanied by an undercurrent of seductive provocativeness, which were refractory to his tentative attempts to set limits. Mary behaved more appropriately with her mother, but she appeared to stifle her excitement toward her father when her mother was present. Mary's sexual fantasies were not limited to her father, but extended to many of her nursery school classmates, and she was quite seductive and hyperactive with the male evaluator. There was little change in Mary's affect when she was asked to describe the nature of the sexual contact with her father. She gleefully spoke about touching his penis in the shower. Her response to the anatomical dolls was one of excitement about the genitals. Mary denied being genitally touched or fondled by her father.

The failure of the child's therapist to interview the father made it easy to mistakenly attribute the child's sexual preoccupation to a genuine molestation rather than as a response to a seductive and sexually permissive caretaking environment.

"Gentle" Molestation

At the other end of the spectrum, a father or paternal caretaker might intentionally fondle the genitals of a preschool child in the context of routine child care, i.e., dressing and bathing. The fondling may be accomplished in a gentle, soothing manner, without force or threats. The child, under these circumstances, may respond with erotic pleasure, being totally unaware of the deviant nature of the act. If there is no attempt at more invasive sexual practices, such as vaginal penetration, anal intercourse, or fellatio, the child may remain asymptomatic. This type of molestation is often not disclosed until the child becomes older and begins to understand the nature of this behavior, or if the pressure for secrecy becomes an onerous burden. Then symptoms of anxiety, regressive behavior, and somatic symptoms might ensue. In a certain percentage of these cases, the gentle fondling will gradually escalate into a more forceful type of genital contact, leading to more prominent symptoms and disclosure.

Family assessment of this type of molestation might reveal: (a) a positive but seductive interaction between the father and child; (b) confirmation of the abuse by the child through verbalization or reenactment in play and fantasy; and (c) prominent paternal psychopathology and/or evidence of sexual deviancy. "Gentle" molestation will not yield positive physical or laboratory findings.

Case illustration. Mrs. F. observed that her four-year-old son James had become increasingly preoccupied with his anus. The child often inserted his finger into his rectum. He had recently given his mother a jar of cream, lay on her lap with his buttocks exposed and told her to "make my butt." Upon questioning, James told his mother that "poppy stick it in butt" and "poppy stick it in Mary's butt." Mary is the father's current girlfriend. Mrs. F. also reported that James had started to fondle the breasts and genitals of women in the street while walking with his mother.

James' mother and father were currently separated. The parents had begun to argue during Mrs. F.'s pregnancy with James, after Mrs. F. refused to submit to an abortion that Mr. F. requested. Mr. F. moved out when James was five months old. Mr. F. continued to play a major role in caring for James while Mrs. F. was working. He was directly involved in diapering, bathing, and feeding the child, and had him for frequent overnight visits.

During the evaluation, James manifested a marked expressive language disorder. However, he spontaneously identified the genitals of the anatomically correct dolls and inserted the father doll's hand in the boy's anus, stating "poppy stick it in butt" and directed his own finger towards his buttocks. When asked about his father, James became animated and stated that he wanted to see him.

When the visit was arranged between James and Mr. F., the child greeted his father warmly and effusively. Mr. F. and James hugged and caressed one another in a loving manner, and Mr. F. swept the child into his arms and pressed him to his chest. In an attempt to demonstrate James' improved verbal skills, his father instructed him to name various objects in the playroom, and to name the parts of his body that Mr. F. pointed out. Beginning with his head and working down, James identified his hair, eyes, nose, mouth, and so forth. As the focus shifted downwards, Mr. F. pointed to the child's penis and James identified his "pee-pee." Mr. F. then asked the child to show him his "pee-pee," and James promptly unzipped his pants and pulled out his erect penis. This took place before the evaluator and the child's therapist. When Mr. F. was questioned about the appropriateness of asking James to display his penis, he claimed that he wanted to show the evaluator that the child was not "sexually" afraid of him. In addition to Mr. F.'s overt sexual stimulation of the child, the sexual molestation was deemed likely because of James' ability to describe the event and re-enact it in the doll play. James' sexually aggressive and provocative behavior with other adults, including his mother, also tended to confirm the molestation. Examination of the child's anus was unremarkable, suggesting a digital anal manipulation by Mr. F. rather than sodomy.

Another category of allegations is one in which there is a kernel of truth, but in the course of multiple interrogations and parental pressures the allegation becomes embellished. Thus one may be dealing simultaneously with true and false allegations. This may occur when the child views repeated questions as demands for more information, when she is eager to please the examiner, when leading questions are used, or when she is exposed to allegations made by other victims.

SEQUELAE OF FALSE ACCUSATIONS

The Alleged Perpetrator

Allegations of sexual abuse make front pages of newspapers, weekly magazines, and television news, and the name of the perpetrator is announced to the community. Unfortunately, in these situations there is no presumption of innocence. Professional reputations may be destroyed by false allegations. Friends abandon the alleged perpetrator, and all of his personal and financial resources become focused on his defense.

The Victim

We have now seen several children who are in psychotherapy for an event that probably did not occur. The therapist has taken the parental allegation as truth and may be creating a new iatrogenic illness in the child, and insists she remain in treatment until she "admits" what happened. The therapist who mistakenly confirms a "false" sexual abuse allegation, and in turn treats the child, is oblivious of the ensuing ethical conflict. Certainly a child in therapy for sexual abuse will experience conflicting feelings, if not hatred, for the alleged parent perpetrator, especially if she perceives the therapist's biased feelings towards that parent. A previously healthy parent-child relationship may be disrupted, if not terminated. At the very least, the child will be bewildered. Additional traumas arise when a child is forced to testify against a parent regarding events that never occurred.

The Mental Health Professional

A mental health professional who repeatedly finds sexual abuse in all cases evaluated will be rapidly labeled as nonobjective in his or her community. Many professionals seem to either always or never find sexual abuse and have developed idiosyncratic techniques for interviewing children. They often use anatomical dolls and play material to substantiate what seems to be predetermined conclusions and as a shortcut to a thorough evaluation. A professional who is considered nonobjective runs the risk of soon losing referrals from all but a select group who are interested in having an expert who will be certain to support a given case.

SUMMARY

The striking increase in the number of children referred for psychiatric evaluation because of alleged sexual molestation that can never be substantiated makes it imperative for mental health professionals to familiarize themselves with the types of parent-child interactions that may lead to "false" reporting of sexual abuse. The examiners must obtain relevant information from the evaluation which will enable them to differentiate actual from unfounded cases of sexual abuse. A typology of unsubstantiated or "false" cases of sexual abuse initiated by parents, children, or third parties has been outlined. "Gray areas" in the spectrum of sexualized contact between parents and children further complicate the task of the evaluator. The "gentle" fondling of a preschool child might produce minimal signs and symptoms of sexual molestation, while a child who is sexually overstimulated rather than sexually abused might resemble his or her sexually abused peers. Erroneous "validation" of a false allegation of sexual abuse bears serious consequences for the wrongfully accused "perpetrator," the child, and the evaluator.

It should be stressed that in a small percentage of cases, even the best trained experts in child sexual abuse will be unable to render a definitive opinion about whether or not a molestation has taken place. In these cases it behooves the therapist to take steps to protect the child. Recommendations might include supervised visitation, continued evaluation, or therapy for the child and parents.

REFERENCES

Benedek, E., & Schetky, D. (1985). Allegations of sexual abuse in child custody and visitation disputes. In D. Schetky & E. Benedek (Eds.), *Emerging Issues in Child Psychiatry and the Law*. New York: Brunner/Mazel, pp. 145-146.

Brant, R., & Sink, F. (1984). Dilemmas in court-ordered evaluation of sexual abuse charges during custody and visitation proceedings. Paper presented at the 31st Annual Meeting of the American Academy of Child Psychiatry, Toronto, Canada, October 12, 1984.

Freud, S. (1917). Introductory lectures on psychoanalysis. *Standard Edition*, 16: 369. London: Hogarth Press, 1963.

Goodwin, J., Sahd, D., & Rada, R. (1978). Incest hoax: False accusations, false denials. *Bull. Amer. Acad. Psychiat. & Law*, 6:269-276.

Green, A. (1986). True and false allegations of sexual abuse in child custody disputes. *J. Amer. Acad. Child Psychiat.*, 25:449-456.

Guyer, M., & Ash, P. (1986). Child abuse allegations in the context of adversarial divorce. Paper presented at the Annual Meeting of the American Academy of Psychiatry and the Law, Los Angeles, October 17.

Jones, D. (1987, in press). Reliable and fictitious accounts of sexual abuse to children. *J. of Interpersonal Violence*.

Kaplan, S., & Kaplan, S. (1981). The child's accusation of sexual abuse during a divorce and custody struggle. *The Hillside Journal of Clinical Psychiatry*, 3:81-95.

Norris, J., & Potter, J. (1986). The devil made me do it. *Penthouse*, January.

Peters, J. (1976). Children who are victims of sexual assault and the psychology of offenders. *Amer. J. Psychother.*, 30:398-421.

Reitman, M., & Robson, K. (1987). Erotic aspects of normal parenting. Paper presented at the 34th annual meeting of The American Academy of Child and Adolescent Psychiatry, Washington, DC, October 23.

Rosenfeld, A., Bailey, R., Siegel, B., & Bailey, G. (1986). Determining incestuous contact between parent and child: Frequency of children touching parents' genitals in a nonclinical population. *J. Amer. Acad. Child Psychiat.*, 25:481–484.

Schuman, D. (1986). False accusations of physical and sexual abuse. *Bull. Amer. Acad. Psychiat. & Law*, 14(1):5–21.

Summit, R. (1986). No one invented McMartin "secret." *Los Angeles Times*, February 5.

Weiss, E. (1983). Incest accusation: Assessing credibility. *J. of Psychiatry & Law*, 305–317.

Yates, A., & Musty, T. (1987). Young children's false allegations of molestation. Paper presented at the 140th Annual Meeting of the American Psychiatric Association, Chicago, IL, May 12.

7

Special Issues in Child Sexual Abuse

Arthur H. Green

MALE VICTIMS OF SEXUAL ABUSE

Retrospective surveys of college students and adults indicate that from 2.5%–5% of these men had been sexually abused during childhood. Finkelhor (1979) reported that 4.1% of a male college student sample experienced sexual contact with adults before the age of 13. Fritz, Stoll, and Wagner (1981) found that 4.8% of a population of college students described at least one sexual encounter with an adult before puberty. A random sample of Texas residents studied by Kercher and McShane (1983) indicated that 3% of the males had been sexually abused during childhood. Bell and Weinberg (1981) discovered that 2.5% of a random sample of heterosexual men in San Francisco had been sexually victimized before puberty, while 4.9% of a cohort of homosexual men reported sexual molestation.

Based on these surveys, Finkelhor (1984) projects that 550,000 to 1,100,0000 of currently 22 million boys (2.5%–5%) under 13 would eventually be victimized. Approximately 46,000 to 92,000 new victimizations would have to occur each year to produce this number of victims. Finkelhor also suggests that there might be an underreporting of sexual abuse among boys because of their reluctance to seek help and their concern about the stigma of homosexuality.

Differences in Sexual Abuse of Boys and Girls

According to the American Humane Association study (1981), based upon 1978 statistics, 15 boys are reported for sexual abuse for every 100 girls. The sexual abuse of boys is more likely than that of girls to come from outside the family. Boys were molested by a male nonfamily member 23% of the time, while 14% of the girls were sexually abused by extrafamilial males. The AHA study also demonstrated that boy victims of sexual abuse were much younger than the girls. Thirty-two percent of the boy victims were under six, while only 18% of the girls were that young. Forty-seven percent of the girls were 13 or over, while only 26% of the boys were of this age. Finkelhor (1984) attributes the age difference to the fact that older boys are less likely to disclose their molestation and to the greater incidence of extrafamilial victimization in boys, in which there is a shorter interval between the incident and the time of disclosure. The AHA study also revealed that sexually abused boys are more likely than girls who are molested to be reported to the police than to a child protective agency or hospital. Sexually molested boys are more likely than girls to come from disadvantaged one-parent families and are more likely to be victims of physical abuse.

A survey of 205 cases of child sexual abuse reported to child protective services by Pierce and Pierce (1985) confirmed the findings of the AHA study in that the victimized boys were younger than the girls (8.6 years versus 10.6 years), their fathers were less likely to be employed, and their mothers had less formal education. The abused boys were more likely to be abused by their stepfathers, while the abused girls demonstrated a higher incidence of abuse by fathers.

Reinhart (1987) studied 189 boys who were sexual abuse victims. These boys were between 0 and 17 years of age, and comprised 16.4% of the total population of sexually abused children. The perpetrators of the abuse of the boys were males 96% of the time. Strangers comprised only 4% of the perpetrators. The mean age of these male victims was 5.9 years. The physical findings included genital abnormalities in 5% of the boys' reports, and anal abnormalities in 29% of the boys. Fifty percent of the boys over eight years of age reported anal intercourse. After age two, there was a trend towards increasing penile penetration of the anus and decreasing digital penetration or insertion of objects. Abnormal anogenital findings were more common in the younger children.

Francis (1987) reviewed 536 cases of incest in U.S. Navy families over a five-year period. Thirty-four cases, or 6% of the total, involved father-son incest. Of these perpetrators, 21 were natural fathers and 13 were stepfathers. The victims' age range was between two and 17, with a median age of six. The duration of the incest ranged from one month to eight years. Alcohol abuse was present in 67% of the cases and evidence of multiple incestuous relationships occurred in 71% of the cases. Two-thirds of the perpetrators (where data were available) had been sexually molested during childhood.

Sexual Abuse of Males and the Sexual Offender

In males, there appears to be a correlation between sexual victimization during childhood and subsequent sexually aggressive behavior, based upon retrospective studies of admitted or convicted sexual offenders. Groth and Freeman-Longo (1979) reported that 80% of a sample of convicted sexual offenders, both rapists and child molesters, had been previously sexually abused. Seghorn, Prentky, and Boucher (1987) found that 57% of child molesters had a history of previous sexual abuse. The molesters who had been sexually abused also described a high incidence of psychopathology and social deviancy in their parents, including paternal alcohol/substance abuse and criminality, and psychiatric illness in their mothers and fathers. These investigators also reported that 23% of convicted rapists had been sexually abused as children. The rapists were more frequently victimized by a family member, while the child molesters were more typically victimized by a stranger or casual acquaintance. This suggests that sexual victimization of a child is less contributory to the etiology of rape than it is to the etiology of child molestation. Freeman-Longo (1986) observes that the offenses of the sexual offender might represent a reenactment of his own sexual victimization and an expression of anger towards his abuser, as well as an identification with the aggressor. Freeman-Longo also cites the sexually arousing component of the victimization.

FEMALES AS SEXUAL OFFENDERS

It has been widely assumed, until recently, that very few women were perpetrators of child sexual abuse. This assumption seemed to have been confirmed by early studies based on reported cases. A study by DeFrancis (1969), based on cases referred to the Brooklyn Humane Society, found 3% of the perpetrators to be women. A similar study, based on reports to the San Francisco Police Department, found a 4% incidence of female offenders (Queens Bench Foundation, 1976). DeJong, Hervada, and Emmett (1983) and Griffith and colleagues (1981) reported a 4% and 6% incidence respectively of female perpetrators, with boys referred to hospital-based sexual assault units. More comprehensive studies, however, revealed a higher rate of sexual abuse by females. The National study of incidence and severity of child abuse and neglect (NCCAN, 1981) reported the percentage of female abusers to be 13% in the case of female victims and 24% for male victims. However, Finkelhor (1984) thought these percentages were inflated because they included charges of neglect and complicity on the part of these women, i.e., nonsexual maltreatment. The American Humane Association study (1981) revealed that 14% of the perpetrators against boys and 6% of the perpetrators against girls were females. Although the percentage of female offenders against boys is higher, many more girls are victimized by females because of the large preponderance of girl victims.

Additional data regarding the incidence of female offenders have been compiled in retrospective self-report surveys carried out on college students and adult populations, in order to deal with the problem of underreporting to public agencies. These surveys generally confirm the findings of the case report studies cited above. Finkelhor (1979) reported that 16% of the male victims and 6% of the female victims were molested by females. Russell (1983) found that 4% of a random sample of San Francisco females had been sexually victimized by women. Bell and Weinberg's (1981) samples of homosexual and heterosexual men and women in San Francisco yielded a somewhat higher incidence of female molestation. In their heterosexual sample, 27% of the males and 7% of the females reported molestation by females during their childhood, while 14% of the male homosexuals and 22% of the female homosexuals were victimized by females. One might speculate about the impact of childhood homosexual seduction on the development of subsequent homosexuality in this cohort.

The data generated by the case reports and self-report surveys indicate that a significant number of females are involved in the sexual abuse of children. The percentage of female perpetrators might even be higher because these cases are often unreported. Because of their culturally prescribed physical intimacy with children during routine infant and child care, mothers, maids, and governesses have an opportunity to fondle or sexually stimulate a child so that it could go unnoticed. Sleeping with the child and sexually seductive and exhibitionistic behavior may be associated with more direct forms of sexual abuse.

Descriptions of Incestuous Mothers

In the earlier literature, mothers involved with incest were regarded as severely disturbed, psychotic, or mentally retarded (Lukianowicz, 1972; Meiselman, 1978; Wahl, 1960). More recent studies, however, have failed to describe a specific profile. Renshaw (1982) described incestuous mothers as lonely and emotionally needy. Marvasti (1986) reported on five cases of mother-child incest. These mothers disclosed their incestuous activity during their involvement in individual or group psychotherapy. The molestation was usually subtle, gentle, and nonviolent. None of these women was psychotic, and four of the five had themselves been victims of childhood incest. Three of these women molested boys, and two victimized their daughters. Lukianowicz (1972) studied two cases of aunt-nephew incest. One aunt was described as a hypomanic spinster and the other as promiscuous, and the nephews were teenagers. Lidz and Lidz (1969) reported three cases of mother-daughter incest in which each daughter became schizophrenic.

While it is important to acknowledge that women are quite capable of molesting children, men are much more likely to use children for their own sexual gratification. Finkelhor (1984) offered several hypotheses to account for the lower rates of sexual abuse by women. Women are socialized to choose partners who are older, more powerful, and more dominant than themselves, and they usually do not initiate sexual relationships. Women are less likely to turn to a child for sexual gratification if conventional adult sex is unavailable, as sexual activity appears to be more important in the maintenance of self-esteem in men than in women. Women's more intense involvement with infant and childcare facilitates a protective bonding which is absent in men. This bonding might be incompatible with a sexually intrusive exploitative posture. Finally, women seem to be less promiscuous than men. Their reduced inclination to have multiple sexual partners might inhibit their sexual interest in children.

SIBLING INCEST

Although sexual contact between daughters and their fathers or stepfathers is the most frequently reported incestuous activity, incest between siblings probably occurs more frequently. Finkelhor's (1979) survey of New England college students revealed that while only 1% of the girls were victims of incest with their fathers or stepfathers, 15% had sexual contact with a sibling. Eighty percent of these girls were sexually involved with their brothers, while 20% had homosexual contact with their sisters. None of the boys reported parental incest, while 10% of them participated in sibling incest which was equally divided into brother and sister incest. Ninety percent of the girls and 80% of the boys were 12 or under at the time. The girls reported that 30% of the sibling incest took place under the threat of force.

Russell's (1983) survey of a random sample of San Francisco women indicated that 3% of the sample were sexually abused by siblings, while this sibling abuse represented 19% of all the reported intrafamilial sexual abuse. Weinberg (1955) estimated that sibling abuse comprised 18% of his total incest sample.

This ratio between sibling and parental incest is sharply reversed when official sexual abuse reporting is scrutinized. For example, an analysis of sexual abuse hotline reports by Pierce and Pierce (1985) revealed that fathers and stepfathers were the perpetrators in 62% of the sexual abuse cases, while only 6% of the cases involved sibling incest. How can we explain this discrepancy between the survey and reporting data? One might speculate that sibling incest is less disruptive to the functioning of the family and, therefore, less likely to be discovered. If it should be disclosed, it might be more easily managed within the family. It is also possible that sibling incest is less damaging to the child than parental incest, so that fewer signs and symptoms of traumatization could facilitate maintaining the secret. This concept is supported by a study by Husain and Chapel (1983) of female adolescent incest victims admitted to a psychiatric hospital. A much higher percentage of these psychiatrically disturbed girls had been molested by fathers and stepfathers than by their brothers or other relatives.

Psychodynamics of Sibling Incest

The literature on sibling incest is sparse in comparison to the plethora of descriptions of families involved in father-daughter or father-son incest. The traumatic impact of sibling incest might only be detected in adult life. We know very little about the predisposing factors in the children who participate in sibling incest and the types of families in which this problem typically occurs. The following factors might contribute to the development of sibling incest:

1. Parental and family psychopathology. Parents who physically or sexually abuse their children might act as role models for an older child victim who reenacts his or her molestation with a younger or more vulnerable sibling. Neglecting or absent parents might delegate a parental role to an older child or relinquish their caretaking activities. A sexualized, mutually consenting, dependent relationship between two deprived siblings might represent an attempt to fill the parenting vacuum. On the other hand, a parentified, exploited older child might coerce a younger sibling into a sexual relationship as a means of obtaining revenge against the parents. A recent study by Smith and Israel (1987) seems to confirm parental complicity in sibling incest. Based on observations of 25 sibling incest families, these investigators described physical and emotional unavailability in the parents. The parents also displayed sexually overstimulating behavior; for example, 32% of the fathers had prior incest with their daughters and in 76% of the families the mother or father participated in an extramarital affair.

2. *Sibling psychopathology.* Any child who has been physically or sexually abused is at risk for molesting a younger sibling. The impulse toward reenactment is derived from an identification with the abusing parent and may also be an expression of a post-traumatic stress response, in which the child achieves a sense of mastery over his or her previous victimization by actively repeating the traumatic event which he or she had passively endured. Deprived, lonely children are vulnerable to sexual exploitation by an older sibling because they are willing to exchange sexual contact for dependency gratification. Hyperaggressive, poorly controlled children might sexually victimize a sibling because of a primary aggressive motivation. A homosexually oriented adolescent pedophile will be at risk for molesting a younger brother. Mentally retarded or extremely passive children are at risk for sexual victimization by a domineering sibling.

The traumatic impact of sibling incest will depend on a series of factors including the type of molestation, frequency, duration, and extent of the sexual contact, the degree of coercion and physical force applied, the discrepancy of age between the siblings, and the nature of the sibling relationship. Long-term sibling incest involving coercion and physical threats or violence with a significant difference in age between the perpetrator and victim is likely to be more damaging than a mutually consensual exploratory sexual contact between siblings close in age. Vaginal and anal penetration is likely to produce more serious psychological sequelae than fondling or mutual masturbation. Kaslow et al. (1981) present evidence that homosexual incest may be more pathogenic than heterosexual incest because the former involves the breaching of an additional taboo (homosexuality).

GRANDFATHER-GRANDCHILD INCEST

Grandfather-grandchild incest accounts for about 10% of all reported cases of intrafamilial child sexual abuse (Goodwin, Cormier, & Owen, 1983; Meiselman, 1978; Tsai & Wagner, 1979), but has been largely overlooked in the literature. According to Goodwin et al. (1983), few of these cases are prosecuted or investigated by child protective services because the grandfather and the grandchild usually live apart. Goodwin and colleagues reviewed 10 cases of grandfather-grandchild incest. All of the cases were referred by the mother of the victim. In eight of the cases the grandfather sexually abused victims in the mother's generation. Six of the grandchild victims' mothers had also been victims of sexual molestation by the grandfather. One wonders about the role of these mothers in permitting or facilitating a reenactment of their own incest experience in the new generation. The 17 granddaughters and one grandson who were molested ranged from two to 15 years of age. Half of the grandfather-perpetrators engaged in vaginal intercourse, and the other half were involved in breast and genital fondling. Eight of the grandfathers victimized other children over many years. While only one grandfather used or threatened violence, only two of the 18 victims were symptom free.

If Goodwin and colleagues' sample of grandfather molesters is typical of grandfather-perpetrators throughout the country, cases of grandfather-grandchild incest should be regarded as seriously as cases of incest involving fathers and children. Perhaps the most refractory incestuous fathers continue their abusive practices in the next generation. Goodwin et al.'s study also suggests that a large percentage of these men might be true pedophiles, in that they victimized numerous children, including many from outside their family. Prevention of grandfather-grandchild incest could be achieved by vigorous intervention with these men when they are molesting their own children in the previous generation. Mothers who have been previously molested by their fathers should consider their children to be at risk in the presence of the grandfathers unless there has been successful therapeutic intervention.

CHILD SEXUAL ABUSE IN INSTITUTIONS

Child maltreatment, including child sexual abuse, was initially perceived as a problem largely confined to families until Gil (1973) expanded the concept of child abuse to include children victimized by the society and its institutions. Over 400,000 children live in residential institutions such as psychiatric hospitals, centers for the retarded and developmentally disabled, children's shelters, detention centers, and jails. An additional 400,000 children live in foster homes. A large percentage of these children are intellectually and psychologically handicapped. Therefore, it is shocking to discover that physical and sexual maltreatment of these children could take place in institutions specifically designed to serve them.

Child sexual abuse has also been reported in greater numbers in elementary and high schools, both public and private, and in preschools and day care centers. In 1984, sexual abuse scandals in the McMartin preschool in Manhattan Beach, California (Summit, 1986), and in the Praca daycare center in New York City rocked the nation. A recent investigation of the backgrounds of childcare workers in New York City's daycare centers disclosed that over 50% of these individuals had records of previous arrests, many for sex offenses (Oreskes, 1984). Just as in cases of sexual abuse occurring in families, children usually are unable to report their molestation to their adult caretakers. It is likely that child victims of sexual abuse in schools and institutions will be harmed to a similar extent that child incest victims in families are because the traumatic components of their molestation are similar, i.e., powerlessness, betrayal, and sexual overstimulation at the hands of a trusted adult caretaker. Many of these children might be more vulnerable to sexual abuse because of their prior psychiatric or cognitive impairment. Many of the victims of sexual abuse at the hands of foster parents were previously removed from their homes and placed in the foster care system because of parental sexual molestation.

Prevention

There needs to be a greater public awareness of the high incidence of sexual and physical maltreatment of children in childcare facilities and the schools. Each institution should devise a system for reporting sexual misconduct; these reports should be investigated by independent agencies. There should be more careful screening of applicants for childcare and teaching positions, including previous arrests for sexual offenses, since we know that pedophiles often seek employment in the field of childcare. Childcare personnel should receive specialized training regarding the normal sexual development of children and the impact of institutional care on the child's sexual behavior. They should be taught how to intervene with children who act out sexually, and respect the privacy of children in their care.

RITUALISTIC SEXUAL ABUSE OF CHILDREN

During the past few years, groups of children from various parts of the United States have described to the police and child abuse evaluators frightening experiences of sexual molestation by groups of adults in bizarre settings (Crewdson, 1985; Moss, 1987; Norris & Potter, 1986; Ross, 1986). The children reported involvement in ritualistic practices such as drinking animal or human blood, observing animal and human sacrifice, lying in coffins, being urinated and defecated upon, and witnessing religious rituals performed by robed and hooded adults, accompanied by readings from the satanic bible. The most highly publicized cases involving ritualistic child sexual abuse were reported in Jordan, Minnesota; Bakersfield, California; and at the McMartin Preschool in Manhattan Beach, California. Although criminal charges have been dropped against most of the defendants in these cases due to inconsistencies in the testimony of the children and the failure to uncover evidence for the sadistic rituals (i.e., remains of "sacrificed" victims) after exhaustive searches, some child abuse experts believe that similarity of the experiences of these children in diverse parts of the country is too compelling to ignore (Summit, 1985, 1986). In the McMartin case, the team of sexual abuse evaluators interviewing the children on behalf of the prosecution were maligned by defense attorneys and the press for "leading" and "pressuring" the children into making false allegations. It is likely that the ultimate truth in these cases would surface over time during play therapy or psychotherapy with the child.

REFERENCES

American Humane Association. (1981). National study on child neglect and abuse reporting. Denver: American Humane Association.

Bell, A., & Weinberg, M. (1981). Preliminary data: Childhood and adolescent sexuality San Francisco study. Bloomington, IN: Institute for Sex Research.

Crewdson, J. (1985). Satanism haunts tales of child sex abuse. *Chicago Tribune,* July 29.

De Francis, V. (1969). Protecting the child victim of sex crimes committed by adults. Denver: American Humane Association.

DeJong, A., Hervada, A., & Emmett, G. (1983). Epidemiological variations in childhood sexual abuse. *Child Abuse & Neglect,* 7:155-162.

Finkelhor, D. (1979). *Sexually Victimized Children.* New York: Free Press.

Finkelhor, D. (1984). *Child Sexual Abuse: New Theory and Research.* New York: Free Press.

Francis, J. (1987). Incidence of father-son incest. Paper presented at the 140th Annual Meeting of the American Psychiatric Association, Chicago, Illinois, May.

Freeman-Longo, R. (1986). The impact of sexual victimization on males. *Child Abuse & Neglect,* 10:411-414.

Fritz, G., Stoll, K., & Wagner, N. (1981). A comparison of males and females who were sexually molested as children. *J. Sex & Marital Therapy,* 7:54-59.

Husain, A. & Chapel, J. (1983). History of incest in girls admitted to a psychiatric hospital. *Amer. J. Psychiat.,* 140:591-593.

Gil, D. (1973). *Violence Against Children.* Cambridge: Harvard University Press.

Goodwin, J., Cormier, L., & Owen, J. (1983). Grandfather-granddaughter incest: A trigenerational view. *Child Abuse & Neglect,* 7:163-170.

Griffith, S., Anderson, S., Bach, C., & Paperny, D. (1981). Intrafamilial sexual abuse of male children: An underreported problem. Paper presented at the Third International Congress of Child Abuse and Neglect, Amsterdam, March.

Groth, A., & Freeman-Longo, R. (1979). *Men Who Rape: The Psychology of the Offender.* New York: Plenum.

Kaslow, F., Haupt, D., Arce, A., & Werblowsky, J. (1981). Homosexual incest. *Psychiatric Quarterly,* 53:184-193.

Kercher, G., & McShane, M. (1983). The prevalence of child sexual abuse victimization in an adult sample of Texas residents. Huntsville, TX: Sam Houston State University.

Lidz, R., & Lidz, T. (1969). Homosexual tendencies in mothers of schizophrenic children. *Journal of Nervous and Mental Disease,* 149:229-235.

Lukianowicz, N. (1972). Incest. *Brit. J. Psychiat.,* 120:301-313.

Marvasti, J. (1986). Incestuous mothers. *Amer. J. Forensic Psychiat.,* 7:63-68.

Meiselman, K. (1978). *Incest: A Psychological Study of Causes and Effects with Treatment Recommendations.* San Francisco: Jossey Bass.

Moss, D. (1987). Are the children lying? *American Bar Association Journal,* May 1.

National Center for Child Abuse and Neglect (NCCAN). (1981). Study findings: National study of incidence and severity of child abuse and neglect. Washington, D.C.: DHEW.

Norris, J., & Potter, J. (1986). The devil made me do it. *Penthouse,* January.

Oreskes, M. (1984, August 8). State inquiry set in child abuse at Bronx Center. *The New York Times.*

Pierce, R., & Pierce, L. (1985). The sexually abused child: A comparison of male and female victims. *Child Abuse & Neglect,* 9:191-199.

Queens Bench Foundation. (1976). Sexual abuse of children. San Francisco.

Reinhart, M. (1987). Sexually abused boys. *Child Abuse & Neglect,* 11:229-235.

Renshaw, D. (1982). *Incest: Understanding and Treatment.* Boston: Little, Brown and Co.

Ross, A.S. (1986). "Ritual" child abuse: Is it real? *San Francisco Examiner,* September 29.

Russell, D. (1983). Incidence and prevalence of intrafamilial and extrafamilial sexual abuse of female children. *Child Abuse & Neglect,* 7:133-146.

Seghorn, T., Prentky, R., & Boucher, R. (1987). Childhood sexual abuse in the lives of sexually aggressive offenders. *J. Amer. Acad. Child and Adol. Psychiat.,* 26:262-267.

Smith, H., & Israel, E. (1987). Sibling incest: A study of the dynamics of 25 cases. *Child Abuse & Neglect,* 11:101-108.

Summit, R. (1985). Too terrible to hear: Barriers to perception of child sexual abuse. Testimony before the U.S. Attorney General's Commission on Pornography, Miami, Florida, November 20.

Summit, R. (1986). No one invented McMartin "Secret." *Los Angeles Times,* February 5.

Tsai, M., & Wagner, N. (1979). Incest and molestation: Problems of childhood sexuality. *Resident Staff Physician,* 129-136.

Wahl, C. (1960). The psychodynamics of consummated maternal incest. *Arch. Gen. Psychiat.,* 3:188-193.

Weinberg, S. (1955). *Incest Behavior.* New York: Citadel Press.

8

Assessment and Treatment of the Male Sex Offender

Judith V. Becker and Meg S. Kaplan

There are little data on the prevalence of child sexual abuse, since many crimes are unreported. Estimates are obtained from victim studies and self-report studies of offenders. Estimates obtained from self-report studies of incarcerated offenders differ from self-reports of nonincarcerated offenders. A recent outpatient study suggests that the number of crimes committed by the average child molester is far greater than previous estimates (Abel, Becker, Mittelman, et al., (1987). In this study, pedophiles were divided into four categories. The findings were as follows: 224 men had sexually molested 4,435 female children not related to them; 153 men had sexually molested 22,981 male children not related to them; 159 men had sexually molested 286 female children related to them; and 44 men had molested 75 male children related to them.

DIAGNOSTIC CRITERIA

The Revised Diagnostic and Statistical Manual of Mental Disorders (DSM-III-R) (American Psychiatric Association, 1987) describes the diagnostic class of sexual disorders that include paraphilias or sexual deviations. These are characterized by repetitive sexual acts that involve nonconsenting partners or preference for use of a nonhuman object for sexual arousal. *Pedophilia* describes adults whose preferred or exclusive method of achieving sexual excitement is in the act or fantasy of engaging in sexual activity with prepubescent children (generally age

Judith V. Becker, Ph.D., is Director, Sexual Behavior Clinic at the New York State Psychiatric Institute and Associate Professor of Clinical Psychology in Psychiatry, Columbia University, College of Physicians and Surgeons, New York City. Meg S. Kaplan, Ph.D., is Instructor of Clinical Psychology in Psychiatry and Research Scientist, New York State Psychiatric Institute.

13 or younger). The difference in age between the adult (who must be at least 16 years of age) and the prepubescent child is at least five years. For late adolescents with this disorder, no precise age difference is specified (American Psychiatric Association, 1987, p. 284).

One problem in the area is the lack of an effective typology in the description of child molesters. This is in part due to the heterogenous nature of offenders. Inappropriate sexual behavior is not always characterized as a paraphilia. Isolated acts can be precipitated by marital problems, illness, or loneliness and are not necessarily diagnosed as pedophilia. In order to identify the true paraphiliac, the clinician, in addition to an indepth psychiatric evaluation, should obtain a detailed sexual history. The clinician should also obtain a detailed social history in order to ascertain whether the individual has adequate social skills and sex education to engage in appropriate consensual sexual activity. Social and sexual inadequacy is more frequently encountered among pedophiles who molest strangers than among incest offenders.

The recent literature has found little psychopathology in sex offenders other than paraphilia. A recent study by Abel, Mittelman, and Becker (1985) found no psychopathology in 59.9% of the child molesters. In this study, only 11.69% of the child molesters had antisocial personalities. Another recent study of male incest juvenile sex offenders found that of 19 subjects, 26.3% had no psychiatric disorders other than paraphilia (Becker, Kaplan, Cunningham-Rathner, & Kavoussi, 1986).

One of the difficulties in the diagnosis of sex offenders is that many of them have multiple paraphilias. A recent study by Abel, Becker, Cunningham-Rathner, Mittelman, and Rouleau (1987, in press) found that nearly 50% of their sample of 561 voluntary adult subjects had multiple sexual deviations, even though one paraphilia initially dominated. With the exception of transsexuals, there was a significant incidence of crossing of deviant sexual behaviors, the average in the range of three to five paraphilias per diagnostic category. These findings are at variance with the traditional view of the paraphiliac as having one exclusive sexual deviation, and therefore concern must be taken in diagnosis and treatment of sexual offenders, such as pedophiles. The other specific paraphilias classified in DSM-III-R are as follows:

> *exhibitionism*—repetitive acts of exposing genitals to strangers for the purpose of achieving sexual excitement;
> *voyeurism*—observation of unsuspecting people, usually strangers, who are naked, disrobing, or engaging in a sexual act;
> *fetishism*—use of inanimate objects for sexual purposes;
> *transvestic fetishism*—recurrent, intense sexual urges, in a heterosexual male, involving cross-dressing;

sexual sadism—intentionally inflicted psychological or physical harm in order to produce sexual excitement;
sexual masochism—deriving sexual excitement from being humiliated, bound, beaten, or sexually harmed;
frotteurism—deriving sexual excitement from touching and rubbing against a nonconsenting person.*

Recent research has concentrated on the adolescent sexual offender, since arousal patterns develop as early as 12 or 13 years of age. Results from a research project by Abel, Mittelman, and Becker (1985) indicate that of 411 adult sex offenders seen voluntarily at an outpatient clinic, 58.4% reported that the onset of their deviant sexual arousal occurred prior to the age of 18. Other researchers (Brecher, 1978; Groth & Birnbaum, 1979; Longo & Groth, 1983) have also found that a significant number of adult offenders had the onset of their deviant sexual interest patterns soon after puberty. Recent surveys of juvenile offenders have also found indications that a significant number had committed their first sexual offenses between the ages of 12 and 15 years of age (Awad, Saunders, & Levene, 1979; Longo, 1982).

Several researchers have suggested that the early onset of deviant behavior in adolescent males is due to experimentation, sex play, or normal aggressiveness of adolescents (Finkelhor, 1979; Gagnon, 1965). Recent research suggests otherwise. Groth (1977) found that 86% of his sample of adult offenders had had previous interpersonal sexual experiences prior to the deviant act. Becker, Kaplan, Cunningham-Rathner, and Kavoussi (1986) assessed 22 adolescent males between the ages of 13 and 18 who had been charged with a sexual crime against a family member. Their results indicated that the mean age of onset of nondeviant genital sexual behavior predated the onset of deviant sexual behavior. The findings of this study also challenge the assumption that adolescent sexual offenders are engaging in sexual experimentation. Thus, further research needs to be focused on the development of adolescent offender typologies.

ETIOLOGICAL THEORIES

Psychological Research

Psychoanalytic theory views paraphilia, or perversion, as an expression of unresolved problems in childhood development. Freud first theorized that the choice of an immature sexual object is a result of a fixation at an infantile level or an unresolved oedipus complex. He hypothesized that excessive gratification could stop at one level of childhood development and never allow the advance of adult sexual development. For example, unable to deal with adult heterosexuality because of castration fears, the sexual deviant resorts to safer, more developmentally primitive forms of sexual expression. Freud later emphasized the notion that perversion may be a regression to perverse sexuality, an early state of sensual gratification (Cook & Howells, 1981; Mohr, Turner, & Jerry, 1964). These psychoanalytic writers share the belief that the perversion is a product of "unresolved problems in libidinal and family development" (Stoller, cited in Cook & Howells, 1981, p. 58).

One classification that is explicit throughout the literature is a distinction between offenders whose behavior is situationally induced and occurs in the context of a normal sexual preference structure. According to the psychological literature, sexual offenders do not form a homogenous group (Marmor, 1978) but, rather, fall into groupings which include personality disorders, mentally handicapped individuals, delinquents, situational cases, organic brain cases, and men under the heavy influence of alcohol.

Social Learning Theory

Numerous researchers cite social learning approaches as important contributing factors to the development and maintenance of paraphilia. They emphasize the importance of conditioning experiences rather than intrapsychic processes within psychoanalysis.

Ford and Beach (1955) state that human sexuality is affected by experience in two ways. First, the kinds of situations that become capable of evoking sexual excitement are determined in a large measure by learning. Second, the overt behavior through which this excitement is expressed depends largely upon the individual's previous experience (p. 262).

Kinsey and his colleagues (1953) also concluded that "the sexual capacities which an individual inherits at birth appear to be nothing more than the necessary anatomy and the physiologic capacity to respond to a sufficient physical or psychological stimulus . . . but apart from these few inherent capacities, most other aspects of human sexual behavior appear to be the product of learning and conditioning" (p. 644).

McQuire, Carlisle, and Young (1965) stated: "The theoretical basis for behavior therapy is that the symptom or behavior to be treated has been learned at some time in the past and can be changed by the learning of a new pattern of behavior" (p. 185).

It has been suggested that early sexual behavior with immature peers may play a role in the conditioning of deviant arousal. McQuire, Carlisle, and Young (1965) have postulated that learning is established by the process of fantasizing the initial deviant experience. They theorized that the offender frequently recalls his first sexual experience. The repeated pairing of these fantasies with orgasm results in their acquiring sexually arousing properties, which are reinforced.

In summary, social learning theory views sex offenses as conditioned behavior learned as a result of inappropriate fantasies which can be changed by learning new patterns of behavior.

CRIMINOLOGICAL RESEARCH

The criminally oriented research on child molestation and other sex offenses attempts to identify those offenders most likely to recommit the crime, e.g., those who are most dangerous to society. Marshall and Christie (1981) studied the criminal files of 41 child molesters convicted of sexual crimes against children aged 14 years or younger. Data from the files revealed that 21 had been convicted of nonsexual assault in the past, and 39 of the 41 had used threats or actual physical violence in the sexual crime. Their research suggests that those inmates who did use force were also generally assaultive, although they were observed to be shy and underassertive.

The most extensive work on the dangerousness of child molesters has been reported by Frisbie (1969). She assigned sexual offenders ratings according to "social dangerousness." Situational offenders were given a rating of "1." A rating of "2" was given to subjects who had established patterns of molestation, were unable to control desires for children when drinking, preferred children to adults, and persistently arranged proximity to children. A rating of "3" was given to persons who had victimized many children, were attracted to children under 10, regarded their sexual behavior as acceptable, and had a standardized method of contacting children. Frisbie suggested that the above ratings were related to sexual recidivism and could be used in prediction.

An important concept legally is that of consensuality. Legally, a sexual act is considered consensual when the participants agree to the act. However, a person who is underaged or is mentally or physically disabled cannot agree or legally consent.

ASSESSMENT

In recent years, research has concentrated on assessment techniques to evaluate sexual offenders. Self-report information may be obtained by use of tests that attempt to assess patterns of sexual arousal or sexual attitudes. Psychological testing is commonly used to evaluate a multitude of problems. However, there are minimal tests to describe patterns of deviant sexual arousal. The few currently being used include the following:

- Barlow, Leitenberg, and Agras (1969) devised a card sorting technique in which various sexual scenes are typed on cards. The individual sorts the cards according to strong or low sexual arousal on a scale of 1 to 4 (Tollison & Adams, 1979). The advantage of such a card sort is that some offenders are willing to validly report their arousal patterns (Abel, 1984).
- Several investigators employ sexual experience scales to measure arousal and sexual anxiety (Zuckerman, 1971). These scales are constructed on a hierarchy of sexual activity.
- LoPiccolo and Steger (1978) have devised the sexual interaction inventory which measures sexual functioning and satisfaction. However, because of frequent denial of the severity of the problem by sex offenders and problems of confidentiality, traditionally clinicians have relied on the clinical interview to reveal the patient's sexual interests.

The use of self-report techniques has raised the issue of whether some behaviors are underreported and others overreported during interviews or on questionnaires.

In investigating sexual preference, behaviorists have made rapid advancements in assessment techniques in order to have valid objective measures of sexual arousal, rather than relying solely on assessment by verbal report or attitudinal measure (Barlow & Abel, 1976). A number of investigators have arrived at the conclusion that the measurement of penile erection is the most valid objective assessment of male sexual arousal known (Abel, Blanchard, Barlow, & Mavissakalian, 1975; Barlow, 1977; Barlow & Abel, 1976; Freund, 1963; Freund, Langevin, & Barlow, 1974; Zuckerman, 1971).

This method involves direct measurement of the patient's penis size while presenting him sexual stimuli (audiotape descriptions, slides or videotapes) depicting specific paraphiliac behaviors. The patient wears

a penile transducer while alone in a laboratory; the transducer measures
the extent of his erection. The patient's penile tumescence responses
to these deviant stimuli are then compared to his responses to nondeviant or socially acceptable sexual stimuli. Several researchers have
reported the use of the penile transducer with paraphiliac populations
(Abel et al., 1975, 1978; Abel, Becker, & Skinner, 1980; Abel, Blanchard,
& Barlow, 1981).

It should be noted that this form of assessment is not without
problems. Penile response is subject to some degree of voluntary control
or faking and must be taken into account during any assessment (Abel,
Blanchard, & Barlow, 1981; Barlow, 1977; Quinsey & Carrigan, 1978).
Another major problem is that it is possible to identify interests outside
of the patient's awareness, e.g., by measuring arousal responses of 1%-
5% of a full erection. This sensitivity makes it more difficult for the
offender to give consent to such assessment, since he is unaware of the
response being measured (Abel, Rouleau, & Cunningham-Rathner, 1985).
Nevertheless, although there are difficulties, the objective measurement
of sexual arousal is an important assessment technique with this population.

A recent study by Abel, Cunningham-Rathner, Becker, and McHugh
(1983) examined the validity of traditional clinical interviews by confronting paraphiliacs with the results of subsequent evaluations. These
confrontations revealed that 50 subjects (55.5%) admitted to an additional 92 paraphiliac diagnoses. The results demonstrate that at least
55.5% of traditional clinical interviews with paraphiliacs are invalid,
since various confrontation procedures (card sort 118.9%, reinterview
20.0%, erection measures 62.9%) can lead subjects to reveal a large
number of new additional paraphilias. The findings also revealed that
the erection measurements can be counted on in 58.9% of cases to yield
additional paraphiliac diagnoses during the confrontation process. Because of frequent use of denial in this population, any assessment should
rely on as much information as possible from various sources. These
include the clinical interview, paper and pencil tests, psychophysiologic
assessment, as well as victim reports, family reports, criminal justice
system information, and any other relevant sources.

TREATING SEXUAL OFFENDERS

Historically, sex offenders were seen within the criminal justice system
without much input from the mental health system. Incarceration was
utilized as the method to deter recidivism. Although incarceration
reduces the risk of reoffending while the offender remains in prison,

incarceration per se is relatively ineffective in deterring sex crimes. As Abel, Mittelman, and Becker (1985) have noted: 1) most sexual crimes are not reported and, as a consequence, no steps can be taken to bring about the arrest of the sex offender; 2) if arrest does occur, conviction and incarceration are exceedingly uncommon. In a study of 250 cases of child sexual abuse reported to protective services, DeFrancis (1969) found that less than 3% of the offenders were incarcerated, and that less than one-third were incarcerated with a conviction of child abuse. In addition, the high recidivism rates of individuals after serving prison terms suggest that this method of deterrence is ineffective.

Since a variety of theoretical orientations have been generated to explain the development of deviant sexual interest patterns, treatment strategies have evolved based on those theories. Traditionally, psychoanalysis has been the treatment for the paraphilias. This theory seeks to undo the repression that is believed to be the cause. Treatment is usually along the lines of reconstructive psychotherapy. Unfortunately, measuring results is extremely complicated since there are no common standards of measurement. Several investigators have reported disappointment with the results of psychoanalysis and psychotherapy as the sole form of treatment in cases of deviant sexual behavior (Cook & Howells, 1981). Those adhering to biological models treat the paraphiliac by reducing sexual drive through surgical or chemical castration (Bancroft, Tennet, Loveas, & Cass, 1974; Berlin & Meinecke, 1981). Giaretto, Giaretto, and Sgroi (1978) describe a coordinated community treatment program for incest offenders which also focuses on treatment of the family.

More recently, a behavioral approach based on social learning theory has been utilized (Bandura, 1973). This approach addresses the development of deviant sexual interest patterns as well as assessment and treatment (Abel, Blanchard, Barlow, & Mavissakalian, 1975; Barlow & Abel, 1976; Abel, Barlow, Blanchard, & Guild, 1977; Abel, Blanchard, Becker, & Djenderedjian, 1978). The behavioral approach has as a major focus teaching the sex offender control over his deviant sexual interest pattern. All paraphiliacs need treatment to eliminate their excessive arousal and interest in paraphiliac behaviors. Sex offenders commit crimes primarily because of the excessive interest in, or arousal by, deviant objects or behavior. For example, pedophiles engage in sexual activities with children because they are sexually aroused by children. Rapists rape because they are aroused by sex in a climate of aggression.

At the Sexual Behavior Clinic of the New York State Psychiatric Institute, a multicomponent treatment strategy is utilized in the treatment of sexual offenders (Abel, Becker, Cunningham-Rathner, Rouleau,

Kaplan, & Reich, 1984; Abel, Mittelman, & Becker, 1985). The treatment format teaches the offender control over his deviant sexual interest pattern utilizing the following techniques:

1. Satiation. This technique was first described by Marshall (1973). It teaches the offender how to use his deviant fantasies postorgasm in a repetitive manner to the point of satiating himself with the very stimuli that he used to become aroused by. Patients are given precise instructions about how to carry out the treatment at home. The treatment consists of having the patient repeat for a prolonged period of time his deviant fantasies, which are tape-recorded and checked by the therapist. Self-administered satiation is particularly useful because it can be used by the offender any time reduction of deviant arousal is necessary.

2. Covert sensitization. The second treatment component to decrease deviant arousal is covert sensitization. This technique is utilized to disrupt the behaviors that are antecedent to the offender's actually coming in contact with his victim. Covert sensitization involves having the offender imagine the various feelings or experiences that begin to lead him toward committing a deviant sexual act and then immediately bringing to mind very aversive images that reflect the negative consequences of proceeding in that direction. Covert sensitization appears to sensitize the offender to those behaviors early in the chain of events that lead to his paraphilic act. It may be that some offenders will never be able to completely eliminate their arousal by deviant acts and may consequently always need to be able to disrupt the very behaviors that lead them toward commission of the act. As with satiation, covert sensitization is self-administered at home. The patient records the session and the therapist checks the tapes to ensure compliance and refine the antecedents and consequences.

Both satiation and covert sensitization are self-control procedures that patients are instructed to use when they experience deviant fantasies or urges.

Our experience in teaching sexual offenders has indicated that a number of them experience difficulty in carrying out functional social interactions with adult partners. Consequently, therapy also focuses on skills training to ensure that the offender has the requisite skills to relate to adult partners.

3. Social skills training. Without appropriate social skills, the offender would make inappropriate aggressive sexual advances toward adults and would continue to be involved with children, with whom appropriate social skills are less necessary. Social skills training involves a role rehearsal procedure that allows the offender to model appropriate social skills from the therapist, practice those skills in his real world, get feedback from the therapist about his performance, and then learn more complicated skills by a similar process.

4. Assertiveness skills training. Some sex offenders lack appropriate assertive skills. Some child molesters, for example, are anxious and inhibited in expressing positive feelings towards women. They then appear to direct these sexual feelings inappropriately towards children. Offenders having assertive deficits need assertive training that involves modeling, rehearsal, and social feedback, similar to the social skills training described above.

It is important to note that while all offenders are in need of treatment to decrease their deviant sexual arousal, some offenders have satisfactory social and/or assertiveness skills, and consequently would not be in need of skills training. A comprehensive assessment will help the therapist identify those in need of skills training.

5. Cognitive restructuring. The majority of sex offenders know that their deviant behavior was contrary to the morals and ethics of our society, yet they gave themselves permission to engage in such deviant behavior. These "permission-giving statements" are cognitive distortions used by sex offenders to justify their behaviors. Examples of such statements include: "A man is justified in having sex with his children or stepchildren if his wife doesn't like sex" or "If a woman says 'no,' she really means 'yes.' "

Treatment for sex offenders' distortions requires their being educated about how cognitive distortions develop and why it is essential that they recognize that their own distortions have allowed them to accept their deviant behavior. Patients with cognitive distortions are confronted through role playing. Patients are asked to take the role of members of the victim's family, the victim, and criminal justice personnel, while the therapist role plays the cognitive distortion. The patient then has to confront the beliefs role played by the therapist. This process of role reversal appears to be highly effective in getting the sex offender to see the inappropriateness of his thinking.

6. Sexual knowledge and sex dysfunctions. Some sex offenders lack knowledge about what is considered appropriate sexual behavior in our culture and, consequently, have involved themselves in paraphiliac behavior. Other offenders fail to involve themselves in appropriate sexual behavior with consenting adults because of specific sexual dysfunctions that preclude these activities.

Treatment involves providing the patient with standard sex education and treating whatever sexual dysfunctions are present. This treatment program is described in detail by Abel and colleagues (1984).

The treatment program described above can be utilized in either a group or individual format. Abel and his associates (1984) utilized this format in the treatment of child molesters. Patients were seen as outpatients in a group format and received the six components over 30, one-and-one-half-hour therapy sessions. Patients were reevaluated immediately post-therapy and at six- and 12-month follow-ups. Data on the 87 offenders who completed treatment indicated that the success rate as defined by lack of recidivism was 98.9% immediately post-treatment. At six months post-treatment, the success rate was 88.6% and 80% at one-year follow-up.

A modified version of this treatment package is presently being utilized in the treatment of adolescent sexual offenders at the New York State Psychiatric Institute. Although long-term follow-up data are not yet available, it appears that the treatment is equally effective with adolescent sex offenders.

SUMMARY

Throughout this chapter our focus has been on the assessment and treatment of the offender. People who commit sexual crimes, however, do not reside in a vacuum and their behavior also impacts on their family members. Although we feel that it is imperative that the offender be held responsible for his behavior and that he learn to control his deviant sexual interest patterns, we also feel that it is important that significant others and family members receive counseling to help them deal with the impact of the offender's behavior, as well as to address any issues within the family that may serve as stressors to the offender and serve to weaken his control.

Although a body of knowledge is beginning to accumulate on the assessment and treatment of sexual offenders, many questions remain unanswered. If sex crimes are to be prevented, we need to develop a better understanding of how deviant sexual interest patterns develop and how we can identify and provide services to those most at risk for the development of these aberrant arousal patterns.

REFERENCES

Abel, G.G. (1984). A clinical evaluation of possible sex offenders. In *The Incest Offender, The Victim, The Family: New Treatment Approaches.* White Plains, N.Y.: Westchester County Mental Health Association.

Abel, G.G., Barlow, D., Blanchard, E., & Guild, D. (1977). The components of rapists' sexual arousal. *Arch. Gen. Psychiat.,* 34:895-903.

Abel, G.G., Becker, J.V., Blanchard, E., & Flanagan, B. (1981A). The behavioral assessment of rapists. In J. Hays, J. Roberts, & K. Solway (Eds.), *Violence and the Violent Individual,* New York: Spectrum.

Abel, G.G., Becker, J.V., Cunningham-Rathner, J., Mittelman, M., & Rouleau, J. (1987, in press). *Multiple Paraphilic Diagnoses Among Sex Offenders.*

Abel, G.G., Becker, J.V., Cunningham-Rathner, J., Rouleau, J., Kaplan, M., & Reich, J. (1984). The treatment of child molesters: A manual. Unpublished manuscript.

Abel, G.G., Becker, J.V., Mittelman, M., Cunningham-Rathner, J., Rouleau, J., & Murphy, W. (1987). Self-reported sex crimes of non-incarcerated paraphiliacs. *Journal of Interpersonal Violence,* I (1):3-25.

Abel, G.G., Becker, J.V., & Skinner, L.J. (1980). Aggressive behavior and sex. *Psychiat. Clin. North America,* 3:133-155.

Abel, G.G., Blanchard, E.B., & Barlow, D. (1981B). The effects of stimulus modality, instructional set and stimulus content on the objective measurement of sexual arousal in several paraphilias. *Beh. Res. Ther.,* 19:25-33.

Abel, G.G., Blanchard, E.B., Barlow, D.H., & Mavissakalian, M. (1975). Identifying specific erotic cues in sexual deviation by audio-taped descriptions. *J. Applied Beh. Analysis,* 8:247-260.

Abel, G.G., Blanchard, E.B., Becker, J.V., & Djenderedjian, A. (1978). Differentiating sexual aggressives with penile measures. *Criminal Justice and Behavior,* 5:315-332.

Abel, G.G., Cunningham-Rathner, J., Becker, J.V., & McHugh, J. (1983). Motivating sex offenders for treatment with feedback of their psychophysiologic assessment. Paper presented at the World Congress of Behavior Therapy, Washington, D.C.

Abel, G.G., Mittelman, M., & Becker, J.V. (1985). Sex offenders: Results of assessment and recommendations for treatment. In H. Ben-Aron, S. Hucker, & C. Webster (Eds.), *Clinical Criminology: Current Concepts.* Toronto: M & M Graphics.

Abel, G.G., Rouleau, J., & Cunningham-Rathner, J. (1985). Sexually aggressive behavior. In W. Curran, A. McGarry, & S. Shah (Eds.), *Modern Legal Psychiatry and Psychology.* Philadelphia: F.A. Davis.

American Psychiatric Association. (1987). *Diagnostic and Statistical Manual of Mental Disorders* (Third edition, revised). Washington, D.C.: American Psychiatric Association.

Awad, G.A., Saunders, E., & Levene, J. (1979). A clinical study of male adolescent sex offenders. *Int. J. Offender Therapy and Comparative Criminology,* 28 (2):105-116.

Bandura, A. (1973). *Aggression: A Social Learning Analysis.* Englewood Cliffs, N.J.: Prentice-Hall.

Bancroft, J.A., Tennet, G., Loveas, G., & Cass, J. (1974). The control of deviant sexual behavior by drugs: Behavioral changes following estrogens and anti-androgens. *Br. J. Psychiat.,* 25:310-315.

Barbaree, H.E., Marshall, W.L., & Lanthier, R.D. (1979). Deviant sexual arousal in rapists. *Beh. Res. Ther.,* 17:215-222.

Barlow, D.H., Leitenberg, H., & Agras, W.S. (1969). The experimental control of sexual deviations through manipulation of the noxious scene in covert sensitization. *J. Abnormal Psychol.,* 74:596-601.

Barlow, D.H., & Abel, G.G. (1976). Sexual deviation. In W. Craigshead, A. Kazdin, & M. Mahoney (Eds.), *Behavior Modification.* Atlanta, GA: Houghton-Mifflin.

Barlow, D.H. (1977). Assessment of sexual behavior. In A.R. Ciminero, K.S. Calhoun, & H.E. Adams (Eds.), *Handbook of Behavioral Assessment.* New York: John Wiley & Sons.

Barlow, D.H., & Abel, G.G. (1976). Sexual deviation. In W. Craigshead, A. Kazdin, & M. Mahoney (Eds.), *Behavior Modification.* Boston: Houghton-Mifflin.

Becker, J.V., Cunningham-Rathner, J., & Kaplan, M.S. (1986). Adolescent sexual offenders: Demographics, criminal and sexual histories, and recommendations for reducing future offenses. *Journal of Interpersonal Violence,* 1 (4):431-445.

Becker, J.V., Kaplan, M.S., Cunningham-Rathner, J., & Kavoussi, R. (1986). Characteristics of adolescent incest sexual perpetrators: Preliminary findings. *Journal of Family Violence,* 1:85-97.

Berlin, F.S., & Meinecke, C. (1981). Treatment of sex offenders with antiandrogenic medication: Conceptualization, review of treatment modalities, and preliminary findings. *Amer. J. Psychiat.,* 138:601-607.

Brecher, E. (1978). *Treatment Programs for Sex Offenders.* Washington, D.C.: U.S. Department of Justice.

Brownmiller, S. (1975). *Against Our Will: Men, Women and Rape.* New York: Simon & Schuster.

Cook, M., & Howells, K. (Eds.). (1981). *Adult Sexual Interest in Children.* New York: Academic Press.

DeFrancis, V. (1969). *Protecting the Child Victim of Sex Crimes Committed by Adults.* Denver: American Humane Association.

Donnerstein, E. (1980). Pornography and violence against women: Experimental studies. *Ann. N.Y. Acad. Sci.,* 347:277-288.

Finkelhor, D. (1979). *Sexually Victimized Children,* New York: The Free Press.

Ford, C., & Beach, F. (1955). *Patterns of Sexual Behavior.* New York: Harper & Row.

Freund, K. (1963). A laboratory method for diagnosing predominance of homo or hetero-erotic interest in the male. *Beh. Ther.,* 1:85-93.

Freund, K., Langevin, R., & Barlow, D. (1974). Comparison of two penile measures of erotic arousal. *Brit. J. Psychiat.,* 124.

Frisbie, L.V. (1969). Another look at sex offenders in California. *California Mental Health and Research Monograph,* No. 12.

Gagnon, J.H. (1965). Sexuality and sexual learning in the child. *Psychiatry,* 28(3):212-228.

Gebhard, P., Gagnon, G., Pomeroy, W., & Christenson, C. (1965). *Sex Offenders.* New York: Harper & Row.

Giarretto, H., Giarretto, A., & Sgroi, S. (1978). Coordinated community treatment of incest. In A. Burgess, A. Groth, L. Holmstrom, & S. Sgroi (Eds.), *Sexual Assault of Children and Adolescents*. Lexington, MA: Lexington Books.

Groth, A.N.(1977). The adolescent sex offender and his prey. *Int. J. Offender Therapy and Comparative Criminology*, 21(3):249-254.

Groth, A.N., with Birnbaum, H.J. (1979). *Men Who Rape: The Psychology of the Offender*. New York: Plenum Press.

Groth, A.N., & Hobson, W.F. (1983). The dynamics of sexual assault. In L. Schlesinger & E. Revitch (Eds.), *Sexual Dynamics of Antisocial Behavior*. Springfield, IL: Charles C Thomas.

Kinsey, A., Pomeroy, W., Martin, C., & Gebhard, P. (1953). *Sexual Behavior in the Human Female*. Philadelphia: W.B. Saunders.

Langevin, R. (1983). *Sexual Strands: Understanding and Treating Sexual Anomalies in Men*. Hillside, N.J.: Lawrence Erlbaum.

Lansky, D., & Wilson, G.T. (1981). Alcohol, expectations and sexual arousal in males: An information processing analysis. *J. Abnormal Psychol.*, 90:35-45.

LoPiccolo, J., & Steger, J. (1978). The sexual interaction inventory: A new instrument for assessment of sexual dysfunction. In J. LoPiccolo and J. LoPiccolo (Eds.), *Handbook of Sex Therapy*. New York: Plenum Press.

Longo, R.E. (1982). Sexual learning and experience among adolescent offenders. *Int. J. Offender Therapy and Comparative Criminology*, 26(3):235-241.

Longo, R.E., & Groth, A.N. (1983). Juvenile sexual offenses in the history of adult rapists and child molesters. *Int. J. Offender Therapy and Comparative Criminology*, 27(2):150-155.

Malamuth, N., Feshbach, S., & Jaffe, Y. (1977). Sexual arousal and aggression: Recent experimental and theoretical issues. *J. Social Issues*, 33:110-133.

Marmor, J. (1978). Sexual deviancy, part I. *J. Continuing Ed. in Psychiatry*, 39:23-31.

Marshall, W.L. (1973). The modification of sexual fantasies: A combined treatment approach to the reduction of deviant sexual behavior. *Beh. Res. Ther.*, 11:557-564.

Marshall, W.L., & Christie, M.M. (1981). Pedophilia and aggression. *Criminal Justice and Behavior*, 8(2):145-158.

McQuire, R., Carlisle, J., & Young, B. (1965). Sexual deviations as conditioned behavior: A hypothesis. *Beh. Res. Ther.*, 2:185-190.

Mohr, J., Turner, R., & Jerry, J. (1964). *Pedophilia and Exhibitionism*. Toronto: University of Toronto Press.

Quinsey, V.L. (1984). Sexual aggression: Studies of offenders against women. In D. Weisstub (Ed.), *Law and Mental Health: International Perspectives, Vol. 1*. New York: Pergamon Press.

Quinsey, V.L., & Carrigan, W.F. (1978). Penile responses to visual stimuli: Instructional control with and without auditory sexual fantasy correlates. *Criminal Justice and Behavior*, 5:333-342.

Stoller, R.J. (1979). *Sexual Excitement*. New York: Pantheon Books.

Tollison, D., & Adams, H. (1979). *Sexual Disorders: Treatment, Theory and Research*. New York: Gardner Press.

Zuckerman, M. (1971). Physiological measures of sexual arousal in the human. *Psychol. Bull.*, 75:297-329.

Section III

LEGAL ISSUES

9

Child Pornography and Prostitution

Diane H. Schetky

Child pornography and child prostitution are becoming prevalent forms of sexual exploitation of children and are often conducted with a profit motive. With the possible exception of juvenile male prostitutes, it is rarely the child who profits either emotionally or materially from these transactions. Child pornography and child prostitution are closely related. Pornography is often a sideline to prostitution and drug dealing and may lead children into prostitution and other sexually abusive situations.

PORNOGRAPHY

Before discussing child pornography, we need to look at society's response to pornography in general. The U.S. Supreme Court has struggled with trying to define obscenity; as early as 1896 it was defined as "sexual impurity" (*Swearingen v. U.S. 161 U.S. 446*, 1896). In 1933, the case involving Joyce's *Ulysses* introduced the concept that literary merit need be balanced with potential harm to the average man (*U.S. v. One Book*, 1933). Former Justice Potter is often quoted as saying he could not define obscenity but that he knew it when he saw it. Justice Brennan in 1957 put forth the following test of obscenity: "Whether to the average person applying contemporary community standards the dominant theme of the material taken as a whole appeals to prurient interests" (*Roth v. U.S. 354 U.S. 476*, 1957). The court further declared that obscenity falls outside of First Amendment protection. Current definitions of obscenity require that it appeals to prurient interests, offensively depicts sexual conduct prohibited by state law, and lacks literary, artistic, scientific, or political value.

The Commission on Obscenity and Pornography was established in

1968 by President Johnson to study the effects of pornography on the public and minors and to determine whether it had any relationship to crime. Many of the studies the Commission relied upon in reaching its decision were based upon soft core pornography of the 1960s rather than the hard core, aggressive, and sadistic pornography that now dominates the market. The Commission concluded that pornography did not have any antisocial effects. Numerous studies have since shown that nonviolent pornography does not under most situations increase violence against women (Donnerstein, 1984).

These studies are not particularly relevant to the new genre of pornography which degrades, dehumanizes, and subordinates women. NCTV reviewed 360 X-rated films in 1985, and could find none that could be considered mere erotica; rather, all contained elements of violence toward women (*NCTV Press Release,* September 12, 1985). Such films now account for 20% of all video sales, and nearly 40% of VCR owners bought or rented an X-rated cassette within the year studied (*Newsweek,* March 18, 1985, p. 61). *Playboy, Penthouse,* and *Hustler* sell 15 million copies per month and pornography constitutes an $8 billion dollar per year business (*News for Women in Psychiatry,* 4(1), September 1985, p. 3). Two million families subscribe to pornographic cable television. Themes of sexual sadism are also becoming standard fare on rock videos.

Malamuth (1984) feels strongly that the mass media can contribute to a cultural climate that is more accepting of aggression toward women. Numerous studies have demonstrated that even a single exposure to aggressive pornography can influence respondents' attitudes and behavior and may result in increased arousal, rape fantasies, decreased sensitivity toward rape, and more acceptance of rape myths and violence toward women (Donnerstein, 1984). However, these studies have been conducted under laboratory conditions and it is not clear for how long these attitudinal changes persist. Donnerstein concludes that it is not the sexual content per se but rather the aggressive content in pornography that contributes to violence against women. Baron and Straus (1984) compared rape rates within the U.S. and found a correlation between high circulation of sex magazines and high rape rates. These authors also believe that it is not sex in the media per se but violence that contributes to rape.

CHILD PORNOGRAPHY

"Child pornography is defined as any visual reproduction of the sexual abuse of children" (Schoettle, 1980, p. 289). Although illegal, child pornography constitutes about 7% of the pornography market. Densen-Gerber and Hutchinson (1979) note there are at least 264 different magazines being sold each month that deal with sexual acts between adults and children. Some such as *Coming with Daddy, Lust for Children, How to Deflower Your Daughter,* and *School Girls* are primers in child sexual abuse. Child pornography may also be used to lure children into sexual activity and instruct them, since young children who view such material may be led to believe that this is acceptable behavior. In addition to decreasing inhibitions, this material may cause sexual arousal in some children.

Rush (1981) believes that child pornography is central to pedophiliac psychology, social orientation, and behavior. Lanning (1986) observes that pedophiles almost always collect child pornography or child erotica. Further, he notes "the only way you can produce child pornography is to molest a child" and that "child pornography exists primarily for the consumption of pedophiles. If there were no pedophiles there would be little or no child pornography" (p. 50). Some pedophiles develop elaborate videotape systems and even computerize their collections and sex acts and exchange data with other pedophiles. The trading of pornography with other pedophiles may lead to exchanging victims for their sexual services (Lanning & Burgess, 1984). Pedophiles also keep records and souvenirs of their victims which, as noted by Lanning (1986), can be very incriminating in investigations. For example, in a recent investigation of child pornography and molestation in the Chicago public schools, a search of a teacher's home turned up 200 photos of nude boys, an international mailing list, fliers advertising young boys in an escort service, and copies of a pornographic magazine believed to have been published by the accused. Further raids of homes of those on the customer list revealed several crates of videotapes, photographs, and magazines related to child pornography (*New York Times,* March 25, 1986).

Lanning (1986) believes pedophiles compulsively collect child pornography out of a need to validate and legitimize their behavior. He speculates that, because there can be no long-term relationship with the child and the child inevitably grows older and becomes less attractive to the pedophile, photographs become a way of keeping the victim young forever. As the victim enters puberty and the pedophile loses interest in the child, he may try to end the relationship by moving the child into prostitution. Burgess and Clark (1984) note:

There are strong indications that the pictures allow the collector a connection with earlier traumatic experiences when he himself was victimized. Rather than confronting the victimization, the collector preserves psychological integrity by producing pornographic material that attempts to justify and normalize the abuse while safeguarding aggressive and libidinal drives. The pornography becomes the confirming evidence against the argument that child exploitation and molestation is not harmful and is justified because the child has aggressive and sexual drives. Pornography endorses the belief patterns that ultimately justify violence toward children. (p. 109)

Pornography may also be used as blackmail against children to ensure their continued participation in the sexual activity and the secrecy that surrounds it. While pedophiles use child pornography primarily to satisfy their own needs, others capitalize on their appetite for it and, although not necessarily consumers themselves, may make considerable profit through the sale of child pornography. Some pornographers may even use their own children, pay parents for the use of their children, or pay needy runaways to pose.

Children involved in child pornography are often seduced by the abuser's caring and fatherlike attitude toward them. The pedophile is adept at choosing children who are particularly needy and in turn relates well to them. Gifts and special favors are common early in the relationship. He may operate on a one-to-one relationship with the victim or be simultaneously involved with a number of children who are aware of each other's sexual activities in what is known as a sex ring. Burgess, Groth, and McCausland (1981) note that the offender's presence in the lives of children involved in sex rings usually appears legitimate as he often occupies a position of authority and is familiar to the children involved. Initiation into sexual activities usually progresses from observing to exhibiting to direct physical sexual activity. The leader of the ring controls and manipulates the child through peer pressure, competition, and threats, as well as rewards. Children who become involved in sex rings are most likely to be male, and the pedophile may encourage them to turn on one another and take vicarious pleasure in their sadism. Because the child has come to trust the pedophile and care about him, the child is understandably ambivalent about the relationship. His embarrassment over his participation, as well as bonding to the pedophile, makes it difficult for him to reveal the secret. The pedophile may operate solo or as part of a more organized, syndicated sex ring in which children are recruited, pornography produced, and sexual services delivered to a wide network of customers (Burgess & Clark, 1984).

Burgess, Groth, and McCausland (1984) are among the few who have studied children involved in child pornography and sex rings. They noted four different response patterns which they termed: 1) avoidance of the event; 2) repetition of symptoms, which included repeated victimization; 3) identification with the exploiter, which included minimizing the significance of the experience and often exploiting other children; and 4) integration of the event, which was the healthiest outcome. Those children who integrated the event held the adult responsible for what occurred and had positive views re criminal prosecution. Burgess et al. noted that many of the 66 children whom they studied were symptomatic prior to disclosure with genital complaints, other somatic complaints, or behavioral changes. Following disclosure, post-traumatic stress responses were common and many new symptoms emerged. Those children who had the longest involvement in sex rings and child pornography were most likely to be bound into an exploitative cycle. Most of the children in their study had been involved with sexual activities for over a year. Those involved only with pornography were most likely to identify with the exploiter. Additional features of these children included intrusive thoughts, gender identity conflicts, avoidant behavior, and stylized sexual behavior (Lanning & Burgess, 1984).

Schoettle (1980) discusses the treatment of a pubescent girl involved in a sex ring and comments on her guilt, role confusion, anxiety, sense of betrayal, loss of self-esteem, and the "flood of emotion" that accompanied disclosure. He notes the child's disturbed early parent-child relationship and how her quest for a father figure contributed to her vulnerability.

Legal Issues

In 1977, the Protection of Children against Sexual Exploitation Act was passed. This act prohibits the participation of children in obscene performances, the transportation for purposes of sale of materials depicting children in sexual conduct, and the interstate transport of children for purposes of prostitution or obscene performances. Further, state laws exist regarding sexual exploitation of minors and sex offense statutes. However, considerable differences exist regarding definitions, penalties, and age of child protected (see Burgess & Clark, 1984).

Much of the public continues to view pornography as a victimless crime, and this attitude undoubtedly contributes toward public apathy about the problem. A 1985 *Newsweek* poll found that most Americans do not want greater restrictions on sexually explicit material but that 68% favor a ban on pornography that features violence (*Newsweek,*

March 18, 1985, p. 60). Feminists have recently taken the approach that the pornographer's right to free speech must be weighed against a woman's right to be free from harm. The city of Indianapolis succeeded in passing an ordinance that defined and penalized pornography as discriminating against women. The ordinance defined pornography as "the graphic sexually explicit subordination of women through pictures and/or words" (*Newsweek,* April 18, 1985, p. 47). Similar laws were passed in Cambridge, Massachusetts, and Suffolk County, Long Island (New York). However, in February 1986, the U.S. Supreme Court declared the Indianapolis ordinance unconstitutional because it violated the First Amendment right of free speech (*New York Times,* February 25, 1986, p. A1). Other current approaches to curtailing pornography include developing stricter zoning laws that restrict where adult book stores and movie theaters may operate.

The public needs to become more aware of how pornography harms women and children and should be urged to protest and picket those (theaters, bookstores, film producers, magazines, etc.) who profit from it. The public can also advocate for stiffer penalties for those found guilty of producing and distributing child pornography.

President Reagan urged a fresh look at the conclusions of the Committee on Obscenity and Pornography and in 1984 established a new commission to study the problem. The Commission has recommended that state laws be changed to make possession of child pornography a crime. Currently, the sale of child pornography is banned throughout the country but possession remains legal in some states. Commission members also favored restrictions on violent pornography, implying it was linked to violent crime (Attorney General's Commission on Pornography, *Final Report,* 1986). Dissenting opinions were expressed by several Commission members who felt the Commission's methods hindered the adequate pursuit of information. Specifically mentioned were the limitation imposed by hearings taking place in a public forum, time and money constraints, lack of evidence supporting a link between nonviolent, degrading, and humiliating pornography and sexual violence, and hasty debate with limited discussion of most issues other than child pornography (Becker & Levine, 1986). These authors also point out how rudimentary our knowledge is about the impact of sexually explicit material on children.

President Reagan also signed legislation raising the penalties for those convicted of producing or distributing child pornography and eliminating the requirement to prove obscenity before obtaining convictions. The new legislation goes beyond commercial child pornography and encompasses reproduction of such materials and permits authorities to seize pornographic materials (*New York Times,* May 5, 1986, p. A20).

CHILD PROSTITUTION

Child prostitution involves the sexual exploitation of children for profit and the use of minor children in sexual acts with adults where no force is present. Payment for sexual services usually takes the form of money, food, clothing, or drugs. Lloyd (1976) estimates that between .5 and 1.2 million children are involved in child prostitution and that there are at least 300,000 male prostitutes under age 16. The peak age for entering into prostitution seems to be about 14 (Enablers, 1978; Gray, 1973; James, 1980) and the average age of prostitutes arrested is dropping (*Newsweek*, July 17, 1978, p. 72). Silbert and Pines (1981) found that 78% of the 200 prostitutes they studied had started as juveniles.

Juvenile prostitutes come from all walks of life and the most common pathway into prostitution is running away. In the Silbert and Pines study mentioned above, 96% of the prostitutes had been runaways. A similar correlation has been found for male juvenile prostitutes (Weisberg, 1985). Reasons for leaving home include neglect and abuse (Bracey, 1979; Brown, 1979; Deisher, Robinson, & Boyer, 1982; Weisberg, 1985), and feelings of not being wanted. Studies repeatedly show a high incidence of prior sexual abuse, often incestuous among both male and female prostitutes (Enablers, 1978; James, 1980; James & Myerding, 1977; Silbert, 1980; Silbert & Pines, 1981; Weisberg, 1985). Other common denominators include passivity, low self-esteem, vulnerability, dependency needs, family conflict, broken homes and alienation from family, low education levels, and poor vocational skills (Gandy & Deisher, 1970; Satterfield, 1981; Wooden, 1976).

Females are often recruited into prostitution by pimps who frequent bus depots looking for runaways. Early on, the pimp plays upon the runaway's dependency needs and emphasizes the nonsexual side of their relationship while offering her understanding, affection, and protection. According to Bracey (1979), the "classic" pimp rarely occupies himself with juveniles as they are regarded as "small change"; he does not want to take the legal risk nor does he want to play the father role. The pimp who chooses to become involved with minors usually supplies them with false identification. He controls his girls—or "stable" as they are known—with just the right amount of affection and intimidation. For the prostitute he offers protection from harassment, supplies her with shelter, outfits her, offers her instruction, and even the pretense of love or paternal affection, and pays her bail and legal fees. Bracey (1979) contends that the pimp does not encourage her to use drugs because it drains his finances and hampers her performance. Others find there is a positive correlation between prostitution and drug abuse.

Gray (1973) comments on the parallel between the pimp-prostitute relationship and conventional marital behavior, i.e., the pimp serves as the major decision-maker and controller of funds in return for which women provide him with emotional support and earn money for him. Most juvenile prostitutes turn all of their earnings over to their pimp and few save any money.

Sereny (1985) describes the rigorously defined and mutually accepted convention that exists between pimp and prostitute in which the prostitute denies that he cheats her and she never cheats him for fear of punishment. Their lovemaking, which is make-believe on both sides, is also part of the pact. Sereny believes that "dishonesty and corruption damages the girl as much as physical harm" (p. 70). Sereny notes that understanding the girl's vulnerability is the pimp's stock and trade. Black pimps prefer to deal with white girls possibly because black girls are too streetwise and would fight back and insist on a percentage of their earnings. Other motives are suggested by Sereny, who quotes a pimp saying, "Can you think of a better way of getting back at whitey than to deal with his kids?" (p. 104). Sereny also notes pimps' basic contempt for the women they use. Most teenage prostitutes become disillusioned with their pimps and tend to move on to others, which are also short-term relationships.

Other routes into prostitution include recruitment by peers, which was noted in 60% of those studied by Bracey (1979), who suggests recruitment becomes a way for a prostitute to ingratiate herself with her pimp. The promise of friendship with other girls may also lure some into prostitution. Finally, the financial enterprise holds strong appeal, considering most who enter the field are poorly educated and lack job skills.

MacVicar and Dillon (1980) found considerable psychopathology in the 10 adolescent and young adult female prostitutes they studied, three of whom were diagnosed as schizophrenic and seven of whom were diagnosed as borderline personalities. MacVicar and Dillon felt that prostitution served as a means of preserving some vestige of object relations and noted the tendency of the prostitutes to use splitting, viewing the pimp as all good and the customer as bad. They describe the prostitute's masochistic submission to the idealized object-pimp and her belief that supporting him is a way of feeling good about herself.

A rather different profile emerges in studies of male juvenile prostitutes, in that many are situational rather than full-time hustlers who do it out of enjoyment of their sexuality or for adventure (Weisberg, 1985). They are not governed by a pimp and in this regard they are not as exploited as the female prostitute and have less negative attitudes about prostitution than do their female counterparts. Many are bisexual or homosexual in their orientation and engage in prostitution as a way of interacting with other gays (Weisberg, 1985). Allen (1980) found a high incidence of polydrug use among adolescent male prostitutes. In contrast to female counterparts, the juvenile male prostitute may have an ongoing relationship with a steady customer often referred to as his "Sugar Daddy." Caukins and Coombs (1976) note that the male prostitute seeks approval and affection from his customers, yet at the same time feels disdain and antagonism toward them. Often the relationship is held together by elaborate fantasy and role playing on each side. Weisberg (1985) found 27% of her sample of juvenile male prostitutes had been involved with pornography, whereas James (1980) found only 10% of her sample had.

A final difference between male and female adolescent prostitutes is that males are much less likely to be arrested for prostitution than are females. Female prostitutes usually get arrested by male undercover police officers posing as customers; Deisher, Robinson, and Boyer (1982) suggest that police may be uncomfortable posing as homosexual customers of male prostitutes, hence the lower arrest rate. Female prostitutes also tend to be more visible than male prostitutes on the street. Following arrest and brief detention, both male and female juvenile prostitutes are likely to be released to their parents and charges are often dismissed (Harlan, Rodgers, & Slatter, 1981). Sereny (1985) observes: "These children present a problem which virtually no police force anywhere in the Western world has been able to handle. They are children who cannot bear to live with their families and who will not stay in institutions. There is no place for them to go" (p. 13).

The juvenile prostitute is hesitant to seek medical care because of embarrassment, fear, and antiauthoritarian attitudes. Deisher, Robinson, and Boyer (1982) note that physicians often err in assuming that juveniles involved in prostitution are knowledgeable about sexuality, venereal disease, and birth control; in fact, this is rarely the case. Additional problems may stem from the prostitute's poor communication skills and physicians' judgmental statements which the adolescent may interpret as bias. Deisher and colleagues advise, for instance, referring to the male prostitute's "lover" rather than "girlfriend." This population is not likely to return for follow-up visits and hence they urge the use of outreach workers.

Bracey (1979) notes that inadequate nutrition and clothing may predispose female prostitutes to health problems. Venereal disease is the most prevalent health problem among this population. Suicidal thoughts and attempts are also common (Deisher, Eisner, & Sulzbacher,

1969; Harlan, Rodgers, & Slatter, 1981), and self-esteem is easily threatened if relationship of female prostitutes with their pimp goes awry (MacVicar & Dillon, 1980). Sereny (1985) aptly describes the low self-esteem of these youths, commenting that

> defeated by the loneliness of their decision to run and stay away they feel valueless as children in a world of adults who cannot help them and valueless as sons and daughters of parents whose lives they are convinced they hinder rather than enrich. Their value as children—their right to be protected—have been taken away and they feel worthless as human beings. Prostitution, the act of extreme self-abasement, serves to both fuel their self-contempt and vengefully express their anger and fear stored up against those who caused it—their parents. (p. 251)

Both male and female juvenile prostitutes are dehumanized by the experience in which they are only valued for their sex organs, which they come to view as a commodity. Disillusionment is inevitable as they soon realize there is no such thing as instant wealth and that selling their bodies cannot win them love and security. Further damage is done as they miss out on education and normal adolescent experiences that would help them prepare to deal with the real world as adults. Exiting the system is not easy when they have no other skills to fall back on other than hustling and few support systems to which they can turn. Age usually cuts short their careers in prostitution, with most leaving after 10 years. Some may turn to crime, others to drugs (Allen 1980; James, 1980).

Most authors are bleak regarding the prognosis for juvenile prostitutes. Experience has led prostitutes to believe that they cannot get anything good from another person and they are not likely to trust a therapist. MacVicar and Dillon (1980) feel that the prostitute's contempt for her therapist stems from envy. They note that her tendency toward immediate gratification and lack of future orientation may also make it difficult for her to break away from prostitution. They believe that the best time to reach the juvenile prostitute is before she gets involved with a pimp. Sereny (1985), in contrast, seems more hopeful, based on her firsthand encounters with juvenile prostitutes in several foreign countries.

Prevention and Rehabilitation

Primary prevention involves attacking problems within the family that predispose youngsters to run away and developing programs that encourage at-risk children to remain in school. Once on the street, it becomes much more difficult to deal with runaways. While cracking down on pimps would seem to be an obvious solution, it is far from simple; many prostitutes remain loyal to their pimps, refuse to testify against them, and in spite of mistreatment return to them when released following arrest. The most promising approach to the problem seems to be the development of runaway youth shelters, as exemplified by Covenant House in New York City, The Bridge in Boston, and Huckleberry House in San Francisco. The Runaway Youth Act in 1974 provided federal funding to various local and state organizations to furnish services to runaways, although currently only six states are budgeted for such programs (*Parade Magazine*, August 18, 1986, p. 6). In addition, private funding for shelters is being raised by the National Network of Runaway and Youth Services, and two hotlines for runaways have been established: The National Runaway Switchboard, 1-800-621-4000, and National Runaway Hotline, 1-800-392-3352. The Trailways Corporation provides free rides home to runaways and has assisted more than 4,500 of them. Ideally, shelters should have components that offer outreach services and medical, psychiatric, vocational, and brief family counseling.

Specially trained youth officers should be assigned to juvenile prostitutes. They need to be sensitized to the dynamics of child sexual abuse and helped to view juvenile prostitutes as victims rather than perpetrators of crime. They also need to be made aware of community resources. Finally, Weisberg (1985) suggests their efforts should be centered on arresting customers and pimps rather than prostitutes.

Legislative responses to the problem have included:

1. The Protection of Children Against Sexual Exploitation Act, which amended the Mann Act to prohibit the interstate transportation of minor males for prostitution.
2. The Child Abuse Prevention and Treatment Act of 1977, which provided for programs directed at preventing and treating child abuse and neglect and the establishment of the National Center of Child Abuse and Neglect.
3. The Runaway and Homeless Youth Act of 1974, which in addition to funding shelters acknowledged that many runaway youths are "throwaways" who have been abandoned by their familes.
4. The Missing Children Act, which established a national clearinghouse to help locate missing children.

In addition, states have their own legislation governing prostitution, which, as noted by Weisberg (1985), tends to have many limitations in its applications to juveniles. Weisberg also observes the difficulties in curtailing juvenile male prostitutes since most are self-employed and are not likely to be transported across state lines or be employed by pimps. The Justice Department's Advisory Board on Missing Children has recommended that state and local laws be changed to allow police to detain runaways and neglected and missing children; the Advisory Board notes that children "do not have a right to freedom from custody" (*New York Times*, March 8, 1986, p. 8).

In summary, there are no easy answers to these problems, although greater awareness on the part of the public, professionals, and legislators is certainly the first step toward finding means of curbing child pornography and prostitution.

REFERENCES

Allen, D. (1980). Young male prostitutes: A psychosocial study. *Arch. Sex. Beh.*, 9(5):399–426.

Attorney General's Commission on Pornography. (1986). *Final Report, Vols. I & II.* Washington, DC: U.S. Government Printing Office.

Baron, L., & Straus, M.A. (1984). Sexual stratification, pornography and rape in the U.S.A. In N.M. Malamuth & E. Donnerstein (Eds.), *Pornography and Sexual Aggression.* New York: Academic Press.

Becker, J., & Levine, L. (1986). XXX/ On Attorney General's Commission on Pornography: Final Report, Vols. *I & II.* In *Readings*, 1(3):12–15.

Bracey, D.H. (1979). *Baby Pros: Preliminary Profiles of Juvenile Prostitutes.* New York: John Jay Press.

Brown, M.E. (1979). Teenage prostitution. *Adolescence*, 14(56):665–679.

Burgess, A.W. (1984). Response patterns of children and adolescents exploited through sex rings and pornography. *Am. J. Psychiat.*, 141(5):656–662.

Burgess, A.W., & Clark, M.L. (1984). *Child Pornography and Sex Rings.* Lexington, MA: Lexington Books.

Burgess, A.W., Groth, A.N., & McCausland, M. (1981). Child sex initiation rings. *Amer. J. Orthopsychiat.*, 51(1):110–119.

Caukins, S., & Coombs, N. (1976). The psychodynamics of male prostitution. *Am. J. Psychother.*, 30:441–451.

Deisher, R.W., Eisner, C., & Sulzbacher, S. (1969). The young male prostitute. *Pediatrics*, 43(6):936–941.

Deisher, R.W., Robinson, G., & Boyer, D. (1982). The adolescent female and male prostitute. *Pediatric Annals*, 11(10):819–825.

Densen-Gerber, J., & Hutchinson, S. (1979). Sexual and commercial exploitation of children: Legislative response and treatment challenge. *Child Abuse and Neglect*, 3:61–66.

Donnerstein, E. (1984). Pornography: Its effect on violence against women. In N.M. Malamuth & E. Donnerstein (Eds.), *Pornography and Sexual Aggression.* New York: Academic Press, pp. 53–81.

Enablers (1979). *Juvenile Prostitution in Minneapolis, Minn.* St. Paul: Enablers, Inc.

Gandy, P., & Deisher, R. (1970). Young male prostitutes: The physician's role in social rehabilitation. *J.A.M.A.,* 212(10):1661–1666.

Gray, D. (1973). Turning out: A study of teenage prostitution. *Urban Life and Culture,* 1(4):401–425.

Harlan, S., Rodgers, L.L., & Slatter, B. (1981). Male and female prostitution: Huckleberry House sexual minority youth service project. Washington, D.C.: Youth Dev. Bureau, U.S. Department of Health and Human Services.

James, J. (1980). *Entrance into Juvenile Prostitution.* Washington, D.C.: NIMH.

James, J., & Myerding, J. (1977). Early sexual experience as a factor in prostitution. *Arch. Sex. Beh.,* 17(1):31–42.

Lanning, K. (1986). *Child Molesters: A Behavioral Analysis for Law Enforcement.* Quantico, VA: U.S. Department of Justice, F.B.I.

Lanning, K., & Burgess, A.W. (1984). Child pornography and sex rings. *F.B.I. Law Enforcement Bulletin,* January, pp. 1–7.

Lloyd, R. (1976). *For Money or Love: Boy Prostitution in America.* New York: Vanguard.

MacVicar, K., & Dillon, M. (1980). Childhood and adolescent development of ten female prostitutes. *J. Am. Acad. Ch. Psych.,* 19:145–159.

Malamuth, N.M. (1984). Aggression against women: Cultural and individual causes. In N.M. Malamuth & E. Donnerstein (Eds.), *Pornography and Sexual Aggression.* New York: Academic Press.

Roth v. U.S. (1957) 354 U.S. 476.

Rush, F. (1981). *The Best Kept Secret (Sexual Abuse of Children).* New York: McGraw-Hill Paperback.

Satterfield, S.B. (1981). Clinical aspects of juvenile prostitution. *Medical Aspects of Human Sexuality,* 15(19):126–132.

Schoettle, U.S. (1980). Child exploitation: A study of pornography. *J. Am. Acad. Ch. Psych.,* 19:289–299.

Sereny, G. (1985). *Invisible Children: Child Prostitution in America, W. Germany and Great Britain.* New York: Alfred Knopf.

Silbert, M. (1980). *Sexual Assault of Prostitutes. Phase One.* Washington, D.C.: National Center for Prevention and Control of Rape, N.I.M.H.

Silbert, M.H., & Pines, A.M. (1981). Sexual child abuse as an antecedent to prostitution. *Child Abuse and Neglect,* 5:407–411.

Swearingen v. U.S. (1896) 161 U.S. 446.

U.S. v. One Book called "Ulysses" (S.D.N.Y. 1933) 5F Supp. 182.

Weisberg, K. (1985). *Children of the Night: A Study of Adolescent Prostitution.* Lexington, MA: Lexington Books.

Wooden, K. (1976). *Weeping in the Playtime of Others: America's Incarcerated Children.* New York: McGraw-Hill.

10

The Child as Witness

Diane H. Schetky

HISTORICAL BACKGROUND

In ancient common law, children below the age of 9 or 10 were not allowed to testify as witnesses (*Rex v. Travers,* 1726). Statutory law regarding the child as a witness did not come into effect until 1778 in England with the case of *Rex v. Brasier* (1779). In this case, which involved the sexual abuse of a child under 7 years of age, the lower court convicted the defendant on the basis of hearsay testimony because it held the young child to be incompetent to give testimony. The Appellate Court reversed the lower court decision and held that in criminal cases a child was competent if he possessed sufficient knowledge of the nature and obligation of the oath. There followed no specific age restrictions governing a child's testimony.

In the U.S. during the Salem Witch Trials in 1692, children were permitted to serve as witnesses and even encouraged to become witnesses against their parents. Almost all of the arrests made were based on the testimony of 10 afflicted girls, some of whom did not even know the people they professed to be witches. Leading questions were permitted, e.g., "How long has thee been a witch?" (Upham, 1969, p. 209), and children were pressured by adults to say who was bewitching them. As noted by Upham (1969), "Becoming objects of such notice they were stimulated to vary and expand the manifestations of the extraordinary influence that was upon them" (p. 7).

In 1895, a 5 ½-year-old-boy was declared competent to testify at his father's murder trial *(Wheeler v. United States).* Factors considered in determining his competency included his intelligence, appreciation of the difference between truth and falsehood, and the child's sense of duty to tell the truth. Statutory requirements of most states have followed the lead of Wheeler, adhering to similar criteria. In 12 states the child is presumed competent to testify at age 14 or older, and in

166

10 states a child under 10 may not testify unless he "has the capacity to receive just impressions and communicate them truthfully," in which case the determination of competency is left to the discretion of the court (Melton, Bulkley, & Wulkan, 1985). Thus, in general, the competency of a child to be a witness must be established on a case-by-case basis. Differences of opinion exist as to the need for a child witness to take an oath, and Wigmore (1940) suggests merely putting the child on the stand and allowing the jury to decide on the credibility of the child's testimony.

Particularly in cases of sexual abuse, the trend has been to see more and more very young children take the witness stand. These cases pose unique problems, including the question of whether or not the preschool child possesses the degree of abstract thinking necessary to comprehend the concept of an oath and the truth. There have been several reports of 4-year-olds testifying in court. One 4-year-old, believed to be the youngest prosecution witness in Allegheny County, testified as to how he had been sexually abused. The child underwent a 30-minute competency hearing, and it was determined that he had sufficient memory and appreciation of the truth. However, when it was time for him to take the stand for the trial, he became cranky and fell asleep and his testimony had to be postponed to the following day (*Pittsburgh Press*, November 18, 1979, p. A1). In New Jersey, a 4-year-old child who was alleged to have been sodomized was allowed to take the stand when he acknowledged that God would punish him if he did not tell the truth (*New York Times*, February 1, 1979, p. B2).

In another New Jersey case, a 4-year-old testified in a proceeding to determine the delinquency of a minor. The case was appealed and reversed by the Superior Appellate Court Division on the grounds that the child had not been given the traditional oath and hence had not been properly sworn in. The Supreme Court reversed the Appellate Court decision, arguing that New Jersey rules of evidence required administration of an oath rather than "the" oath and that no particular words needed to be used in the oath as long as it conveyed the obligation to speak the truth. The court further argued that the requirement of possessing independent recollection of events should not affect the admissibility of evidence but rather the weight given to it (*State v. Interests of R.R., A Juvenile*, 1976).

Another problem concerns lapse of time between events witnessed and actual testimony. In *Macale v. Lynch* (1920), the defendant was convicted based on testimony of a 6-year-old who had recovered after a period of prolonged hospitalization. The State Supreme Court reversed the lower court's decision, arguing that the child had been exposed to multiple discussions with parents, attorney, and medical personnel and could not relate the facts accurately after such a long time interval. In contrast, a New Jersey court allowed a 4-year-old girl to testify against her father in regard to alleged sexual abuse said to have occurred at age 2½. Further, she was allowed to sit on her mother's lap while testifying, a situation the defense attorney described as "akin to having Charlie McCarthy testify on Edgar Bergen's lap" (*Washington Post,* June 16, 1985, p. A6). Nonetheless, the Appellate Division of the Superior Court voted to allow the testimony.

This author was involved in a trial in Massachusetts in which the child witness who turned 4 during the proceedings was deemed competent to testify about alleged sexual abuse by his father said to have occurred some six months earlier. Although the child was technically competent, no one had assessed the child's ability to cooperate and this rather oppositional little boy proceeded to run circles around the court, refusing to enter the courtroom. When finally coaxed in, he refused to answer questions, clung to his mother who was allowed to sit next to him, and pleaded to go home. The prosecution failed to get him to produce any evidence and the boy's father was acquitted.

Connecticut has recently passed legislation (Public Act No. 85–587, 1986) that states, "No witness shall be automatically adjudged incompetent to testify because of age and any child who is a victim of assault, sexual assault or abuse shall be competent to testify without prior qualifications" (p. 1). The problem with this provision is that the child witness is presumed to be a victim without any preliminary findings of fact; thus, the presumption of innocence is violated and an element of prejudgment introduced.

EVALUATING COMPETENCY

As outlined by Stafford (1962), there are four basic elements to testimonial capacity.

1. The child's capacity to communicate, observe, and remember matter about which testimony is being sought.
2. The child's mental capacity at the time of the occurrence in question and ability to observe and register such occurrence.
3. Memory sufficient to retain an independent recollection of the observations made.
4. Capacity to translate into words the memory of such observations.

As was apparent in the cases mentioned above, the legal criteria for competence to testify do not take into consideration such factors as the child's temperament, ability to cooperate, and present reality testing, all of which may affect performance in court. Often it will be advisable to have a child psychiatric forensic examination performed on the child solely for purposes of assessing competency, although in our experience this is rarely requested and little has been written about how to perform such an evaluation on a child. The basic questions to be addressed in a competency evaluation concern: 1) whether there is a mental disease or defect present which affects judgment or decision-making behavior; and 2) whether this mental disease or defect directly impairs the individual's performance on a specific task. Quinn (1986) provides an excellent discussion on how to conduct such an evaluation. She stresses the need to be aware of the current legal standard of competence in one's jurisdiction and that detailed exploration of the allegation should be avoided so as not to contaminate the interview. She mentions the need to use DSM-III diagnoses as well as behavior descriptions that will convey the child's ability or inability to be a witness. Quinn recommends exploring the child's willingness to testify and the option of recommending modification of the legal proceedings so as to enhance the child's cooperation and performance.

DECIDING WHETHER OR NOT A CHILD SHOULD TESTIFY

In addition to the issue of whether or not a child is competent to testify, one needs to consider whether or not it is in the child's interests to testify. Berliner and Barbieri (1984) offer guidelines from a prosecutor's standpoint stating, "The child victim should testify only when that testimony will substantially increase the chance of conviction and will not do serious harm to the child" (p. 134). An additional concern is how effective the child will be as a witness. Claman and colleagues (1986) list numerous factors to be considered, such as the child's appearance and appeal, ability to relate positively, ability to express self and describe the abuse, willingness to testify, and ability to deal with loyalty conflicts. It is necessary to weigh the pros and cons as well as the need to protect the child and others from future victimization.

The trauma of having a child testify is likely to be greatest when the child is a victim of the crime or was in the zone of danger either emotionally or physically, e.g., witnessing the assault of a parent. If the victim had significant ties to the defendant, she will probably be more conflicted about testifying than if he was a stranger. Another important variable has to do with how much support the child has received from her family and agency personnel and whether she feels believed.

Common fears expressed by child witnesses are: 1) the fear of retaliation by the defendant, particularly if he has made threats to her in the past; 2) the fear, often valid, that she will not be believed; 3) feeling as if she is on trial, often reinforced by aggressive cross-examination, or guilt if she blames herself for what happened; and 4) humiliation and embarrassment from the nature of questions asked and the presence of the jury and press. Some authors believe that detailed questions about the crime may retraumatize the child. A realistic concern has to do with the inevitable postponements and delays, the need for repeated questioning in the pretrial phase, and the disruptive effect this has on the child's life. Perhaps most devastating is a trial that ends in acquittal, which leaves the child feeling unbelieved and unprotected.

On the positive side, testifying may allow the child to take an active role in a step toward mastering a trauma. It offers her the chance to be believed and see justice work. It may also provide a constructive outlet for her anger. Many children will find reassurance in knowing that by testifying they may be protecting other potential victims and forcing the defendant to get help.

LEGAL AND CONSTITUTIONAL ISSUES

In order to understand why witnesses and defendants are treated as they are in court, we need to understand the constitutional and legal issues that govern how a trial proceeds. Child witnesses—and, for that matter, all witnesses—have no constitutional rights afforded to them in court. There is no right to counsel and no right to remain silent. The defendant, in contrast, has the right to legal representation, the right to remain silent, and the protection of the 1st, 6th, and 14th Amendments of the Constitution. The 14th Amendment affords the accused due process rights, which include the right to obtain witnesses on his behalf, the right to cross-examination, and the right to legal representation to protect his interests during the trial.

The confrontation clause of the 6th Amendment provides that "the accused shall enjoy the right to be confronted with the witness against him." This amendment to the Constitution in 1791 was made in part in response to the trial of Sir Walter Raleigh for treason, in which evidence was presented against him in the form of written depositions; Raleigh's repeated requests to confront the witnesses went unheeded (Stephens, 1919). It is felt that the process of face-to-face confrontation affects recall, veracity, and communication. In addition, the confrontation clause serves to allow for effective cross-examination and ensures that the witness testifies under oath. The question of admissibility of videotaped deposition was taken up by the Supreme Court in *U.S. v. Benfield* (1979): the court ruled that such a procedure was constitutionally infirm when the defendant was not permitted to be an active participant in the video deposition and that the procedural substitute is constitutionally inferior.

Nonetheless, exceptions do exist. Recent legislation in many states permits child victims of sexual abuse to testify on closed-circuit TV and/or use of videotaped testimony (Heeney, 1985). In addition, two states (New York and California) specify the use of two-way closed-circuit TV so that the child may also view the defendant. Terr (1986) cautions that closed-circuit television may

> lull courts into thinking that sexually abused children will automatically tell the truth on television, when in fact there are far deeper reasons (besides embarrassment and fear about telling a story to all of those people including the perpetrator, in the open courtroom) that may interfere with a child's forthrightness (p. 469).

Further, Terr believes that in some instances it may be helpful for the child to take the witness stand against the defendant.

In Texas the legislature enacted a law which allows for the videotaping of a child and admissibility of that tape provided "the child is available to testify if the accused so desires" (Art. 38.071(2) of Texas Criminal Procedure). In the event that a witness is "unavailable," videotaped testimony may be introduced as hearsay (*Ohio v. Roberts,* 1980). Graham (1985) cites several situations in which this might be invoked, including mental or physical illness, privilege, lack of memory, and death. Graham notes several states have enacted statutes in which the finding that the child would suffer moderate emotional or mental distress is sufficient grounds on which to declare the child unavailable.

Hearsay statements are generally excluded from court because they are not made under oath and because they are not subject to cross-examination or the scrutiny of the jury. However, several exceptions exist concerning extrajudicial rape complaints (see Kenmore, 1984). The one most often invoked in regard to victims of child sexual abuse is the theory of excited utterance or res gestae. The court finds spontaneous utterances more trustworthy than other extrajudicial statements but requires that a shocking event must have occurred, that the declarant must have made the statement while under the influence of the shocking event, and that the statement must relate to the event in question.

Another issue concerns the child's right to privacy versus the defendant's right to a public trial as stipulated in the 1st Amendment and the public's right to know. The intent of this amendment is to provide checks and balances on the criminal justice system, while also allowing the public to see that justice is being done. Two important legal cases have addressed this issue. In *Richmond Newspapers, Inc. v. Virginia* (1980), the U.S. Supreme Court disallowed closed hearings, noting that public access was guaranteed by the 1st Amendment. *Globe Newspaper Co. v. Superior Court* (1980) questioned the constitutionality of barring anyone who did not have direct interest in a case involving a minor victim of sexual abuse. The Superior Judicial Court of Massachusetts supported exclusion of the press, feeling it encouraged young victims to come forward. The Globe appealed to the U.S. Supreme Court, which remanded the case in light of Richmond Newspapers, and the Massachusetts Supreme Court affirmed the earlier decision (*Globe Newspaper Co. v. Superior Court*, 1982a). The Globe again appealed to the U.S. Supreme Court, and Justice Brennan held the statute to be in violation of the 1st Amendment and that there was insufficient justification for mandating a closed courtroom (*Globe Newspaper Co. v. Superior Court*, 1982b).

Dissenters noted that states are permitted to close proceedings involving 17-year-olds charged with rape but not to protect children who have been raped. Melton (1984) comments, "Justice Brennan argued that a mandatory closure statute could be justified only if it could be shown that 'closure would improve the quality of testimony of all minor victims'—an impossible task" (p. 117). It should be noted that in other countries, such as England and Israel, the court has the discretion to close the courtroom to the public when a child victim is testifying (*Courts Law;* The Children and Young Person's Act, 1933).

DEVELOPMENTAL FACTORS AFFECTING CHILDREN'S PERCEPTION AND RECALL OF EVENTS AND THE INTERVIEWING OF CHILDREN

In spite of the fact that courts have tended to treat child witnesses much the way they do adults, we know that children have unique ways of perceiving, reacting to, and relating traumatic experiences. Some of the developmental factors that account for these differences include the following:

Cognitive Factors

1. Predominance of primary process thinking. Young children show a relative weakness of secondary process or logical thinking compared to the strength of their impulses and fantasies until about age 4 to 6 years when logical thinking and ability to postpone immediate gratification of instincts take over. They may, in some situations, confuse fact with fantasy. Johnson and Foley (1984) studied young children and found they had some difficulty in discriminating between what they had done and what they had thought of doing. However, they concluded the children were able to differentiate their own thoughts from another person's actions.

2. Sexual immaturity.   Children will interpret sexual events according to where they are in their own psychosexual development. Thus, the young child may perceive a sexual assault as an aggressive attack or violation of her body rather than a sexual act per se. The degree of their awareness of social mores will also affect how they perceive the abuse and how much guilt they experience.

3. Language.   Language problems may often be the source of confused communications between children and adults. Aside from articulation problems, many young children are concrete in their thinking. The child's literal thinking may cast doubts on his credibility, as in the case of the child who was asked if he had ever been in the defendant's home and he replied no because he had been in his apartment, not his house.

4. Time sense.   Young children do not share adults' sense of time or even units for measuring time, yet may be quite correct if allowed to describe events in relation to holidays, seasons, birthdays, meals, or TV programs. Children have been shown to be quite accurate with regard to frequency of occurrence or temporal order of events (Brown, 1975; Hasher & Zacks, 1979).

However, as noted by Terr (1983), following psychic trauma, distortions of time and time-related phenomena may occur. Such distortions commonly take the form of lengthening the actual duration of the traumatic experience and perceiving time as more drawn out. Terr (1984) speculates that this subjective durational prolongation may have a self-protective function in that it makes possible a larger number of potentially effective actions within a short period of time. She also found that a few children had trouble with proper sequencing of events during trauma or a tendency to condense events. Terr concluded that children under 8 years of age, and those who had been exposed to sensory deprivation or suffered mild concussions, were most likely to experience time confusion.

5. *Memory.* Studies have shown that children's memories tend to be more fragmented and less complete than adults' memories (Johnson & Foley, 1984). Children make more errors of omission than do adults, yet at the same time are likely to notice things that adults do not, which may prove very useful in court (Neisser, 1979). Reasons speculated for these discrepancies include the fact that younger children are not able to deal with memory tasks in a linear fashion and that children do not have relevant prior knowledge that allows them to relate one set of events to another and organize disparate elements into a cohesive whole (Johnson & Foley, 1984). However, as noted by Kobasigawa (1974), if given external prompts or cues children perform well on recall, which may be the rationale for allowing attorneys to lead child witnesses. It should be noted that adults are also suggestible, although more latitude is permitted regarding posing leading questions to the child witness in court.

Dale, Loftus, and Rathburn (1978) found that the presence of leading questions increased the likelihood that subjects of all ages would incorporate this information into answers given two weeks later. Similar findings are reported by Cohen and Harnick (1980) and Murray (1983). However, these studies were conducted in laboratory conditions. In an attempt to observe children in a more lifelike setting, Goodman and colleagues (1987) studied children receiving inoculations in their doctors' offices. They found the children to be highly accurate in their recall of events, but found the 3- and 4-year-olds to be more suggestible than the 5- and 6-year-olds. The latter showed some suggestibility but mostly to detail about the room rather than to information about persons or actions involved.

Another type of memory involves facial recognition, and here children have more difficulty than do adults according to the studies of Chance and Goldstein (1984). They found that the accuracy of correct identification of strangers increases with age, with the accuracy at kindergarten level being only 35%-40%, at ages 6 to 8 50%-58%, at ages 9 to 11 60%-70%, and at ages 12 to 14 70%-80%, which corresponds with the adult range. However, it should be noted that these findings apply only to laboratory conditions. Goodman and colleagues (1987), following up on the children they studied receiving inoculations, found the 3- and 4-year-olds to be weak on facial recognition after a period of a week. In contrast, Marin and colleagues (1979) found children to be as accurate as adults in answering objective questions and identifying photos of a confederate.

Children, in contrast to adults, are not amnestic for traumatic events, although both may experience lapse of memory over time. Terr (1985) describes the fascinating persistence of memory in children who were traumatized prior to the acquisition of verbal skills. These children, who had no verbal memory of their traumas when evaluated, nonetheless demonstrated through their play a "perceptual memory" of what occurred.

Emotional Factors

1. Dependency on caretaker. Young children are taught to believe their parents and regard them as authority figures. Given the young child's emotional and physical dependency on her parents and wish to please them, it may be exceedingly difficult for her to challenge her parents' perception of events when they differ from her own. When a child is repeatedly told that something did not occur which in fact did, she may come to doubt her own perceptions. Thus, 11-year-old Nicole retracted her former allegations that her stepfather had tickled her private parts, saying, "My mother says it didn't happen. She must be right. I must have been mistaken." As noted by Summit (1983), child victims of ongoing sexual abuse often come to doubt their own perceptions when they receive no validation from adults around them.

2. Loyalty conflicts. Children quite naturally feel compelled to protect their parents even when abused by them. Conflicts intensify if the child has been threatened by family disruption or the prospect of a parent going to jail. Loyalty conflicts also occur outside of the family as children may identify with the abuser (particularly if abuse is ongoing) and have positive feelings toward the abuser in spite of what has transpired.

3. Ego impairment. Terr (1980) described misperception as a defense in children who were severely traumatized. She noted that among the children of the Chowchilla kidnapping, five out of 23 misidentified the man who had kidnapped them yet could recall with great accuracy other details of their ordeal. Fish-Murray, Koby, and van der Kolk (1987) reported cognitive impairment in children who had been physically abused when they were confronted with affective stimuli that interfere with perception and interpretation of information at hand. These children may demonstrate adequate reality testing in daily life or in the courtroom during voir dire, but decompensate when confronted with a highly charged emotional situation that brings back an earlier trauma such as confronting the offender.

Other forms of ego impairment that may interfere with a child testifying include mental retardation or psychosis.

4. Interviewer factors. How the child is questioned will affect the child's responses. Failure to establish rapport with the child and use of coercive, threatening, repetitive, tricky, or biased questions will render the child confused and less cooperative; in addition, such questions are likely to have a negative impact on the jury.

JURORS' REACTIONS TO CHILD WITNESSES

Goodman, Golding, and Haith (1984) believe that most jurors have many doubts about the credibility of child witnesses but note that research into this area has been scant. However, they feel that juror bias may be overcome by sufficient evidence. Jurors will react most favorably to witnesses who demonstrate trustworthiness, consistency, certainty, confidence, and objectivity. Goodman et al. observe that inconsistency and lack of confidence may undermine a child's credibility. Further, they comment that children are apt to be less powerful than adults in their style of delivering testimony. Goodman and colleagues (1984) found that jurors were reluctant to judge a person's innocence or guilt solely on a child's statements and that they looked for more supporting evidence. Jurors were more likely to make negative comments about a 6-year-old's testimony to a simple perceptual event than to an adult testifying to the same event. Goodman et al. conclude, "The influence of children's testimony is greater than one would predict given their perceived credibility, but corroborating evidence may play a key role in determining the influence of children's statements" (p. 153).

RECOMMENDED CHANGES IN THE TREATMENT OF CHILD WITNESSES

Numerous authors have called for changes in the way in which child victims of sexual abuse are dealt with by investigators and the court (Bauer, 1983; Berliner & Barbieri, 1984; Libai, 1969; Parker, 1982; Weiss & Berg, 1982; Whitcomb, 1985; Yates, 1987). The American Academy of Child and Adolescent Psychiatry has drawn up recommendations for protecting children undergoing abuse investigations. Measures that can be taken to minimize additional trauma to the child witness and help support the child through testifying will be discussed below.

Pretrial Phase

Children should only be interviewed by specially trained investigatory personnel who possess a knowledge of child development, the family dynamics of child sexual abuse, the acute and long-term effects of child sexual abuse, and age-appropriate techniques for interviewing children. They need to be aware of their own feelings and on guard against bias, leading questions, or interrogatory techniques that have no place in the interview of a child and that may contaminate or even invalidate it. Parker (1982) recommends appointing a Child Hearing Officer (CHO) who would be a specially trained attorney to act as counsel and advocate for the child witness and who would be employed by the state. The CHO would perform the initial investigation instead of the police and accompany the child to any medical examinations, pretrial hearings, and grand jury or voir dire appearances, and have the power to request medical or psychiatric evaluation of the witness for purposes of protecting the child's health. By assuming so many functions, the CHO minimizes the number of people and interviews the child witness must face, while at the same time providing the child with support and continuity. Similar but less comprehensive support may be provided by victim advocate programs that prepare the child for what lies ahead, including visits to the courtroom and role playing.

The initial interview should, when possible, be videotaped to minimize duplication of efforts and perhaps spare the child an appearance before the grand jury. The videotaped interview also becomes a check on the professionalism of the interview should questions later arise about how it was conducted.

Cases involving child witnesses need to be prioritized on the court docket in order to allow the child to proceed with her life and to preserve the freshness of her recollections. Libai (1969) proposes taking the child's testimony in a special child courtroom immediately after the accused has been apprehended and before the trial has begun. The purpose of the special hearing would be to take the child's testimony for submission of evidence to the trial and thus limit cross-examination.

Trial Phase

Courtrooms need to be scaled down to the child's size and modes of expression. Steps in this direction include providing child-sized furniture, and dolls, paper and markers as alternate means of expression. Further, it is vital to take into consideration the child's physiological needs. Fatigue, hunger, need to urinate, and brief attention span will all affect testimony and should be treated with due respect and frequent breaks.

Libai, in 1969, was the first to suggest designing special courtrooms for children. He proposed allowing the jury, the accused, and the audience to sit behind a one-way glass which would separate them from the judge's room but allow them to observe and hear everything. The accused would have a microphone and earphones so as to enable him to communicate with his counsel. The only persons in the courtroom with the child would be the judge, prosecutor, defense counsel, and child examiner.

Although these suggestions have not been adopted in all states, those that have been implemented in some states include the use of closed-circuit, two-way TV, whereby victim and defendant are in separate rooms but can see each other on TV. This author was involved in one such case in Massachusetts where the witness was a 4-year-old child. No one took the trouble to explain to the child what his father was doing on TV and as he got bored with the proceedings, he turned to the judge and asked her, "Could we please change channels and watch cartoons?"

The uses and limitations of videotapes have already been discussed. If it is deemed necessary for the child to testify before the defendant and jury, she should not have to appear alone, but rather should be accompanied by a trusted but impartial adult. Following testimony, the child should be allowed to talk about the experience; it should not be assumed that just because the testifying is over the trauma is now all behind the child.

Statutory and Procedural Changes

To reiterate earlier discussion, these would include closing courtrooms to the public and press during a child's testimony, establishing rules to determine competency, and altering hearsay rules to permit out-of-court statements made by the child.

SUMMARY

As more and more children come before the court, the legal system—which was designed for adults and not children—needs to become more flexible and accommodate to the special needs of children, while not abrogating the constitutional rights of the defendant. Given the right circumstances and proper supports, children can be credible and effective witnesses and the experience need not traumatize them.

REFERENCES

American Academy of Child and Adolescent Psychiatry. (1986). Statement on protecting children undergoing abuse investigations and testimony. AACAP, 3615 Wisconsin Avenue, NW, Washington, DC, 20016.

Bauer, H. (1983). Preparation of the sexually abused child for court testimony. *Bull. Am. Acd. Psych. & Law,* II(3):287-291.

Berliner, L., & Barbieri, M. (1984). The testimony of the child victim of sexual assault. *J. Soc. Issues,* 40(2):125-137.

Brown, A.K. (1975). The development of memory: Knowing, knowing about and knowing how to know. In H.W. Reese (Ed.), *Advances in Child Development and Behavior, Vol. 10.* New York: Academic Press, pp. 105-152.

Chance, J.E., & Goldstein, A.F. (1984). Face recognition memory: Implications for children's eyewitness testimony. *J. Soc. Issues,* 40(2):69-85.

Claman, L., Harris, J.C., Bernstein, A.G., & Lovett, R. (1986). The adolescent as a witness in a case of incest: Assessment and outcome. *J. Am. Acad. Child. Psych.,* 25(4):457-461.

Courts Law 5717-197 38(6). England.

Cohen, R.L., & Harnick, A.H. (1980). The susceptibility of child witnesses to suggestion. *Law and Human Behavior,* 4(3):201-210.

Dale, P.S., Loftus, E., & Rathburn, R. (1978). The influence of the form of the question of eyewitness testimony of preschool children. *J. Psycholinguistic Research,* 7:269-277.

Fish-Murray, C., Koby, E., & van der Kolk, B.A. (1987). Evolving ideas: The effect of abuse on children's thought. In B.A. van der Kolk (Ed.), *Psychological Trauma.* Washington, DC: American Psychiatric Press.

Globe Newspaper Co. v. Superior Court (1980) 379 Mass. 846. 401 N.E.

Globe Newspaper Co. v. Superior Court (1982a) 457 U.S. 596.

Globe Newspaper Co. v. Superior Court (1982b) 2613 102 S. Ct.

Goodman, G.S. (1984). The child witness: Conclusions and future directions for research and legal practice. *J. Soc. Issues,* 40(2):157-175.

Goodman, G.S., Aman, C., & Hirschman, J. (1987). Child sexual and physical abuse: Children's testimony. In S. Ceci, M.P. Toglia, & D. Ross (Eds.), *Children's Eyewitness Memory.* New York: Springer-Verlag.

Goodman, G.S., Golding, J.M., & Haith, M.M. (1984). Jurors' reactions to child witnesses. *J. Soc. Issues,* 40(2):139-156.

Graham, M. (1985). Difficult times for the constitution: Child testimony absent face-to-face confrontation. *The Champion,* August, pp. 18-21.

Hasher, L., & Zacks, R.T. (1979). Automatic and effortful process in memory. *J. Experimental Psychol. General,* 108:356-388.

Heeney, L. (1985). Coping with "the abuse of child abuse prosecutions." The criminal defense lawyer's viewpoint. *The Champion,* August, p. 17.

Johnson, M.K., & Foley, M.A. (1984). Differentiating fact from fantasy: The reliability of children's memories. *J. Soc. Issues,* 40(2):33-49.

Kenmore, C. (1984). The admissibility of extrajudicial rape complaints. *B.U. Law Review,* 64:199-240.

Kobasigawa, A. (1974). Utilization of retrieval cues by children to recall. *Child Development,* 45:127-134.

Libai, D. (1969). The protection of the child victim of a sexual offense in the criminal justice system. *Wayne Law Review,* 15:977-995.

Macale v. Lynch (1920) 110 Wash. 444, 188, P517.

Marin, B.V., Holmes, D.L., Guth, M., & Kovac, P. (1979). The potential of children as eyewitnesses: A comparison of children and adults on eyewitness tasks. *Law and Human Behavior,* 13:295-305.

Melton, G. (1984). Child witnesses and the first amendment: A psychological dilemma. *J. Soc. Issues,* 40(2):109-123.

Melton, G., Bulkley, J., & Wulkan, D. (1985). Competency of children as witnesses. In J. Bulkley (Ed.), *Child Sexual Abuse and the Law*. Washington: ABA Press, pp. 125-139.

Murray, S. (1983). The effect of post-event information on children's memories for an illustrated story. Unpublished paper. Aberdeen, Scotland.

Neisser, U. (1979). The control of information pickup in selective looking. In A.D. Pick (Ed.), *Perception and Its Development*. Hillsdale, N.J.: Lawrence Erlbaum Associates, pp. 201-219.

Ohio v. Roberts (1980) 488 U.S. 56, 100 S. Ct. 2531.

Parker, J.Y. (1982). The rights of child witnesses: Is the court a protector or perpetrator? *New England Law Review*, 17:643-717.

Quinn, K. (1986). Competency to be a witness. *Bull. Am. Acad. Psychiatry and Law*, 14(4):311-321.

Rex v. Brasier (1779) 1 Leach 199, 168 Eng. Rep. 202.

Rex v. Travers (1726) 2 Str. 700 93 Eng. Rep. 793.

Richmond Newspapers, Inc. v. Virginia (1980) 448 U.S. 555.

Stafford, C.F. (1962). The child as a witness. *Washington Law Review*, 13(3):303-324.

State v. Interests of R.R. A Juvenile (1976) 79 N.J. 97, 398 A 2d.76.

Stephens, H. (1919). The trial of Sir Walter Raleigh, 2. *Transactions of the Royal Historical Society*, 172. London.

Summit, R.C. (1983). The child sexual abuse accommodation syndrome. *Child Abuse & Neglect*, 7:177-193.

Terr, L. (1980). Personal injury to children: The court suit claiming psychic traumas. In D.H. Schetky & E.P. Benedek (Eds.), *Child Psychiatry and the Law*. New York: Brunner/Mazel.

Terr, L. (1983). Time sense following psychic trauma. *Amer. J. Orthopsychiat.*, 53:244-261.

Terr, L. (1984). Time and trauma. *Psychoanalytic Study of the Child*, 39:633-665.

Terr, L. (1985). Children traumatized in small groups. In S. Eth & R. Pynoos (Eds.), *Post-Traumatic Stress Disorder in Children*. Washington, D.C.: APA Press.

Terr, L. (1986). The child psychiatrist and the child witness: Traveling companions by necessity if not design. *J. Am. Acad. Child Psych.*, 25(4):462-472.

The Children and Young Person's Act (1933) Geo 5 c 212 42. Israel.

Upham, C.W. (1969). *Witchcraft at Salem Village, Vol II*. New York: Frederick Ungar.

U.S. v. Benfield (1979) 593k F 2d 815 (8th Cir.).

Weiss, E.H., & Berg, F.R. (1982). Child victims of sexual assault: Impact of court procedures. *J. Am. Acad. Child Psych.*, 21(5):513-518.

Wheeler v. United States (1895) 199 U.S. 523.

Whitcomb, D. (1985). Prosecution of child sexual abuse. Innovations in practice. Testimony before Subcommittee on Children, Family, Drugs, and Alcohol. Committee on Labor and Human Resources, U.S. Senate, May 2, 1985.

Wigmore, J.H. (1940). A treatise on the Anglo-American system of evidence. In *Trials at Common Law Vol. 2*, (3rd ed.). Boston: Little, Brown.

Yates, A. (1987). Should young children testify in cases of sexual abuse? *Am. J. Psychiatry*, 144(4):476-480.

11

The Expert as Witness

Diane H. Schetky

Anyone who evaluates children for sexual abuse should be prepared for the possibility of being asked to testify in court regarding his findings. This chapter is addressed to the relative novice who may not have had much experience in testifying in court. Testifying is a logical extension of our role as an advocate for the child. Further, the pediatrician or mental health professional is often in the position of knowing more about the case than others involved in it and, because of his credentials, his testimony may carry a great deal of weight. Resistance to appearing in court may stem from reality factors such as frequent delays, disruption to one's schedule, and difficulty getting paid. However, it is just as likely to result from ignorance regarding what is expected of the health professional in the role of expert witness and how the court functions, as well as distaste for having one's opinions challenged. This chapter will try to familiarize the reader with what is expected of the expert witness and thus help make testifying a less intimidating experience.

Being qualified as an expert witness means that one possesses an area of special knowledge beyond that of the average person. Further, the expert is permitted to draw inferences from facts which a jury would not be able to do (McCormick, 1972). If the court determines that the expert possesses special knowledge, he is then permitted to testify as to opinion, in contrast to the ordinary witness who may only testify as to fact or observation. The expert is entitled to compensation for time lost from work, whereas the ordinary witness receives no remuneration for time spent in court.

TYPES OF INVOLVEMENT

Family Court

The expert witness involved with child sexual abuse cases is most likely to testify in family court around issues of neglect or abuse. Entry into the court is often at the request of the state's attorney, the guardian ad litem for the child, or the child's attorney if one has been appointed. If custody is an issue, the expert may also be approached by the attorney for either parent or may be court-appointed. It is important to realize the limitation in doing unilateral custody evaluations and spell this out to all parties involved, i.e., that one cannot make any comparisons between parents if both have not been seen nor can one offer opinions on parties one has not seen. Further, it is important to stress that the court is likely to view such evaluations as biased; thus, they are of limited value and may result in the court ordering the family to have yet another evaluation. It is far preferable to have parents agree to be seen by one expert at the onset and better yet to be court appointed, which confers more neutrality.

Questions put to the expert will usually focus on evidence for abuse, its impact on the child, and disposition and treatment.

Civil Court

Increasingly, we are hearing of victims of sexual abuse filing civil suits for damages related to the abuse. Suits may be brought against the offender, against state agencies acting in the role of surrogate parent (as with the child who is abused in foster care), against day care agencies and schools, and even landlords (e.g., for defective locks which allowed the rapist access to his victim) and home owner's insurance policies. Another area concerns suits against physicians and therapists for sexual misconduct. Although such suits are not likely to involve children, there is a strong parallel to child sexual abuse in that a breach of a fiduciary relationship is involved and, like the child, the patient is not in a position to give informed consent to a sexual relationship with the therapist. (It is precisely because of this that we, as child specialists, may be called upon to testify in such cases.) In order to prove liability in malpractice cases, it must be shown that a duty existed, that it was violated, and that there was a proximate effect between this violation and the plaintiff's injuries.

In child sexual abuse, the most serious damages are usually psychic rather than physical, and it is the expert's role to demonstrate the extent of damages and how they are or are not related to the sexual trauma. The expert may be asked to examine the plaintiff by either the prosecution or the defense attorney. Such evaluations need to be extremely comprehensive and are likely to be subjected to rigorous cross-examination because, in contrast to cases heard in family court, large sums of money are at stake. It is important to get a careful history, with documentation from others where possible, of both premorbid and current functioning. Corroboration from other sources will strengthen the expert's stance. Questions asked of the expert typically have to do with present damages as well as the likelihood of future pain and suffering and the need for therapy. Attorneys will often break down damages into general (i.e., damaged sense of self and depression) as well as specific (i.e., loss of wages secondary to inability to work because of depression).

It is customary to submit a preliminary report which may undergo several modifications as the expert works with the attorney. In many instances the attorney may prefer not to have a written report as it may be discoverable and used in cross-examination of the witness. Involvement in these cases, in contrast to family court, is adversarial and if the attorney does not like the expert's report, she is free to seek another opinion. It is not unusual for years to elapse between the time of evaluation and the time the case finally comes to court. This is yet another reason for preparing a detailed and comprehensive report, which may also serve to refresh one's memory.

Criminal Court

The involvement of child mental health experts in criminal trials involving allegations of child sexual abuse has typically been limited in the past to preparing and supporting the child witness. Rules of evidence have prevented mental health professionals from testifying in such cases since statements made out of court by the child are considered hearsay (see Chapter 10 for exceptions to this rule). In contrast, the pediatrician may be asked to testify to physical findings. More recently, expert witnesses have been called upon to testify about hypotheticals or educate the court and jury about the dynamics and aftereffects of child sexual abuse and how one goes about evaluating allegations of sexual abuse. Three routes by which expert testimony may be introduced in these cases include: 1) as commentary on the witness's credibility; 2) as support of the child's testimony; and 3) as rebuttal against defense attorneys' attempts to discredit the child's testimony (Whitcomb, 1985).

Many psychiatrists and psychologists are loath to confer with defense attorneys in these cases and view such consultation as aiding and abetting the enemy. They may be operating on the false assumption that the defendant is guilty before any finding of fact. One needs to be aware, especially in child custody cases, of the possibility of false allegations and consider how detrimental these may be to the child as well as to the defendant and his relationship with his child. A second rationale for becoming involved with defense cases concerns the problem of improper evaluation of child sexual abuse, which may result in the case being dropped, acquittals, or innocent people being convicted. The attorney may need the help of the expert to interpret prior evaluations and findings and comment on the professionalism of the evaluation.

The expert may also be asked to comment on the child's credibility or possible dynamics of the case based on review of secondary materials such as transcripts of interviews or videotapes. It is important to proceed with caution in these cases and not exceed one's data base (Schetky & Benedek, 1986). Access to key documents and the child may not be possible, hence the importance of qualifying statements. Further, the expert needs to remember that if his impressions of the case are not favorable to the defendant (which is often the case), then his opinions will not be sought out in court. On the other hand, an unfavorable report may help the defense attorney decide how to proceed with the case and may even encourage the defendant to plead guilty.

Two major differences between criminal and family court are the standard of evidence, which in criminal court is higher (i.e., beyond a reasonable doubt), and the presence of a jury. The latter introduces a whole new element into testifying and takes some getting used to. The expert needs to try to establish rapport with the jury, which is not always easy if not much is known about their background. The author approaches juries as one would an audience to whom she is making a presentation, trying to pitch her delivery at a level that is neither too erudite nor too condescending. The jury will be concerned with how credible the witness is, whether he is consistent and has a thorough knowledge of the case, and above all whether he is fair. Arrogance and cockiness are likely to alienate a jury, whereas humility and candor may win points with the jury.

PREPARING A WRITTEN REPORT

If asked to prepare a report the expert should be responsive to the questions asked, e.g., Was the child abused? Is it safe for her to return home? Should she have any contact with the defendant and, if so, under what conditions? Is treatment indicated and if so what kind? The report should provide and document the basis of one's opinions. Data about when, where, and for how long the various parties were seen should be included, as well as what other sources of information were relied upon in forming one's opinions. The date of the report should also be included.

Direct observations and quotes are extremely helpful in bringing reports to life and refreshing the examiner's memory when the case finally comes to court. It is important to carefully choose one's language, striving for objective terms and avoiding any statements that might be viewed as pejorative. Each statement should be examined in terms of how it will stand up under cross-examination. Speculative statements and generalities are of little use and carry no weight in court.

Children's drawings may be very useful and may be included along with an explanation about the context in which they were drawn (i.e., spontaneous or on request). Inasmuch as the court may wish to enter them in evidence along with the report, it is prudent to prepare extra copies so as not to be left emptyhanded in court.

A signed consent form for release of the report should always be obtained, even when the evaluation is court-ordered. It should specify the purpose of the evaluation, to whom it will be released, the fact that it is not confidential, and that it will be released without the parties having the opportunity to read it. In the author's experience, attorneys and their clients will resort to a variety of tactics in an attempt to suppress an unfavorable report. These tactics have included invoking privilege on the grounds that the client was coming for therapy not an evaluation; that the psychiatrist had forged the patient's name on a release (when possible it is advisable to have signatures witnessed); and in one case that the court had ordered a psychological evaluation and that the examiner did not qualify because she was a psychiatrist. One attorney even cried discrimination on the basis of her client's indigent status, i.e., because the state had paid for the psychiatric consultation for the defense this enabled the district attorney's office to find out about the evaluation and in turn subpoena the defense psychiatrist whose evaluation was not favorable to the defendant. In this case, the court ruled that the child's best interests prevailed and allowed the psychiatrist, who had only reviewed the records, to testify for the prosecution based on a prior agreement between attorneys to share materials.

PRETRIAL CONFERENCE WITH THE ATTORNEY

A pretrial conference with the referring attorney is extremely helpful but is often overlooked in abuse and neglect hearings where the attorney's preparation may be last minute and remuneration is such that it is tempting to cut corners. In contrast, in civil and criminal cases the time spent in conferring with attorneys may exceed time spent with the patient. The pretrial conference allows the attorney to prepare the expert for probable lines of questioning and as attorneys are taught never to ask questions in court to which they do not know the answers, it enables them to anticipate the witness's responses. The pretrial conference further allows the expert to point out important areas or questions that should be brought out in court. It is also an effective way of alleviating the expert's anxieties about testifying. Finally, it is helpful if the witness can be briefed on the cast of characters and any particular foibles, techniques, or philosophies of the judge and opposing attorney.

THE SUBPOENA

A subpoena is a document served on the witness in person, usually by a sheriff, summoning him to appear in court on a certain date. The time specified usually refers to the time at which the trial is scheduled to commence, not necessarily when the expert will be needed, hence the importance of clarifying this with the attorney whose name appears on the document. Most courts respect the busy schedules of physicians and psychologists and will try to accommodate to the best of their ability. However, few courts run on schedule and it is wise to come fortified with work to do in the event that there are delays.

A duces tecum subpoena is a demand for medical records. In some cases this will be sent directly to the hospital's department of medical records, but if the expert is in private practice and the patient is an outpatient, the expert will be expected to produce his records on the patient. Anything the expert brings with him to court may be examined by the attorney for the opposing side and submitted into the court record as an exhibit. If release of sensitive material is potentially damaging to the patient, the expert may take this up with the court or confer with an attorney.

PREPARING FOR COURT

Anxiety about testifying in court is normal and is best handled by careful preparation. Prior to going to court, records should be organized and reviewed. Preparing a flow sheet that accentuates important factual material, dates seen, and findings avoids the need to fumble through notes in the courtroom. Audio-visual materials such as photos, charts, and drawings may be effectively used to augment verbal testimony.

DEPOSITIONS

In civil cases it is customary to depose the expert prior to trial. This involves the opposing attorney questioning the expert about his findings so as to help her prepare her case for trial. The questioning is similar to that which occurs in court with the exception of no judge being present to intercede when objections are raised. The attorney for whom the expert is consulting will be present and may be consulted during the proceedings. There is no need for spontaneity in these procedures since there is no jury present and it is important to wait and think through answers before giving them. Depositions are duly recorded and the written transcript should be reviewed for errors prior to trial as a reminder of what was said since reference will be made to the deposition during the actual trial.

TESTIFYING IN COURT

Testifying in court has been discussed at length elsewhere (American Psychiatric Association, 1984; Benedek, 1980; Gutheil & Appelbaum, 1982; Sadoff, 1975) and will be only briefly reiterated here. The first step in testifying is being sworn in, after which the expert is queried about his credentials. Lawyers may need help ahead of time in sorting out what is important in the expert's curriculum vitae from what is not; for example, they often are more likely to emphasize state licensure than board certification. Providing the attorney with a resumé with salient points underscored may assist her in qualifying the expert. An additional copy for the court stenographer may enhance correct spellings.

After credentials have been acknowledged and expertise conferred, direct examination by the attorney for whom the expert is appearing begins. This is usually rather benign and follows the rehearsed lines of questioning. Often the attorney is eager to jump to the expert's conclusions and it is important that the expert be given the opportunity to articulate how he arrived at his findings. Usually the attorney will refer directly to the written report, but the expert may elaborate upon material within the report. Typically, direct questioning will be interrupted by numerous objections from the opposing attorney related to the rules of evidence. When this occurs the witness must stop until the judge rules on the objection and directs the witness to resume testifying.

Direct examination is followed by cross-examination. The novice in this situation may feel as if he is on trial, particularly when aggressive tactics are employed. It is the job of the opposing attorney to try to discredit the witness's testimony. If she fails in this endeavor, she may resort to attacking the expert's profession or his person. When this occurs, it is important to realize that the opposing attorney probably does not have a very good case and to remain composed. In the event of harassment or inappropriate personal questions, the expert may appeal to the judge for intervention. Sarcasm or anger in such situations are never appropriate responses, although occasionally humor may be used judiciously; for example, in response to "Doctor, what are you being paid for your testimony today?" the reply might be, "That depends on how long you keep me on the witness stand."

During cross-examination, it is important for the expert to pause before responding, to keep answers brief, and to not volunteer more than is requested. If one does not know the answer or cannot respond with a yes or no, one should say so. If questions are confusing or nonsensical, it is perfectly appropriate to request that they be repeated or rephrased. Often confusing are questions having to do with possibility and probability. Anything is possible, whereas probable implies a greater than 50% likelihood of something occurring. Hypothetical questions may be introduced that seem to have no bearing on the case. They should be answered to the best of one's ability and one may point out the lack of parallels to the case at hand. If new information is introduced that is grounds for altering a prior opinion, one must be prepared to modify one's position in court.

REDIRECT EXAMINATION

Redirect examination provides the opportunity for both attorneys to seek clarification of what has been said or question further regarding new information that has emerged during testimony. Following this, the judge may also wish to ask questions of the witness, after which the witness is usually excused from the courtroom.

FOLLOW-UP

Often requested but rarely volunteered are follow-ups on the outcome of the proceedings. It is important to know whether the expert's recommendations were followed and, if not, what other factors affected the outcome of the case. Expert witnesses tend to have much narcissism at stake and must realize that they are but one cog in the wheel and that the adversary system operates on evidentiary theory, which at times may be contrary to our vested interests in seeing done what we believe is correct. Second, a follow-up with the attorney for whom the expert testified allows for feedback on his testimony and may provide him with helpful pointers to use in future appearances as an expert witness.

SUMMARY

Testifying in court can be a stimulating experience in thinking on one's feet and effectively communicating one's findings. It is an opportunity to educate, to advocate, and to have a role in seeing justice done. It is hoped that the reader will not shirk from this experience but rather approach it as a chance to develop and master new skills.

REFERENCES

American Psychiatric Association (1984). Report of the Task Force on Clinical Assessment in Child Custody. In *Issues in Forensic Psychiatry*. Washington, D.C.: APA Press.

Benedek, E.P. (1980). The expert witness. In D.H. Schetky & E.P. Benedek (Eds.), *Child Psychiatry and the Law*. New York: Brunner/Mazel.

Gutheil, T.G., & Appelbaum, P.S. (1982). The clinician in court. In T.G. Gutheil & P.S. Appelbaum (Eds.), *Clinical Handbook of Psychiatry and the Law*. New York: McGraw-Hill.

McCormick (1972). Evidence 13 1t 29. St. Paul, MN: West Publishing Co.

Sadoff, R.L. (1975). The psychiatrist in the courtroom. In R.L. Sadoff (Ed.), *Forensic Psychiatry*. Springfield, IL: Charles C Thomas.

Schetky, D.H., & Benedek, E.P. (1986). The role of the child psychiatrist as expert witness for the defense in cases of alleged child sexual abuse. Paper presented at the Annual Meeting of the American Academy of Child and Adolescent Psychiatry, October 17, 1986.

Whitcomb, D. (1985). Prosecution of child sexual abuse. Innovations in practice. Testimony before Subcommittee on Children, Family, Drugs, and Alcohol. Committee on Labor and Human Resources, U.S. Senate, May 2, 1985.

Section IV

TREATMENT AND PREVENTION

12

Treatment of the Sexually Abused Child

Diane H. Schetky

Before discussing models of intervention and treatment of child sexual abuse, it is important to consider the rationale for them. In terms of the offender, prevention of further sexual abuse and protection of the victim and other children at risk are top priorities. This presumes the willingness of the offender to enter into a treatment program if he is not incarcerated.

The child will need help in handling her immediate feelings about the sexual abuse and getting back on track in her emotional development. In many cases, treatment of underlying problems that may have predisposed the child to becoming a victim (i.e., neediness, low self-esteem, need to please others, and inability to assert herself) will also be indicated. Finally, it is hoped that treatment may prevent some of the long-term sequelae that have been associated with sexual abuse in childhood, including repeated victimization or identification with the aggressor.

In cases of incest, goals for the family include preserving and strengthening the family or what is left of it, restoring roles and self-esteem, allowing the child to experience the parenting she has lacked, and helping parents assume more protective roles in regard to the child victim. Salvaging the marriage should not always be a goal, especially when treatment prospects for the offender are not favorable.

VICTIM TO PATIENT PROCESS

In order to understand how to treat symptoms related to child sexual abuse, it is necessary to understand their origins and functions. Based on their work with adult inpatients who experienced childhood sexual

193

abuse (90% were abused by a relative), Rieker and Carmen (1986) delineate what they term the *victim to patient process.* They describe the fragmented identity that results from the victim's attempt to accommodate to a family's refusal to recognize the abuse. As a survival strategy, the victim turns to altered affectual responses and denial, thereby changing the meaning of the abuse. Meanwhile, the victim's perceptions about what occurred and her self-confidence are undermined by the denial of those around her, which counters her reality testing. In a similar vein, Summit (1983) describes the sexual accommodation syndrome which occurs in child victims of incest and consists of 1) secrecy, 2) helplessness, 3) entrapment and accommodation, 4) delayed and unconvincing disclosure, and 5) retraction. Additional measures the child may use in order to adapt include domestic martyrdom, splitting of reality, altered consciousness, hysterical phenomena, projection or rage, and self-mutilation.

The parents' disbelief and rejection increase the child's sense of helplessness, and she may turn to self-blame as a way of trying to make sense out of what is going on. Shengold (1979) elaborates on the splitting process that occurs and states that, in cases of incest, the child needs to see the abusing parent as good because the image of a good parent mitigates the intensity of her fear and rage. Often her anger gets turned inward into self-loathing and self-destructive behavior.

The victim feels she is expected to sacrifice herself and gratify the needs of the abusing adult at the expense of having any rights to privacy or experiencing her own needs as separate from those of the adult. Rieker and Carmen (1986) feel that this, combined with the fact that the victim is conditioned to please others and is devoid of any self-protective mechanisms, leads her to being vulnerable to repeated abuse. Many victims will learn to handle the excessive, premature sexual stimulation by turning off feelings, which may lead to dissociative reactions, feelings of detachment, and frigidity in later life.

The secrecy that surrounds the sexual abuse "is both the source of fear and the promise of safety" (Summit, 1983, p. 181) as the child is lulled into believing that everything will be all right if she does not tell. Summit (1983) believes that unless the child shares the secret, she "is likely to spend a lifetime in what comes to be a self-imposed exile from intimacy, trust and self-validation" (p. 182). At the same time, however, the secrecy confers a certain amount of power and the child realizes she has "the power to destroy the family and the responsibility to keep it together" (p. 185), hence her reluctance to reveal the sexual abuse.

MODELS OF INTERVENTION AND TREATMENT FOR VICTIM AND OFFENDER

Legal

The legal system seeks to punish the offender and protect society. Incarceration may also be used to set an example to others, although its value as a deterrent to sexual abuse has never been proven. The emphasis is on removing the offender from the home and community, but in the process the needs of other family members may be overlooked. The victim is regarded as a potential witness and the need to obtain and present evidence may exacerbate the trauma she is experiencing, although innovative techniques may minimize the impact of some of these proceedings (see Chapter 10).

The offender who is incarcerated may or may not enter a sex offenders treatment program, depending on his willingness to participate and the availability of programs. Some courts have made use of mandated outpatient treatment programs with a deferred sentence for selected offenders who appear to be highly motivated. Such programs typically involve extensive commitment to family, group, and individual therapy over a period of several years. In spite of the low recidivism rates claimed by these programs, many judges are reluctant to use them, and some attorneys may fear noncompliance on the part of their client and so opt for a short-term jail sentence instead. Imprisonment alone, however, does not attack underlying problems. Further, it lowers the offender's impaired self-esteem and only adds to the multiple problems confronting the family.

Protective Services

The emphasis of protective services is on crisis intervention and protection of the child. Caseworkers play a critical role in the initial evaluation of the child and validation of sexual abuse. Their contributions include bringing the abuse out into the open, authoritative protection through legal intervention, and support to the family during the period of crisis. Caseworkers must make critical decisions, such as whether to place the child outside of the family, whether the state should take temporary custody or even move for termination of parental rights, and when it is safe for the child to return home. They also follow the family while the case is active and are in a position to coordinate services to the family.

Unfortunately, many protective services agencies are understaffed, and high staff turnover is likely to result in inadequate or interrupted services to families. Further, many caseworkers are not trained to deal with sexual abuse nor are they given adequate supervision and support. The emphasis remains on intervention rather than prevention or treatment; too often, removal of the offender is viewed as a solution to the problem and the treatment needs of the victim and her family get overlooked (Adams-Tucker, 1984).

Family Systems/Family Therapy Approach to Incest

This approach operates on the assumption that incest is a symptom of family dysfunction. Pioneered by Giarretto (1982) in its application to sexually abusive families, this systems approach combines couples, marital, family, and dyad therapy with self-help groups and community supports. Offenders who wish to enter into therapy are selected on the basis of their willingness to accept responsibility for what they have done and a commitment to saving their marriages. Goals of therapy include preserving the family, getting the offender to accept responsibility for what he did and the nonoffender to admit to being a poor parent, dealing openly with family conflict, and restoring family roles. Issues dealt with in therapy include abuse of power, lack of empathy, role reversal and blurring of boundaries, isolation, poor communication, low self-esteem, and controls and limit setting (Giarretto, 1982).

Giarretto's program has served as a model of effective liaison with the criminal justice system and has demonstrated the efficacy of mandated treatment of the offender as an alternative to jail. Giarretto (1976) claims to have a recidivism rate of only 1% in his program and that 90% of victims are reunited with their families within the first month.

Critics of family therapy are many. The Group for Advancement of Psychiatry report (GAP, 1970) cited the lack of consensus regarding goals of family therapy. McDermott and Char (1974) feel that it "arbitrarily forces the child to fit the system and in practice all too often seems to neglect the real needs of children" (p. 427). They further caution, "Knowing the whole does not mean that we understand all the parts, particularly a developing and unfolding one, and this applies especially to those who are not trained and oriented in working with children" (p. 430). Many would agree with McDermott and Char that it is impractical to try to engage a child under the age of 12, and before the state of formal operations, into an adult system of communication.

Regarding the use of family therapy for incest victims Adams-Tucker (1984) refers to it as a "clinical cop-out," subsuming the needs of the child within a systems approach to the family, and points out the risk that the child's needs may remain peripheral. Meiselman (1978) expresses concern that family therapy may heighten the child's guilt if the therapist assumes that all family members are equally responsible for what occurred. The presence of children may inhibit parents from discussing sexual problems or feed into the problem of blurred boundaries. Of particular concern in dealing with incestuous families are the hazards of plunging in without doing an adequate diagnostic assessment, given the known risks of suicide (Goodwin, 1980) and other acting-out behaviors in this population. Family therapy is also contraindicated if family members are too disorganized to reap benefit (Boatman, Borkan, & Schetky, 1981).

Group Therapy

This is a particularly useful therapeutic modality for adolescent and preadolescent victims of sexual abuse because of its potential for offering peer support. Group therapy also facilitates discussion of sensitive areas and helps participants overcome their sense of isolation. To date, most groups described have consisted entirely of female victims. If a male co-therapist is used in such a group, his presence may afford participants the opportunity to overcome their distrust of males and learn to relate in nonsexual ways. Most groups are time-limited and will not alter the underlying psychopathology in the child that may have preceded the sexual abuse; hence, the value of group therapy for this population is primarily one of support and education. Group therapy is often contraindicated for the child with severe ego impairment (i.e., borderline, psychotic, or retarded) or for the child with high potential for acting out, as this becomes too disruptive to the group.

Individual Therapy

The rationale for individual therapy for child victims is that the sexual abuse and conditions that may have predisposed it have resulted in sufficient internal conflict and dysfunction to warrant individual treatment. Goals typically involve resolving conflict, restoring function, and allowing the child to move forward in her emotional development. The advantages of the individual approach are that in-depth, long-term therapy may be catered to the victim's specific needs. Individual therapy offers the child the opportunity to experience intimacy in a nonsexualized relationship with an adult and develop a sense of trust. The therapy focuses on her rather than the family so her needs do not become diluted, and it deals with the total child not just the sexual abuse. Individual therapy alone, however, may not help the victim overcome her sense of isolation and being deviant. A more practical concern is that it may not be possible to keep the patient in treatment owing to resistance from family and agencies, as well as her need to flee as therapy gets into highly conflicted areas. In the author's opinion, individual therapy is the preferred choice of treatment for the young child; with the older child, it may be used alone or in conjunction with family or group therapy.

The spectrum of theoretical orientations used in individual therapy of victims of sexual abuse ranges from traditional analytic to feminist, with most therapies falling somewhere in between. The feminist approach, as typified by Herman and Hirschman (1977) and Brownmiller (1975), views the problem of sexual abuse as stemming from male supremacy and patriarchal families. The feminist emphasis is on consciousness raising, greater criminal sanctions for sex offenses, and ending male supremacy. This rather simplistic formulation fails to explain the fact that women can also sexually abuse children, and it tends to neglect family dynamics. However, the feminist movement has been a tremendous source of support for women in terms of encouraging them to speak out about sexual harassment and to become more assertive. Particularly successful have been victim advocate and compensation programs. Feminists view traditional psychoanalytic therapy as futile and condemn it for its emphasis on the victim's guilt and inadequacy and its tendency to isolate the victim. Their assumptions that all psychoanalysts are passive, nonempathic, and sexist in their thinking are unduly harsh and stereotypic.

Therapy for the Nonabusing Parent in Incestuous Families

Such therapy may often be indicated to focus on problems in the nonabusing parent (usually the mother) or within the family that may have predisposed to sexual abuse (e.g., depression, denial, feelings of inadequacy, separation fears, and role reversal). If the nonabusing parent experienced sexual abuse as a child, feelings about this will undoubtedly be activated and need to be dealt with. The parent will need support in coping with the aftermath of the revelation of sexual abuse and in assuming a more protective role toward the victim. She will also need to deal with her guilt about what occurred and with her anger at her spouse; indeed, she will have to decide whether or not she wishes to try to save the marriage. Her jealousy and anger toward her daughter may also be an issue. These women are often very needy and have long-standing difficulties that are best managed through individual psychotherapy. However, group therapy has also proven useful for this population (Damon & Waterman, 1986).

Support for Parents or Foster Parents in Nonabusing Families

Parents whose children have been abused outside of the family will need support dealing with their rage, guilt, and feelings of helplessness. Often they may wish to repress the entire experience and they need help allowing the child to discuss it. Some may respond by becoming overprotective toward the child and they need to be encouraged to allow the child to get on with her life. Foster parents also need help in dealing with their feelings about sexual abuse and the child's family, and in managing the abused child in their care who is acting out sexually. Such help is pivotal in assuring the success of the placement, as all too often the needs of foster parents are overlooked. They may be seen in support groups or individually in conjunction with the child's therapy.

TREATMENT RECOMMENDATIONS FOR CHILD SEXUAL ABUSE VICTIMS AND THEIR FAMILIES

Several factors will enter into treatment recommendations. The first is whether treatment is intended to be supportive or long-term and uncovering. In essence, is treatment intended to deal with the aftereffects of sexual abuse and restore baseline functioning or to treat the problems that may have predisposed the child to becoming a victim as well? How disturbed is the child? She may look relatively healthy compared to the rest of the family but still be a far cry from the norms for her age. Pseudomaturity may mask unmet needs, and for some victims one of the goals is helping them to become a child again. It is safe to assume that most sexually abused children suffer from some form of ego damage, i.e., poor self-esteem and peer relations and limited or maladaptive coping skills. In some victims there may be an organic deficit based on prior physical abuse.

The second question to ask concerns the likelihood of sustaining treatment. Motivation, finances, mobility, work schedules, and whether or not treatment is mandated by the court and supported by protective services are all factors to consider. For instance, a child in foster care may participate in a group, then be precipitously returned home to parents who are threatened by the group and will not support their child attending it. Such a situation is unfair to both the child and group.

Availability of community resources is a major determinant of who gets referred where. It is helpful to think in terms of optimal and feasible plans and have contingencies on which to fall back when referrals do not go as hoped for.

An inpatient admission or residential treatment may be indicated for some victims if the child's behavior is out of control to the point of harming others or herself or if she is too incapacitated emotionally to function in a less restrictive environment. Hospitalization may also be useful for a brief period of evaluation during the time of crisis intervention, particularly if the family appears to be at risk for acting-out behaviors.

The choice of a male or female therapist will be an issue if the patient has strong feelings that would preclude engaging with one or the other. While a female victim of sexual abuse may find it easier to talk with a woman, seeing a male therapist offers her the opportunity for a corrective experience.

A final question concerns the matter of which family members to involve in treatment and in what form. In all likelihood the recommendation will be a combination of treatment modalities that meet the needs of child and parents. If family therapy is contraindicated, it is imperative that the parents receive some sort of help either in the form of individual therapy, parent guidance, or conjoint sessions with the child. Unfortunately, no studies exist comparing the efficacy of various forms of treatment that might aid us in the selection process. Preliminary results of one study suggest that victims who received individual therapy from members of a sex abuse team had a good outcome (Sauzier, 1987).

INDIVIDUAL THERAPY WITH CHILD VICTIMS OF SEXUAL ABUSE

Play therapy is the most natural form of therapy for the young child and, as noted by Erikson (1950), play is the child's natural medium of exchange. Many severely traumatized children will reenact their trauma repetitively in play. Such play is often not therapeutic because in contrast to ordinary play it fails to allay anxiety and gives no relief. Terr (1981, 1983) speculates on the reasons for this, noting that the child is unable to totally identify with the offender because he is so malicious and at the same time she cannot identify with the victim because she is too ineffective. The child ends up being stuck being herself and thus fails to gain any emotional distance from the situation. Anxiety is generated, which re-creates the traumatic events and in turn aggravates rather than calms the child. Terr believes there is no possibility of a happy ending in post-traumatic play because the ending is never satisfying, but the child persists as if determined to find a better ending the next time around. Terr reminds us that play is far more effective in dealing with fantasied ills than real events and concludes that traumatic play fails because it attempts to deal with external events rather than internal ones.

The therapist can help the child break this vicious cycle by linking sex play with actual experiences and helping the child discover other ways of dealing with her feelings. The therapist may encourage areas of mastery that serve to help the child ward off feelings of helplessness and discover acceptable outlets for her aggression. Terr (1983) recommends the use of corrective dénouement play with traumatized children. This involves providing the child with a real rather than magical solution to her problem by allowing her to realize that "1) (s)he could not have avoided the traumatic event because (s)he did not know how and 2) that now (s)he has the coping skills to deal with a similar event should it occur in the future" (p. 346). Once again the emphasis is on mastery and relieving guilt and fear. Lamb (1985), counter to what many therapists advocate, advises against telling the child the abuse was not her fault because she believes this serves to reinforce the child's victim status. Like Terr, Lamb emphasizes the need to help the child understand the abuse situation in the context of choices.

Children who have been highly eroticized present therapists with a different set of problems. As noted by Yates (1982), such children are easily aroused by physical or psychological closeness and therapists must be careful about the possibility of these children misinterpreting their actions. Because the erotic behavior is pleasurable and ingrained, it is often difficult to modify in spite of the adverse social situations it generates. Therapists may need to take an educational approach, e.g., encouraging the child to limit masturbation to her bedroom, and teach her the concept that genitals are private and off limits to others.

When so much energy is channeled into traumatic play or sexual activity, there is often little left over for learning. Further, aggressive drives, which in latency become sublimated into learning, may be inhibited in sexually abused children because aggression has become associated with the offender and the victims fear that if they unleash their aggression they may become like the offender.

Therapists need to recognize the magnitude of the traumas endured by some young victims, particularly where sexual abuse has been accompanied by physical and emotional abuse and neglect in the absence of any sort of empathic adult response. If the immature ego of a 2-year-old is repeatedly assaulted, it soon becomes overwhelmed. The child's foremost concern will be with mere physical survival, and the usual developmental tasks of this age are of necessity put aside. Added to the difficulty of working with the very young child is the fact that recollections of the abuse may be at a preverbal level. When treating such children the therapist may find it necessary to temper therapeutic goals, since these children demand the utmost patience, and the therapist may not be rewarded with change for some time. Further, these children are likely to be passive and not particularly creative or imaginative, so they may not endear themselves to the therapist.

Useful materials to make available to the child in the playroom include dolls, puppets, a doll house, a doctor's kit, and a toy hospital. It is not necessary to invest in expensive and often uninviting anatomically correct dolls; more simple dolls may serve just as well during therapy. Clay and drawing materials should be available to the child. Also useful are children's books on sexual abuse to be read with the child or loaned out (see Appendix).

GROUP THERAPY WITH CHILD VICTIMS OF SEXUAL ABUSE

Although little has been written about group therapy for victims of child sexual abuse, it is an extremely effective treatment modality. Issues to consider in planning a group are whether it should be open or closed, time-limited or not, structured or unstructured, the age range of participants, and whether or not it should be coeducational and limited to victims of sexual abuse. Screening procedures need to be set up and a disposition system for those not suitable for the group. Support services will need to be provided to other members of the family. Consideration should be given to choice of therapists in terms of their experience and ability to work together. Having opposite-sexed therapists may offer certain advantages but can also be a source of resistance for patients who feel more comfortable with a woman. The group should be large enough to ensure group process and continuity in the face of absences or dropouts but not so large that individual needs get overlooked. A group size of six to eight children is probably optimal.

An example of a structured group is that offered by the Pulaski County Sexual Abuse Treatment Project in Arkansas to eight children ranging from 7 to 12 years (Sturkie, 1983). The group met eight times and covered a different theme in each session. These included:

1. Believability
2. Guilt and responsibility

3. Body integrity
4. Secrecy and sharing
5. Anger
6. Powerlessness and identifying areas of control
7. Other life crises
8. Court appearances

The ninth and final session was set aside for special activities. Rules for the group included confidentiality, not having to talk, and only one person talking at a time.

An example of semistructured groups were two run at the University of Oregon Health Sciences Center for adolescent and preadolescent girls who were victims of incest (Boatman, Borkan, & Schetky, 1981). There was no set agenda and the girls controlled the pace in terms of what they wanted to discuss and when. Interestingly, they covered almost the same areas as did the structured group referred to above. Initial issues dealt with included anxiety about being in the group, establishing group cohesiveness, overcoming secrecy, and emphasizing that the secret was really the offender's not theirs. One group member compared the experience of sharing with others in the group to "a flower opening up in the light and closing when it leaves."

Guilt emerged around police interrogations and the physical exam which some viewed as punishment, and one girl feared she, too, might go to jail with her father. The girls acknowledged that they had a special relationship with their fathers, and guilt over competition with their mothers was evident. It was emphasized that their fathers were responsible for what occurred and they were not. Anger at their mothers over lack of protection and for having treated them like "little mothers" was freely expressed. Some feared becoming inadequate mothers like their own, whereas others who were in foster care began to idealize their absent mothers. Part of the group process involved trying to allow the girls to accept their mothers' limitations.

The girls had a harder time dealing with their relationships with their fathers and tended to avoid the topic or to express much ambivalence toward them. Some were able to acknowledge that the incest was not all bad and that they missed the special attention they had received from their fathers and the power that went along with the relationship. Many tried to deal with the incest intellectually, seeking explanations for their fathers' behavior. Some concluded aptly that their fathers were basically "little boys."

Concerns about sexuality and heterosexual relationships emerged, including such issues as Were they still virgins? Should they tell their boyfriends? Would this have happened to them if they were boys? How would the experience affect their sexual adjustment as adults? Would other men treat them this way? The therapists offered them some sex education and structured role-play situations that allowed them to practice saying no. This exercise seemed to carry over into their outside lives as one girl gleefully related to the group how she had been able to tell her stepfather to stay out of the bathroom while she was showering.

Additional issues covered included being in foster care and having to testify in court. Emphasis remained on helping the girls reestablish control over their lives and become more assertive and aware of their options. One group composed a letter to the local paper complaining about having their family names printed in conjunction with their fathers' trials. Ironically, the paper refused to publish it because the girls would not sign their names to the letter!

Termination involved the girls recognizing the limits of what the group could do for them and that it could not meet all of their needs. In some instances, the girls acknowledged feeling that they had changed more than their parents had.

In working with children in groups it is useful to provide them with activities that serve to engage their interest, promote group process, and help them open up. An ice breaker for an initial session may be "mushrooming," in which the girls pair off in twos, find out everything they can about each other in two minutes, and then introduce one another to the group. Name games involve having the child print her name backwards, then free associate to it. For instance, in one group, Sharon spelled her name backwards as "norash" and said it reminded her of "big black clouds, it starts to rain and everybody runs away. A tornado comes and rips up all the houses." Gina said that Anig "reminds me of respect but I don't get any." Fantasy trips may involve having the child close her eyes and imagine wandering down a street and telling where she ends up. Anita told the group, "I was a loaf of bread, french moldy bread, wet and soggy because of no roof." The sharing of these fantasies led to a group discussion of how damaged and unprotected they all felt.

Other techniques suggested by Blick and Porter (1982) include a group ice breaker, in which the group tries to find a shared common experience, and a group go-around, in which each member gives a synopsis of her week's experiences. Blick and Porter also focus on increasing awareness of body language and movements, reinforcing expression of feelings, and immediate verbal praise for positive behavior. Symbolic nurturance may be provided to the group by snack breaks, and group members may share the responsibility for bringing in refreshments.

TERMINATION OF THERAPY

MacFarlane and Waterman (1986) provide useful criteria for deciding when a child is ready to stop treatment. These criteria include whether or not the child has resolved her feelings about the abuse and has come to terms with the offender and her mother. Additional criteria include whether she is able to trust, assert, and protect herself, whether she has regained her self-esteem and control over her life, and whether she understands the difference between sex and affection.

ISSUES FOR THE THERAPIST

Working with sexually abused patients is likely to stir up the therapist's own incestuous feelings either as a child or an adult. It is essential that the therapist treating sexually abused patients come to terms with his own feelings about sex and child sexual abuse. (Boatman, Borkan, & Schetky, 1981; Kreiger, Rosenfeld, Gordon, & Bennett, 1980; Meiselman, 1978; Swanson & Biaggio, 1985). If the therapist does not do so, there is risk that he may communicate his own discomfort to the patient and not allow her to talk about the abuse or he may attempt to ascribe it to fantasy. The result is confusing and upsetting to the patient and risks re-creating the experience she had with the adults around her who failed to validate her sexual experience. The therapist also needs to be prepared to deal with the child's and family's anger, which may become displaced onto the therapist (Solin, 1986).

The female therapist, as noted by Herman (1981), may tend to overidentify with the patient and, in losing her objectivity, may fail to allow the patient to discuss positive feelings toward her father. The therapist may be tempted to get angry for her patient, which is usually futile. The feminist therapist may be tempted to defend the victim's mother and have difficulty facing the degree of estrangement between mother and daughter (Herman & Hirschman, 1980).

The male therapist may find himself blaming the victim or overidentifying with the father (Herman & Hirschman, 1980). There is also the possibility that he may become titillated by the disclosure of details (Swanson & Biaggio, 1985). At times, he must deal with the child's seductive behavior in the office and needs to recognize that this is often a testing maneuver in which the child is trying to determine whether the therapist will respond in a sexual manner as other males in the past have done with her.

Kreiger, Rosenfeld, Gordon, and Bennett (1980) emphasize the importance of the therapist remaining consistent, predictable, and safe. MacVicar (1983) mentions dangerous acting-out behavior toward the female therapist as a means of testing to see if she will protect the child. The child may exhibit seductive behaviors toward the male or female therapist. The therapist needs to explore the meaning of this behavior with the child, set limits, and, if necessary, cut short sessions if the patient becomes too excited. If the child is acting out sexually within therapy (i.e., exposing herself or grabbing at the therapist's genitals), it behooves the therapist to protect himself against possible charges of sexual abuse by making careful notes as to what transpired and apprising parents of these incidents. If the child's seductive behavior persists and the therapist is at a loss as to how to deal with it, he should seek consultation from a colleague.

The therapist needs to avoid presupposing how the child feels and allow her to present her feelings in the order in which she chooses. Anger, sadness, neediness, and alienation almost always take priority over sexual issues, particularly in the young child.

The therapist may become angry and discouraged by the child's passivity and slow progress. He may also find it difficult to empathize with events beyond the domain of his own experience (Kreiger, Rosenfeld, Gordon, & Bennett, 1980). The sexually abused child may re-create in the therapist her own feelings of helplessness, which the therapist needs to recognize so that he may deal with them psycho-therapeutically. Finally, the therapist must recognize that in some instances he is dealing with chronic conditions because of the extent of early deprivation and ego impairment, and that nurturing and sustaining the child may be more realistic goals than cure.

It is recommended that therapists working with sexually abused children avail themselves of individual or peer supervision as a means of fostering greater awareness of their feelings and getting support in the treatment of these difficult cases. It is also vital to coordinate treatment with therapists involved in treating other family members. Finally, it is advisable for therapists to limit the number of sexual abuse cases they are seeing at any one time in order to avoid burnout.

SUMMARY

In summary, this chapter has explored treatment modalities and some of the treatment issues in working with the sexually abused child and her family. It is recognized that the literature on the treatment of child sexual abuse lags behind the proliferation of articles dealing with other aspects of child sexual abuse. We recommend that the clinician avail himself of workshops and continuing education in this area. Further, it is urged that those who deal with large numbers of sexually abused children consider undertaking research concerning what works in therapy with this population and how therapy may modify long-term effects of child sexual abuse.

REFERENCES

Adams-Tucker, C. (1984). The unmet psychiatric needs of sexually abused youths: Referrals from a child protection agency and clinical evaluations. *J. Am. Acad. Child Psych.*, 23(6):659-667.

Blick, L.C., & Porter, F.S. (1982). Group therapy with adolescent incest victims. In S. Sgroi (Ed.), *Handbook of Clinical Intervention in Child Sexual Abuse*. Lexington, MA: Lexington Books.

Boatman, B., Borkan, E., & Schetky, D.H. (1981). Treatment of child victims of incest. *Am. J. Fam. Therapy*, 9(4):43-51.

Brownmiller, S. (1975). *Against Our Will: Men, Women and Rape*. New York: Simon & Schuster.

Damon, L., & Waterman, J. (1986). Parallel group treatment of children and their mothers. In K. MacFarlane & J. Waterman (Eds.), *Sexual Abuse of Young Children: Evaluation and Treatment*. New York: Guilford Press.

Erikson, E. (1950). *Childhood and Society*. New York: W.W. Norton.

Giarretto, H. (1976). The treatment of father-daughter incest: A psycho-social approach. *Children Today*, July-August, pp. 2-35.

Giarretto, H. (1982). A comprehensive child abuse sexual treatment program. *Child Abuse and Neglect*, 6:263-278.

Goodwin, J. (1980). Suicide attempts in sexual abuse victims and their mothers. *Child Abuse and Neglect*, 4:265-276.

Group for the Advancement of Psychiatry (1970). *The Field of Family Therapy* (GAP Report No. 78). New York: Brunner/Mazel.

Herman, J. (1981). *Father-Daughter Incest*. Cambridge, MA: Harvard University Press.

Herman, J., & Hirschman, L. (1977). Father-daughter incest. *Signs: Journal of Women in the Culture and Society*, 2:735-756.

Herman, J., & Hirschman, L. (1980). Father-daughter incest. In U.S. Dept. of Health and Human Services (Ed.), *Sexual Abuse of Children: Selected Readings*. Washington, D.C.: DHHS Publication No. (OHDS) 78-3000161.

Kohan, M.J., Pothier, P., & Norbeck, J.S. (1987). Hospitalized children with a history of sexual abuse: Incidence and care issues. *Am. J. Orthopsychiat.*, 57(2):258-264.

Kreiger, M., Rosenfeld, A., Gordon, A., & Bennett, M. (1980). Problems in psychotherapy of children with histories of incest. *Am. J. Psychotherapy*, 34(1):81-88.

Lamb, S. (1985). Treating sexually abused children: Issues of blame and responsibility. *Am. J. Orthopsychiat.*, 56(2):303-307.

MacVicar, K. (1983). Psychotherapy of sexually abused girls. *J. Am. Acad. Child Psych.*, 22(2):229-308.

MacFarlane, K., & Waterman, J. (Eds.) (1986). *Sexual Abuse of Young Children: Evaluation and Treatment*. New York: Guilford Press.

McDermott, J., & Char, W. (1974). The undeclared war between child and family therapy. *J. Am. Acad. Child Psych.*, 13(2):422-436.

Meiselman, K. (1978). *Incest: A Psychological Study of Causes and Effects with Treatment Recommendations.* San Francisco: Jossey-Bass.

Rieker, P., & Carmen, E. (1986). The victim to patient process. *Am. J. Orthopsychiat.,* 56(3):360-370.

Sauzier, M. (1987). Symposium on the long-term effects of childhood sexual abuse. American Academy of Child and Adolescent Psychiatry. Washington, DC, October 22.

Shengold, L. (1979). Child abuse and deprivation: Soul murder. *J. Am. Psychoanalytic Assoc.,* 27:533-599.

Solin, C. (1986). Displacement of affect in families following incest disclosure. *Am. J. Orthopsychiat.,* 56(4):570-577.

Sturkie, K. (1983). Structured group treatment for sexually abused children. *Health and Social Work,* 8(4):299-308.

Summit, R.C. (1983). The child sexual abuse syndrome. *Child Abuse and Neglect,* 7:177-193.

Swanson, L., & Biaggio, M. (1985). Therapeutic perspectives on father-daughter incest. *Am. J. Psychiat.,* 142(6):667-674.

Terr, L. (1981). Forbidden games: Post-traumatic child's play. *J. Am. Acad. Child Psych.,* 20:741-760.

Terr, L. (1983). Play therapy and psychic trauma. A preliminary report. In C. Schaefer & K. O'Connor (Eds.), *Handbook of Play Therapy.* New York: Wiley Interscience.

Yates, A. (1982). Children eroticized by incest. *Am. J. Psychiat.,* 139(4):482-485.

13

Prevention of Child Sexual Abuse

Diane H. Schetky

Child sexual abuse is a multifaceted problem for which there are no easy answers. In spite of changing cultural mores and attitudes toward children over the past two thousand years, the sexual abuse of children has persisted. This chapter will examine what is being done and can be done about the problem on several levels. Just as child abuse requires a victim and offender, the potential to abuse and be abused, and a facilitating environment, a parallel case can be drawn for child sexual abuse. Thus, to be effective we need to attack the problem at all levels.

THE CHILD

Every child is a potential victim of child sexual abuse. Hopefully, growing up in an emotionally sound family with open communications and education about self-protection may diminish the child's chances of becoming a victim.

Currently in vogue are efforts to educate children about child sexual abuse. This is a relatively new field for which federal funding first became available in the 1980s. Many of these prevention programs are modeled after sex education and substance abuse educational programs used within school systems. Programs may consist of talks by school personnel or outsiders, use of audio-visual materials, discussion groups, role plays, games, workbooks, or even live theater such as The Illusion Theater of Minneapolis. The goals of these programs are to expand the children's knowledge about sexual abuse and give them the power and resources to prevent it. However, a major difference exists in that pressure to experiment with drugs, alcohol, or sexuality usually comes from peers, which with education and assertiveness training may be easier to resist than the psychological coercion, usually from a trusted adult, that accompanies child sexual abuse. A second major difference is that sexual abuse in contrast to substance abuse usually begins at a

210 Child Sexual Abuse

much earlier age, when the child lacks the coping skills that an adolescent has and, further, is often physically and emotionally dependent upon her abuser. At this time it is premature to judge whether indeed these programs will prevent sexual abuse.

Efforts to evaluate prevention programs are just beginning. Binder and McNiel (in press) evaluated a child sexual abuse program involving school-age children. They found that the children did not show any increase in emotional distress after the program and that their knowledge about how to protect themselves increased after the program. Plummer (1984) looked at the effects of a three-day inschool program on 69 fifth graders. She demonstrated that children did gain knowledge about sexual abuse but that on retesting eight months later many showed substantial loss of learning and had reverted to their original notions. These included the need to keep secrets, blaming themselves for abuse, confusing child abuse with sexual abuse, and feeling they were most likely to be molested by a stranger. Conte and colleagues (1985), studying 6-to-10-year-olds, also found that many misperceptions persisted after a three-day inschool training program. This situation is reminiscent of sex education where children cling to their preferred notions of conception to protect their image of asexual parents. Considering how highly charged some of the material is, it is not surprising that anxiety may interfere with the child's processing of the information. It would be of interest to compare how much is retained when it is presented by a stranger in school, or even a teacher, as opposed to information presented by the child's parent.

Educating children about child sexual abuse through parents is another approach. The problem is to first get parents comfortable in raising the subject with their children. If they are able to do so, this then gives the child permission to come to them with sexual questions or concerns. Prevention efforts could be aimed at parent groups in an attempt to both educate and help them become more comfortable in discussing sexuality and child sexual abuse with their children. Parents may also teach their children about privacy, self-assertion, and the need not to keep secrets in a context that has nothing to do with sexual abuse. Education about these matters should begin in the preschool years.

Some critics have raised concern that education programs directed toward children may reach the point of overkill and may make children wary of adults and any physical contact with them. For instance, a little girl seen in psychiatric consultation in preparation for a surgical repair of a congenital narrowing of her vagina was incensed that her trusted doctor had examined her vagina. This very bright child had been taught by her parents that her vagina was private. There is danger that attention to this concept of privacy is being overgeneralized; one remedy, which was mentioned in Chapter 5, is that pediatricians routinely include genital inspection in physical examinations. An unfortunate ripple effect of all the talk about good touch and bad touch is that some parents, especially fathers, are recoiling out of fear that normal displays of affection may be misinterpreted.

Another approach to prevention is to focus on the vulnerable child. Pedophiles have a way of picking their victims and may target the child who is needy, has low self-esteem, is a loner, or is defective in some way. Finkelhor (1986) has pointed out other at-risk factors previously mentioned, and it is clear that girls with stepfathers are at greater risk for sexual abuse. Physicians need to be alert to at-risk families and think of ways in which to build these children's self-esteem and assertiveness and strengthen the family unit. Preventive therapy for new stepfamilies aimed at clarifying boundaries, roles, and expectations and improving communication could be of value to the entire family. Group therapy for vulnerable children can help them work on assertiveness and develop a positive sense of self and may provide a useful forum for sharing concerns about sexuality.

The child who has previously been victimized or abused remains at risk for future victimization or identification with the aggressor, as is the case with many male victims. These children should be a high priority for therapy designed to help them recover from the sexual trauma and get back on the track of normal development.

THE OFFENDER

Just as we have learned to routinely ask female patients about sexual abuse, we need to inquire of male patients about both past sexual abuse and any abusive tendencies. Because of the stigma attached to pedophilia, few are likely to bring up the subject on their own. Clinicians need to be aware of the various treatment modalities available to the sexual offender and their efficacy. Contributing or coexisting emotional disorders should also be treated. More emphasis needs to be placed on the treatment of the adolescent offender. As most offenders are involved with many more victims than they admit to, early intervention following an initial disclosure cuts down on the number of potential victims. Communities need to innovate outpatient treatment programs that will meet the needs of all family members. For selected offenders, mandated participation in these programs may be offered with a suspended sentence in lieu of incarceration. A proposal has been made, in Maine for lighter sentences for those nonviolent offenders who admit their guilt early in proceedings (Alexander, unpublished). If passed, the plan would offer incentive to sex offenders to turn themselves in, admit their guilt, and seek help early on. It would also spare victims from having to testify in court and would encourage treatment of the entire family unit. Although jail satisfies the outraged public and may give an aura of safety to the community, it does nothing for the victim's family and may cause more distress through stigmatization, loss of income, family disruption, and likelihood that the victim will blame herself for all of this. Further, jail alone does not treat the offender's underlying psychopathology. For the repeat offender who has not responded to treatment, prolonged incarceration remains appropriate.

We have much to learn from the early childhood histories of sex offenders. Many were themselves sexually abused, received little by way of empathy, and grew up in an abusive environment yearning for a close relationship with a father who was unavailable. Homosexual pedophiles may try to give a child the love and closeness they never experienced as a child, and they often turn to children to meet unfulfilled needs that are basically nonsexual. Others were taught to view women and girls as sex objects rather than persons in their own right and so they failed to develop a trusting relationship with a woman. While it is tempting to put all the blame for child sexual abuse on men, we must ask what their mothers' roles were in shaping offenders' views of women, sexuality, and their self-concepts. It follows from the above that a child who is reared in a warm, empathic, nurturing environment that fosters a good sense of self and one who is exposed to healthy role models is probably not likely to become a sex offender.

Adult life experiences may also influence proclivity toward sexual abuse. A provocative study by Parker and Parker (1986) of sexually abusive inmates and normal controls found that fathers who took active roles in caring for their daughters in the first three years of life were much less likely to abuse them in later life. The authors believe that "familiarity raises the threshold for sexual excitation by making potential sexual stimuli relatively dull and uninteresting" (p. 535). Parker and Parker found the risk of abuse among stepfathers was almost twice that of natural fathers, which they attributed not to stepfather status per se but rather to their lack of involvement in early childcare. To expand upon their findings, it is possible that nonabusing fathers achieved intimacy in nonsexual ways through bodily care as is postulated to be the case for mothers, that through daily nurturing they achieved more empathy for their children, and that the satisfactions of fathering enhanced their sense of self and competency. (As a corollary, the child who receives good fathering is probably less vulnerable to sexual abuse).

Our society needs to develop more respect for fathers who wish to actively parent their young children. Changes that might encourage more involvement of fathers with their children would include flexible work schedules, paternity leaves, time allowed off for sick children, and more acceptance of men who choose to be househusbands. The field of child development is belatedly looking at the role of fathers in the child's early development, and preliminary studies suggest that their impact is considerable (Pruett, 1983).

THE ENVIRONMENT

The 1980s have witnessed the progressive sexploitation of children by the media. Children are now the highest paid models and routinely appear made up to look older than their years and dressed in provocative outfits. Brooke Shields proclaimed for all on TV, "There is nothing between me and my jeans." An issue of *Life* magazine (February, 1984) celebrated Valentine's day with pictures of naked babies; some, with genitals partially exposed, posed as cupids clad in feathers, black lace, or, in one case, chain mail with a serpent entwined around his leg. The adultification of child has been a popular theme in literature and film, e.g., *Lolita, Paper Moon, Pretty Baby,* and *Taxi Driver.* The more pervasive themes of children satisfying adult sexual fantasies become, the more they sanctify children as legitimate sex objects.

Further blurring of generational boundaries is indicated by the way in which children are dressed to look like adults and don makeup, heels, and stockings at earlier and earlier ages. Meanwhile, adults have adopted youth fads in their dress and strive to look younger. The toy industry is also pressuring children to grow up in a hurry, thrusting Barbie dolls and war toys upon preschoolers. Several authors (Elkind, 1981; Postman, 1982) have voiced concerns about the disappearance of childhood and the pressures being put upon today's children to grow up too quickly. If this situation is confusing to children, it must also be so to adults, who are increasingly receiving mixed messages about children's sexuality. We need to ask whether, in addition to creating enormous psychological pressures on children, the adultification of children is also contributing to their increased vulnerability to sexual abuse.

The media continue to give top billing to sex scandals and stories of sexual abuse involving children. Unfortunately, many reports focus on sensationalism rather than on what can be done about the problem. This often results in invasion of the victim's privacy and insensitive interviews at the scene of the crime. There is also the risk that the public may grow accustomed to these reports, cease to be alarmed by them, or cease to react in a constructive fashion. On the other hand, the media have a duty to inform the public, and some newspapers and TV channels have run in-depth, sensitive programs on the topic of sexual abuse and may be credited with making it a household word. Media attention has helped to educate families, helped them realize they are not alone with the problem, and offered them advice about where to turn for help.

Another concern is that there are some viewers who will try to emulate what they view on TV. Tragically, 37 youths have lost their lives playing Russian Roulette after viewing it on TV in the film, *The Deer Hunter* (*NCTV News*, 1986). A rape scene with a Coca Cola bottle in another film was also emulated in real life. With the advent of Cable TV there is the additional problem of young children viewing R-rated films. When women are repeatedly victims of sexual violence on TV and in the movies, one has to be concerned that repeated viewing of such scenes will eventually erode inhibitions and raise thresholds as to what constitutes an acceptable level of sexual violence (Schetky, 1985). If TV viewers banded together, they could form an effective boycott against the programs and sponsors of shows which rank high in violence and sexual violence.

The women's movement has had a major impact on sexual attitudes. Feminism has done much to encourage abused women to come forth and press charges, has strengthened their credibility, has demanded stiffer sentences for sex offenders, and has fostered victim advocate and rape crisis services. Feminists see the solution to sexual abuse as ending male supremacy, which they believe accounts for the frequent violation of the incest taboo between fathers and daughters. However, as women have gained greater equality, the incidence of reported sexual abuse has continued to rise (59% between 1983 and 1984 according to the Child Welfare League of America [*New York Times*, March 19, 1986]). It is difficult to know whether this increase is real or an artifact of increased case finding and reporting.

A parallel development with the women's movement has been the rising divorce rate. Current estimates are that 45% of all children born in the U.S. in 1983 will experience divorce of their parents and 35% of these children will experience a remarriage. As more and more women have entered the work force, their services as homemakers have been devalued and they are considered capable of supporting themselves. Shifting attitudes toward the roles of men and women have resulted in the popularity of no-fault divorce legislation. The results of this new, presumably progressive legislation have been financially disastrous for many women. As documented by Weitzman (1985), in a 10-year study done in California, in the first year after divorce women experienced a 73% decline in income, while their former husbands experienced a

42% rise. Weitzman also noted that spousal awards to mothers with children under 6 dropped drastically, with only 13% of mothers in this group receiving any award. The implications are that this group may be hard put to find quality day care for their children in an affordable range. As child care in the home becomes a rare commodity and is relatively expensive, more single parents are forced to turn to day care facilities, which they may not thoroughly investigate or they may be lulled into a false sense of security by others who have used questionable programs. As noted in Chapter 4, this group of young children is doubly at risk for sexual abuse by providers of day care and parents' lovers. One remedy is to establish government-funded day care centers or encourage private industry to offer day care for employees.

Another possible backlash of the women's movement may be that some men are threatened by today's new woman and her independence and demands, and may turn to children as more helpless, passive, and submissive sex objects. However, this is purely speculative and has not been borne out by any research. One disturbing trend, reminiscent of the Victorian era, is that fear of AIDS and other sexually transmitted diseases may be encouraging men to seek younger and younger sex partners (*Parade Magazine*, July 20, 1986, p. 4).

One approach to the prevention of sexual abuse is through legislative changes. Screening the histories of day care employees for prior convictions related to sexual abuse would appear to be one step in the right direction. Central files for sex offenders have also been proposed. However, numerous problems exist with this scheme such as Who bears the cost? What guarantees are there about confidentiality? Who keeps the records and for how long and who may have access to them? The obvious problem is that most child molesters do not have prior arrests and even if they do there is nothing to prevent them from applying for a job under a pseudonym.

Effective use of the legislature has been through enactment of mandatory reporting laws for child abuse. Although there are penalties for failure to report, it is not clear how often these are applied. Continued effort needs to be made regarding encouragement of health care personnel to think about, ask about, and report child sexual abuse. Professionals should also be concerned about the possibility of a lawsuit if they fail to report and a child is reinjured.

Legislation could also mandate more funding for victim compensation programs, early intervention programs, runaway shelters, educational programs in the schools geared toward prevention, and more research into the efficacy of these types of interventions and into child sexual abuse in general.

Finally, we need stiffer penalties for persons involved with child kidnapping, pornography, and prostitution. Penalties should apply to consumers of child pornography as well as patrons of juvenile prostitutes.

In summary, there are no easy answers to the problem of child sexual abuse. Before we find the answers, we need to know what questions to ask. It is hoped that this book may stimulate more questions and research in the area of child sexual abuse.

REFERENCES

Alexander (Unpublished). Some thoughts on approaches to handling certain categories of sex offender cases. (Copies may be obtained from Judge Alexander, Kennebec County Courthouse, 95 State Street, Augusta, Maine 04330.)

Binder, R., & McNiel, D. (In press). Evaluation of a school-based sexual abuse prevention program: Cognitive and emotional effects. *Child Abuse and Neglect.*

Conte, J.R., Rosen, C., Saperstein, L., & Shermack, R. (1985). An evaluation of a program to prevent sexual victimization of young children. *Child Abuse and Neglect,* 9:319–328.

Elkind, D. (1981). *The Hurried Child.* Reading, MA: Addison-Wesley.

Finkelhor, D. (1986). High risk children. In D. Finkelhor (Ed.), *Sourcebook on Child Sexual Abuse.* Beverly Hills: Sage Publications.

NCTV News (March, 1986). 7(1–2):10.

Parker, S., & Parker, H. (1986). Father-daughter sexual child abuse: An emerging perspective. *Am. J. Orthopsychiat.,* 56(4):531–549.

Plummer, C. (August, 1984). Preventing sexual abuse: What in-school programs teach children. Paper presented at the 2nd National Conference for Family Violence Researchers, Durham, N.H.

Postman, N. (1982). *The Disappearance of Childhood.* New York: Delacorte Press.

Pruett, K. (1983). Infants of primary nurturing fathers. *Psychoanalytic Study of the Child,* 38:257–287.

Schetky, D.H. (1985). Role models of violence. In D.H. Schetky & E.P. Benedek (Eds.), *Emerging Issues in Child Psychiatry and the Law.* New York: Brunner/Mazel.

Weitzman, L.J. (1985). *The Divorce Revolution: The Unexpected Social and Economic Consequences for Women and Children in America.* New York: Free Press.

Appendix

ANATOMICALLY CORRECT DOLLS

Analeka Industries, Inc.: Show and Tell Mates
Cotton cloth dolls, adults 22″ and juveniles 16″ with fingers. Available in Caucasian, Black, and Native (tan) versions. Colorful clothing with velcro fastenings. Accessories such as additional clothing available.
Comment: No nipples on adults.
Cost: Set of 4 dolls, $149.50.
Address: P.O. Box 141, West Linn, Oregon 97068.

The Child Guidance Center of Greater Cleveland and Dolls Ltd.: The Doll Family
Dolls available in sets of 4 or 8 or individually. Available in Black, Caucasian or Hispanic. Adults are 26″ and children 22″. Dolls are machine washable and hypoallergenic. Clothing is easily removable.
Comment: Faces are not very friendly looking.
Cost: Set of 4 dolls, $275; set of 8 dolls, $500.
Address: Child Guidance Center, 2525 East 22nd St., Cleveland, Ohio 44115.

Hylands Anatomical Dolls, Inc.: Real People Dolls.
Friendly looking dolls with yarn hair. Available in Caucasian, Black, Hispanic, and Asian. Durable cloth construction with painted faces. Clothing easy to remove with velcro closures. Accessories also available.
Cost: $150 per set.
Address: 4455 Torrance Blvd., Suite 310, Torrance, California 90503.

Janon, Inc.: Maple Hill Doll
Sculptured, hand-washable dolls with fingers, wire-wrapped to allow them to bend. They also manufacture a less expensive rag-style, anatomically correct doll whose body is flatter and less realistic. Adults 21″ and children 17″. Available in black and white. Also available are senior-citizen anatomically correct dolls, an anatomical canine "Puddles," and "Baby New Born," which features interchangeable male and female sex organs.
Comment: Very humanlike, appealing dolls.
Cost: Set of 4 dolls, $395.
Set of 4 rag-style "walker" dolls, $185.
Address: 317 E. Front St., Grand Ledge, Michigan 48837.

Migma Designs, Inc.
Soft, pliable dolls with neutral faces and colorful, easily removed clothing. Available in Caucasian, Black, and Native. Comes with manual.

Comment: Small mouths, fingers not separated.
Cost: Set of 4 dolls, $150.
Address: P.O. Box 70064, Eugene, Oregon 97401.

Patient Puppets
Durable cloth dolls available in black and white and other races on request. Adults 22″ and children 16″. Hand washable. Dolls come with day and nighttime wear, which is easily removable. Mouths include movable tongues. Grey-haired dolls also available.
  Comment: $10 from sale of each kit is channeled back into prevention, education, and treatment.
  Cost: Set of 4 dolls, $300.
  Address: 40 Home St., Winnipeg, Manitoba, Canada R3G 1W6.

Teach-A-Bodies
Attractive, well-constructed dolls with much detail, including chest and underarm hair on adult male doll. Female adult comes with a baby with umbilical cord and sanitary napkin and belt. Grandparent dolls also available. Fingers are optional. Available in black and white. Washable. Extra accessories available, including circumcised and uncircumcised exchangeable penises.
  Comment: Dolls suitable for sex education as well.
  Cost: Adult pair, $85.
  Child pair, $70; toddlers, $70.
  Fingers, $10 extra.
  Exchangeable penis, free.
  Puppets, $15 each.
  Address: 2544 Boyd St., Fort Worth, Texas 76109.

BOOKS WRITTEN FOR CHILDREN AND TEENAGERS*

Ageton, S. *Facts About Sexual Assault: A Research Report for Teenagers.* Rockville, MD: NIMH, U.S. Dept. of Health and Human Services, 1985. Factual data based on survey of teenagers. Includes sections on aftermath of sexual assault and reporting, as well as tips on prevention. Very good section on advice to males.

Anderson, D., & Finne, M. *Margaret's Story: Sexual Abuse and Going to Court.* Minneapolis, MN: Dillon Press, 1986. $9.95. This is a straight-forward, informative, and reassuring book about Margaret, a black child, who is molested by a neighbor. It deals openly with the range of Margaret's feelings and shows her mastering the experience of testifying. The book should be helpful to any child who must testify in court, and to parents of victims as well. It is very nicely illustrated. An appendix contains some basic information about child sexual abuse, a glossary

---

* Price of book and year of publication are given where available.

of relevant sexual and legal terminology, and a list of people a child might turn to for help.

Bateman, P. *Acquaintance Rape: Awareness and Prevention for Teenagers.* Alternatives to Fear, 101 Nickerson, Suite 150, Seattle, Washington 98109. This guide is intended to help teenagers identify a potential acquaintance rape situation.

Beaudrey, J., & Ketchum, L. *Carla Goes to Court.* New York: Human Sciences Press, 1983. $12.95. A sensitive, well-written book that deals with a young child's fears and confusions about going to court as a witness to a crime. It emphasizes her ability to master the experience while also explaining court procedures.

Berenstain, S., & Berenstain, J. *The Berenstain Bears Learn about Strangers.* New York: Random House, 1985. $1.95 (paper). Teaches toddlers that strangers are not all good and not all bad and to use common sense.

Boegehold, B. *You Can Say No.* Golden Books. Racine, WI: Western Publishing Co. $4.95. Written for preschoolers. Teaches them how to say no in situations involving both strangers and family members.

Channing, L. *What Every Child Should Know About Sexual Abuse* and *You're in Charge.* So. Deerfield, MA: Bete Co., Inc., 1986. $8.00. Coloring and activity booklets for the young child. Emphasis is on education and teaching the child to say no.

Dayee, F. *Private Zone.* New York: Warner Books, 1984. $2.95. Designed to be read by parent to the young child. Criticized by some as silly and alarmist but contains useful information, such as suggestions to parents on what to do if a child is sexually assaulted.

Fay, J., & Flerchinger, B.J. *Top Secret: Sexual Assault Information for Teenagers Only.* Renton, WA: Network Publishing. King County Rape Relief, 1984. $11.95. Useful information for adolescents with emphasis on self-protection.

Flynn, K. *Some Questions You May Ask About Going to Court.* Hennepin County Public Affairs Dept., Minnesota. Simple but useful information for the child going to court on what happens at a trial and what happens to the offender and victim afterwards. Suggests counseling as a helpful means of dealing with feelings about abuse and trial. Black-and-white photos.

Hubbard, K., & Berlin, E. *Help Yourself to Safety.* Edmonds, WA: Chas. Franklin Press, 1985. $3.50 (paper). Written for school-age children and intended to help them avoid dangerous situations with friends and strangers. Good illustrations and list of safety tips for children and their parents.

Mackey, G., & Swan, H. *Dear Elizabeth.* Children's Institute of Kansas City, 9412 High Dr., Leawood, Kansas 66206. Fictitious account of the sexual abuse of an adolescent presented in the form of a diary. Useful in therapy or in prevention programs.

Marvel Comics Group & NCPCA. *Spider Man and Power Pack.* 1985. Available from National Commission for Prevention of Child Abuse, 332 So. Michigan Ave., Suite 1250, Chicago, Illinois 60604-4357. Stock No. B-84-325, $1.00 each. Even Spider Man experienced sexual abuse as a child. In this episode he helps a young boy tell his parents about an abusive babysitter and counsels a runaway to confide in a trusted adult about an abusive father. Emphasis is on the facts that the child is not to blame and is not helpless.

Playmore Publishers. *It's O.K. to Say No.* New York. $1.95. Coloring book for children ages 2 to 6 and activity book for children ages 6 to 11. Gives children the message that it's all right to say no to adults who make them feel uncomfortable.

Polese, C. *Promise Not to Tell.* New York: Human Sciences Press, 1985. $13.95. Designed for readers ages 8 and up, this well-written novel deals sensitively and honestly with the topic of sexual abuse. Information conveyed is both preventive and therapeutic. Attractive illustrations.

Ruzicka, J. *Kids Go to Court, Too.* Hennepin County Public Affairs Dept., Minnesota. Factual pamphlet on testifying in court with almost no attention to the child's feelings. Stark black-and-white photos.

Wachter, O. *No More Secrets for Me.* Boston: Little, Brown, 1983. $4.95. Four stories about children in a variety of sexually abusive situations.

Williams, J. *Red Flag, Green Flag People.* Fargo, N.D.: Rape and Abuse

Crisis Center, 1980. $4.00. A coloring book for young children focusing primarily on potentially dangerous strangers.

Williams, J. *Annie: Once I was a Little Bit Frightened.* Fargo, N.D.: Rape and Abuse Crisis Center. $2.50. A simple booklet for ages K-8 urging children to tell if an adult is hurting them. Booklet remains vague as to what sort of hurt and avoids explicit sexual references. The obvious problem is that the young child may not associate sexual touching with being hurt.

BOOKS WRITTEN FOR PARENTS

Adams, C., & Fay, J. *No More Secrets: Protecting Your Child From Sexual Assault.* San Luis Obispo, CA: Impact Publishers, 1981. $4.95. Excellent book with focus on prevention and dialoging with children. Recognizes that children are most likely to be abused by someone they know.

Adams, C., Fay, J., & Lorren-Martin, J. *No Is Not Enough: Helping Teenagers Avoid Sexual Assault.* San Louis Obispo, CA: Impact Publishers, 1984. $6.95. A parents' guide to help teenagers avoid victimization. Includes advice on what to say and when.

Ageton, S. *Facts About Sexual Assault: A Research Report for Adults Who Work with Teenagers.* Rockville, MD: NIMH, U.S. Dept. of Health and Human Services, 1985. Surveys a nationally representative sample of teenagers and presents data on female victims and some offenders. Discusses aftereffects of sexual assault and preventive measures.

Bulkley, J., Ensminger, J., Fontana, V., & Summit. *Dealing with Sexual Child Abuse.* National Commission for Prevention of Child Abuse, 1982. NCPCA Publishing, 332 Michigan Ave., Suite 1250, Chicago, IL 60604-4357. Booklet deals with legal, medical, and social aspects of child sexual abuse.

Division of Child Protection, Children's Hospital National Medical Center has the following booklets available:
A Message to Parents About Child Sexual Abuse. $.75.
Public Concern and Personal Action: Child Sexual Abuse. $.75.
Phone 202-745-5685 or send requests to Education and Training Specialist at Division of Child Protection, Children's Hospital Na-

tional Medical Center, 111 Michigan Ave., N.W., Washington, D.C. 20010.

Fay, J. *He Told Me Not to Tell.* Renton, WA: King County Rape Relief, 1979. Useful guideline for parents on how to talk to their children about child sexual abuse.

National Center on Child Abuse and Neglect. *Sexual Abuse of Children: Selected Readings.* Rockville, MD: U.S. Dept. of Health and Human Services, 1980. DHHS Pub. No. (OHDS) 78-30161. Contains a variety of writings covering most aspects of sexual abuse, including articles written by victims. A good overview. Listing of treatment programs is by now dated.

Planned Parenthood. *How to Talk with Your Child About Sexuality: A Parent's Guide.* New York: Doubleday, 1986. $7.95. This helpful guide covers facts for preschoolers through teens, while also addressing values and how to talk with children about sexuality. One chapter discusses how to protect children from sexual abuse. There is a helpful appendix which includes a glossary of sexual terms and facts about contraception and sexually transmitted diseases.

Renshaw, D. *Sex Talk for a Safe Child.* Chicago, IL: American Medical Association, 1984. Order Dept. OP-234/5, P.O. 10946, Chicago, Illinois 60610.

Sanford, L.T. *Come Tell Me Right Away: A Positive Approach to Warning Children About Sexual Abuse.* New York: Ed-U Press, 1982. (P.O. Box 583, Fayetteville, N.Y. 13066.) Emphasizes exploitative and nonsexual aspects of abuse as well as sexual. Discusses dangers of teaching blind obedience. Provides guidelines on how to talk with children about sexual abuse.

Sanford, L.T. *The Silent Children: A Parent's Guide to Prevention of Sexual Abuse.* New York: McGraw-Hill, 1982.

U.S. Dept. of Health and Human Services. *Child Sexual Abuse: Incest, Assault and Sexual Exploitation.* Rockville, MD, 1981. DHHS Pub. No. (OHDS) 81-30166. Provides overview of child sexual abuse, prevention, and treatment.

U.S. Dept. of Health and Human Services. *Child Sexual Abuse Pre-*

vention. Tips to Parents. Rockville, MD, 1984. Useful pamphlet for waiting rooms. Includes sections on listening to your children, choosing a preschool or child care center, and physical and behavioral signs of sexual abuse.

The following booklets are available through the National Committee for Prevention of Child Sexual Abuse Publishing Dept., 332 S. Michigan Ave., Suite 1250, Chicago, IL 60604-4357:

May, G. *Understanding Sexual Child Abuse.* ISBN 0-937906-05-0. Stock No. b-78-303. $3.50 each. The booklet gives an overview of sexual offenses against children with detailed discussion of incest.

Summit, R. *Dealing with Sexual Abuse.* ISBN 0-937906-06-9. Stock No. B-78-304. $3.50 each. Explains roles of those individuals involved in various aspects of the investigation and treatment of child sexual abuse.

Basic Facts about Sexual Child Abuse. 1982. ISBN 0-937906-08-5. Stock No. P-78-401. $1.25 each. Pamphlet answers basic questions about child sexual abuse and discusses factors contributing to incest as well as behavioral and physical symptoms in sexually abused children and what to do if abuse is suspected.

GENERAL

National Committee for Prevention of Child Abuse. *Child Sexual Abuse Prevention Resources,* 1984. ISBN 0-937906-42-5. $2.00 each. Contains references on audio–visual materials, live performance and theater groups, school curricula, games, dolls, prevention programs, and reading materials for children and adults. Available from NCPCA (address listed above).

Inservice Training, Lectures, Workshops, Consultation

Division of Child Protection, Children's Hospital National Medical Center, Washington, D.C., offers Professional Training Programs including speeches, presentations, and workshops for professional and lay audiences. Contact: Education and Training Coordinator, Division of Child Protection, Children's Hospital National Medical Center, 111 Michigan Ave., N.W., Washington, D.C. 20010.

Dr. Nicholas Groth, Forensic Mental Health Association, 29 Lynwood St., Webster, Massachusetts 01570.

Plummer, A. *Preventing Sexual Abuse.* Learning Publications, Inc., 1985. $19.95 (Box 1326, Dept. BA 5678, Holmes Beach, Florida 33509). A resource book for youth workers and educators designed to help develop prevention programs.

Dr. Suzanne Sgroi, New England Clinical Associates, Suite 209, 970 Farmington Ave., W. Hartford, Connecticut 06107.

Simrel, K.O., Lloyd, D.W., & Kanda, M. *Medical Corroborating Evidence in Child Sexual Abuse/Assault Cases.* Available from Division of Child Protection, Children's Hospital National Medical Center, 111 Michigan Ave., N.W., Washington, D.C. 20010. Attn.: Education and Training Specialist. This useful small booklet covers the physical exam and laboratory tests and has a section on sexually transmitted diseases.

FILMS

"The Young Victims of Sexual Abuse: An Interview Protocol." This videotape presents a protocol developed at Cleveland Metropolitan General Hospital, which is a series of questions asked of preschool-age children about body parts and their functions. This film received an award of recognition from the American Academy of Child and Adolescent Psychiatry. Available from Child Guidance Center, 2525 East 22nd St., Cleveland, Ohio 44114. Contact Anne McIntyre at 216-696-5800.

"Incest: The Victim No One Believes." A very powerful film in which three young adult women discuss how incest has affected their lives. Available from MTI Teleprograms, 3710 Commercial Ave., Northbrook, Illinois 60062.

"Breaking Silence." Survivors of childhood incest talk candidly about their experience. Offenders are also interviewed. Available from Film Distribution Center, 1028 Industry Drive, Seattle, Washington 98188. Or call 206-575-1575.

The following list of films was prepared by and is reproduced with permission from the Division of Child Protection, Children's Hospital

National Medical Center, Washington, D.C., for the Fourth National Conference on the Sexual Victimization of Children, 1986:

FILM DESCRIPTIONS

Films and video cassettes have been loosely grouped below to help participants schedule their film viewing time. Please note that most of the 16 mm films are also available in video cassettes. For additional information about particular films, contact the distributor directly.

Films annotated "New" are those not previously shown at a CHNMC National Conference on Sexual Victimization of Children. Older films also are included for balance, particularly films on topics not covered by new releases.

Community and Professional Education

"Child Sexual Abuse: Socio-Cultural and Community Issues"

Unique film presentation geared toward the need for prevention programming and social/institutional change. Addresses religious and ethnic issues. Discusses historical and contemporary myths that can contribute to the phenomena of child victimization. Provides an overview of a conceptual framework for action to bring about social/institutional change. Stresses the need to adopt coordinated prevention programming. Suitable for community groups, teacher training, and other professionals. Part of the Seattle Committee for Children Prevention Curriculum on view in the French Market Exhibit Hall. (New)

Medium:	Video Cassette
Length:	30 minutes
Distributor:	Committee for Children
	Seattle, Washington

"Men Who Molest: Children Who Survive"

Suitable for professional education. Filmed on location at a community-based offender treatment program and at a hospital-based victim treatment program. Offenders candidly discuss the nature and cause of their deviant behavior. Depicts a variety of treatment modalities including behavior modification, confrontation, and group therapy. Two child victims are shown in therapy and confronting their abusers. A powerful and often emotional film that concludes with a realistic discussion of long-term prognosis for various types of offenders. Includes study guide. (New)

Medium: Video Cassette
Length: 52 minutes
Distributor: Filmmakers Library, Inc.

"Secret Sounds Screaming: The Sexual Abuse of Children"

Community activists, survivors, offenders, and parents explore sexual victimization as a power issue. Expresses frustration with legal proceedings and with the eroticization of children by the media. Includes the voices and experiences of people of color, the poor, and working women. Independently produced. (New)
Medium: Video Cassette
Length: 30 minutes
Distributor: Visions in Film

"Silent Shame: The Sexual Abuse of Children"

Documentary produced by NBC. Focuses on the prevalence of child sexual abuse and the connection between child pornography and pedophilia. Addresses current law enforcement programs aimed at restricting production and distribution of child pornography. Interviews with experts are interspersed with interviews and concealed-camera sequences with producers/purveyors of child pornography and professed pedophiles. Interviews with two child victims stress the need for more counseling follow-up and resources. Contains edited or masked examples of child pornography photographs and films. (New)
Medium: Video Cassette
Length: 48 minutes
Distributor: Films Incorporated

"The Touching Problem"

Dramatization of one child's experience with abuse by a relative. Illustrates facts about sexual abuse and abusers, as well as the emotional repercussions on the child and the family.
Medium: 16 mm
Length: 18 minutes
Distributor: Coronet/MTI Films and Video

"To Protect the Children"

This documentary, aired on the Turner Broadcasting System, Inc., contains segments focusing on different aspects of the problem of child sexual abuse. Begins with the reenactment of the trial and sentencing of a chronic pedophile. Second sequence focuses on two sisters who were victimized by their stepfather and includes naturalistic discussions with members of their extended family. A young man, victimized as a child, descibes himself as a survivor after assistance from an adult support group. In an institution for adolescent offenders, three teenagers discuss their own childhood victimization and its impact. Strong emphasis on need for stiffer legal penalties, as well as for more community involvement in prevention.

Medium: Video Cassette
Length: 48 minutes
Distributor: The Lansburg Company

Prevention Programming for Children and Youth

"Better Safe than Sorry III"

Latest in a series of prevention films. Designed for high school students. Actors portraying victims lead into dramatizations of acquaintance rape, incest, and male victimization. Stresses increased responsibility of teens for their own safety as they mature, combined with the message that the victim is not at fault. Script provides suggestions for increasing personal safety, but these are not dramatized. (New)

Format: 16 mm
Length: 19 minutes
Distributor: FilmFair Communications

"Child Molestation: A Crime Against Children"

For older elementary school and junior high children. Interviews with children who have been molested and have been helped through counseling. Provides clear answers to confusing questions like: What is molestation? and What do you do if you think you are going to be molested?

Medium: 16 mm
Length: 11 minutes
Distributor: AIMS Media

"Feeling Yes, Feeling No: The Adult Program"

Discusses the nature and scope of child sexual assault, as well as what an adult should do when a child discloses abuse. Describes the purpose and structure of the "Feeling Yes, Feeling No Prevention Program," which includes three short films and a detailed, 88-page curriculum guide. Suitable for parents and community groups. (New)

Medium: 16 mm
Length: 28 minutes
Distributor: Perennial Education, Inc.

"Feeling Yes, Feeling No: Program One"

Three actors portray scenes about positive and negative touching for a class of young elementary school children. The actors' discussion with the children emphasizes building confidence and the child's right to say "No." Very lively song "My Body's Nobody's Body But Mine." (New)

"Feeling Yes, Feeling No: Program Two"

Reinforces the understanding of "Yes" and "No" feelings and goes on to demonstrate, through skits, how to recognize and deflect suspicious approaches by strangers. (New)

"Feeling Yes, Feeling No: Program Three"

Introduces the subject of sexual assault by a family member or another trusted person. Demonstrates through skits how to get help in the face of such an event. (New)

Medium: 16 mm
Lengths: Program One—14 minutes
                 Program Two—14 minutes
                 Program Three—16 minutes
Distributor: Perennial Education, Inc.

"Little Bear"

For preschoolers and very young elementary grades. Uses actors dressed in animal costumes, a format familiar to young children. Demonstrates nice touches (hugs), hurtful touches (hard squeezes), and confusing touches (on genital areas). Teaches children to recognize, refuse assertively, and report abuse to an authority figure. Stresses that abuse is not the child's fault. Complete prevention package includes Training Video, Teachers Guide, and Coloring Book. (New)

Medium: Video Cassette

Length: 19 minutes
Distributor: Universal Dimensions, Inc.

"Little Bear Training Video"

Part of "Little Bear" prevention package. Suitable both for teachers and for use with community groups, P.T.A.s, and school administrators. Combines general information on the extent and impact of the problem with discussion of the need for prevention programming. Shows and discusses the abusive situation experienced by Little Bear. Provides specific guidelines for teachers. (New)
Medium: Video Cassette
Length: 30 minutes
Distributor: Universal Dimensions, Inc.

"No More Secrets"

Intended for children ages 7 through 12. Explicit but not alarming portrayals of sexual abuse within the family. Children show how to talk about incest to someone they trust and how to say "no" to intrusion. Comes with instructional guide and paperback for parents.
Medium: 16 mm
Length: 13 minutes
Distributor: ODN Productions, Inc.

"Talking Helps"

Training film for "No More Secrets." Shows a discussion among teachers, parents, and administrators planning a prevention program for their school. Addresses concerns about teaching this sensitive topic. (New)
Medium: 16 mm
Length: 27 minutes
Distributor: ODN Productions, Inc.

"Touch"

Intended for elementary school children. Very straightforward, but not alarming presentation that defines sexual abuse and discusses how to cope with a molesting situation. Lively interactions with children responding to questions and between a small group of children and actors of Illusion Theater.

Medium: 16 mm
Length: 33 minutes
Distributor: Coronet/MTI Films and Video

"What Tadoo"

Designed for grades K-3. Combines live action with charming puppets
in a dream visit to the "Land of Lessons" and "Region of Rules" where
a young boy learns to say no, get away, and tell. Shows how strangers
may approach children by using lures, tricks, and pretending. Also
discusses bad or confusing touches. Concludes with upbeat song. (New)
Medium: 16 mm
Length: 18 minutes
Distributor: Coronet/MTI Film and Video

"Yes You Can Say No"

Dramatization of the struggle of one young school-age boy to manage
his feelings about sexual molestation perpetrated by his uncle and to
use his personal resources to address the problem. Shows peer rela-
tionships that encourage assertiveness. Emphasizes the difficulties and
final benefits of telling. Intended for grades 2-6. Part of the Seattle
Committee for Children Prevention Program on view in the French
Market Exhibit Hall. (New)
Medium: Video Cassette
Length: 19 minutes
Distributor: Committee for Children
                Seattle, Washington

Initial Intervention

"A Time for Caring: The School's Response to the Sexually Abused
Child"

For use in teacher training. Provides an overview of the problem and
lists behavioral signs that should alert teachers and other school personnel to the possibility of sexual abuse. Reviews initial interviewing
techniques, reporting, and follow-through. Stresses professional responsibility and multidisciplinary case management.
Medium: 16 mm
Length: 28 minutes
Distributor: Lawren Productions, Inc.

"Identifying, Reporting, and Handling Disclosure of the Sexually Abused Child"

Primarily designed for teachers and other child caregivers. Presents common behavioral indicators and gives illustrations using child actors in a school setting. Provides vignettes of teachers interacting with different child victims during initial disclosures. Emphasizes the legal mandate to report. Part of the Seattle Committee for Children Prevention Program on view in the French Market Exhibit Hall. (New)

Medium: Video Cassette
Length: 25 minutes
Distributor: Committee for Children
               Seattle, Washington

"If I Tell You a Secret: Interviewing the Sexually Abused Child"

Intended for professionals who become involved in case management. Depicts interview techniques useful for social workers, protective service workers, physicians, nurses, police officers, and district attorneys. Members of each of these professions discuss their individual approaches.

Medium: 16 mm, color
Length: 34 minutes
Distributor: Lawren Productions, Inc.

"Response: Child Sexual Abuse—A Medical View"

Developed for physicians. Detailed discussion of how to conduct a sensitive, thorough, and legally valid initial medical evaluation of a child victim of suspected assault. Contains information on use of the colposcope, examples of types of physical changes that might be observed, and very clear instructions on the importance of an accurate medical record. Study guide provided. Also on view in the French Market Exhibit Hall. (New)

Medium: Video Cassette
Length: 30 minutes
Distributor: Child Sexual Abuse Prevention Project
               United Way, Inc.
               Los Angeles, California

"Response: Child Sexual Abuse—The Clinical Interview"

Designed to train mental health professionals to conduct sensitive and effective diagnostic interviews with both known and suspected victims of child sexual abuse. Focuses primarily on very young children. Provides demonstrations of successful interviewing techniques which show in detail how to establish rapport; how to use communication aids such as drawings, puppets, and anatomically correct dolls; and how to assess the child's responses. Also on view in the French Market Exhibit Hall. (New)

Medium:	Video Cassette
Length:	60 minutes
Distributor:	Child Sexual Abuse Prevention Project
	United Way, Inc.
	Los Angeles, California

"Sexually Misused Children: Identification, Documentation, Management"

A basic training film best suited to health care settings. Provides background data and a discussion of common myths. Psychosocial factors addressed focus on familial abuse with an emphasis on father-daughter incest. Information about the physical exam focuses on the female child. Accompanied by a study guide and multiple choice test. (New)

Medium:	Video Cassette
Length:	26 minutes
Distributor:	Media Library
	University of Michigan Medical Center

Law Enforcement Intervention

"Child Abuse: Police Intervention:

Law enforcement personnel attitudinal and behavioral training tool. Two physical abuse cases and one incest case are used to illustrate effective intervention strategies and techniques. A multidisciplinary approach is emphasized.

Medium:	16 mm
Length:	26 minutes
Distributor:	Coronet/MTI Film and Video

"Just Tell the Truth"

Designed to prepare children for appearing in court. Educates and reassures the child that there is nothing to fear. Stresses the importance of telling the truth. Ends with a five-minute sequence for adults in which a therapist presents important pointers regarding the testimony of children. Also available in Spanish. Includes a coloring book. Related materials on display in the French Market Exhibit Hall. (New)

Medium: Video Cassette
Length: 15 minutes
Distributor: Kids Rights

"The Sexually Abused Child: A Protocol for Child Advocacy Through the Criminal Justice System"

For all law enforcement personnel, including judges, attorneys, court personnel, and probation officers, as well as social/protective service workers. Provides guidelines on case management within the law enforcement system. Discusses possible procedural adjustments to lesson negative impacts on child victims.

Medium: 16 mm
Length: 26 minutes
Distributor: Lawren Productions, Inc.

"Double Jeopardy"

Designed to sensitize professionals to the trauma the child victim often experiences during the lengthy judicial proceedings in cases of child sexual abuse. Case histories demonstrate the benefits of an interdisciplinary approach to management of the child and family.

Medium: 16 mm
Length: 40 minutes
Distributor: Coronet/MTI Film and Video

Incest

"Breaking Silence"

Focuses on the reactions of victims using examples of children's drawings and the recollections of adults who were abused as children. Addresses the necessity for and difficulties of breaking silence as an adult and entering into the process of healing through therapy. Intense. (New)

Medium: 16 mm
Length: 58 minutes
Distributor: Film Distribution Center

"Child Sexual Abuse: The Untold Secret"

Five young adolescent girls each discuss aspects of their prior victimization by their fathers or stepfathers. The victims are in shadow.

Candid and poignant sequences address the initiation of abuse, the feelings and behavior problems it engendered, the reasons for and means of disclosure, and the aftermath from the victim's perspective.

Medium: Video Cassette
Length: 30 minutes
Distributor: American Journal of Nursing Company

"Finding Out: Incest and Family Sexual Abuse"

This Canadian film concentrates on the role played by the victim's mother in dealing with incest or family sexual abuse. A former child victim and her mother discuss the long-term impact of incest. Comments by therapists and counselors are interspersed. Stresses that the victim and the mother are not the guilty parties. Useful for community awareness programs and in conjunction with family counseling.

Medium: 16 mm, color
Length: 25 minutes
Distributor: Kinetic

"Not In My Family: Parents Speak Out on Sexual Abuse of Children"

Five mothers in incestuous families speak openly and candidly about their experiences. The group discussion covers topics such as disbelief, denial, anger, and the final development of individual coping mechanisms. For prevention education and intervention programs.

Medium: 16 mm
Length: 34 minutes
Distributor: Lawren Productions, Inc.

DISTRIBUTORS

AIMS Media
6901 Woodley Avenue
Van Nuys, California 91406-4878
(818) 785-4111
(800) 367-2467

American Journal of Nursing
  Company
555 West 57th Street
New York, New York 10019
(212) 582-8820
(1-800) 223-2282

Child Sexual Abuse Prevention
  Project
United Way, Inc.
621 South Virgil Avenue
Los Angeles, California 90005
(213) 736-1300, Ext. 291

Committee for Children
172 20th Avenue
Seattle, Washington 98122
(206) 322-5050

Coronet/MTI Film and Video
108 Wilmot Road
Deerfield, Illinois 60015-9990
(800) 621-2131

Film Distribution Center
1028 Industry Drive
Seattle, Washington 98188
(206) 575-1575

Filmmakers Library, Inc.
133 East 58th Street
New York, New York 10022
(212) 355-6545

FilmFair Communications
10900 Ventura Boulevard
P.O. Box 1728
Studio City, California 91604
(818) 985-0244

Films Incorporated
5547 N. Ravenswood Avenue
Chicago, Illinois 60640-1199
(1-800) 323-4222 Ext. 334

Kids Rights
P.O. Box 851
Mount Dora, Florida 32757
(904) 383-6200
(1-800) 892-KIDS

Kinetic
255 Delaware Avenue
Suite 340
Buffalo, New York 14202
(716) 856-7631

(The) Lansburg Company
Attn: Anne Kahane
1811 West Olympic Boulevard
Los Angeles, California 90064
(213) 478-7878

Lawren Productions, Inc.
P.O. Box 666
Mendocino, California 95460
(707) 937-0536

Media Library
The University of Michigan
Medical Center
R4440 Kresege I/0518
Ann Arbor, Michigan 48109-0518
(313) 763-2074

O.D.N. Productions, Inc.
74 Varick Street
Suite 304
New York, New York 10013
(212) 431-8923

Perennial Education, Inc.
930 Pitner
Evanston, Illinois 60202
(312) 328-6700
(800) 323-9084

Universal Dimensions, Inc.
4603 N. 16th Street, Suite #4
Phoenix, Arizona 85016
(602) 266-4972

Visions in Film
P.O. Box 315
Franklin Lakes, New Jersey 07417
(201) 891-8240

Name Index

237

Subject Index

Abuse history:
  of offenders, 35–36, 127
  of wives of incestuous fathers, 37
Abusers. *See* Offenders
Adolescent(s):
  books for, 218–221
  interviewing, 73
  need for treatment, 67–68
  psychosexual development in, 9–10, 15
Alcohol abuse, father-daughter incest and, 33
Alienation from mother, of daughters abused by fathers, 38
Allegations, 104–123
  case illustrations of, 111–116
  characteristics of, 116
  context of, 63–64
  credibility of, 64–66, 107–110
  evaluation of child and, 107
  evaluation of parents and, 111
  false, 105–110, 113–116, 121–122
  "gentle" molestation and, 120–121
  gray areas in, 116–121
  literature review of, 105–107
  parent-child interactions and, 110–111
  sexual overstimulation and, 117–119
  true, 112–113, 116
Anal phase of development, 12–13
Anal-rectal examination, 90
Anatomically correct dolls:
  in interviewing child, 76–77
  sources of, 217–218
Assertiveness skills training, of offender, 145
Attorney General's Commission on Pornography, 158
Aunt-nephew incest, 129

Babies, psychosexual development of, 5–6, 12
Behavioral problems, in sexually abused children, 46–47
Behavioral symptoms, medical and social evaluation of, 97
Bible, child sexual abuse in, 22–24
Body image, of victims, 42
Borderline personality disorder, in incest victims, 44

Boys. *See* Male *entries*
"Brainwashing," false allegations and, 108

Child Abuse Prevention and Treatment Act of 1977, 163
Child Hearing Officer (CHO), 177
Child pornography, 154–158
Child prostitution, 159–164
  legislative responses to, 163–164
  male-female differences in, 160–161
  prevention of, 162–163
  rehabilitation after, 163
Child sexual abuse. *See also* Incest
  allegations of, 104–123. *See also* Allegations
  boy-girl differences in, 125–126
  clinical evaluation of, 57–79. *See also* Clinical evaluation
  "gentle," 120–121
  in institutions, 132–133
  investigation of, 59–60
  medical evaluation of, 82–101. *See also* Medical evaluation
  overview of literature on, 30–51. *See also* Literature overview
  prevalence of, 30–32
  prevention of, 209–216. *See also* Prevention
  recognition of, 57–59
  ritualistic, 133–134
  validation of, 64–66
  victims of. *See* Male victims; Victim(s)
Child witness(es), 166–178
  child's interests and use of, 169–170
  competency of, 70, 168–169
  constitutional issues concerning, 170–172
  developmental factors affecting, 172–176
  historical background of, 166–168
  jurors' reactions to, 176
  legal issues concerning, 170–172
  recommended changes in treatment of, 176–178
Civil court, expert witnesses in, 182–183
Clinical evaluation, 57–79
  common sources of error in, 78
  of competency to testify, 70
  intervention strategies for, 60–63

51590